T0269752

GROUNDBREAKERS

GROUNDBREAKERS

The Return of Britain's Wild Boar

Chantal Lyons

BLOOMSBURY WILDLIFE
LONDON • OXFORD • NEW YORK • NEW DELHI • SYDNEY

*To Bonne-Maman (may this dedication partly make up
for my being so bad at French)*

BLOOMSBURY WILDLIFE
Bloomsbury Publishing Plc
50 Bedford Square, London, WC1B 3DP, UK
29 Earlsfort Terrace, Dublin 2, Ireland

BLOOMSBURY, BLOOMSBURY WILDLIFE and the Diana logo are trademarks
of Bloomsbury Publishing Plc

First published in the United Kingdom 2024

A catalogue record for this book is available from the British Library

Library of Congress Cataloguing-in-Publication data has been applied for

ISBN: HB: 978-1-3994-0163-0; ePub: 978-1-3994-0161-6; ePDF: 978-1-3994-0162-3

2 4 6 8 10 9 7 5 3 1

Typeset in Bembo Std by Deanta Global Publishing Services, Chennai, India
Printed and bound in Great Britain by CPI Group (UK) Ltd, Croydon CR0 4YY

To find out more about our authors and books visit www.bloomsbury.com
and sign up for our newsletters

Contents

Introduction   7

PART ONE: PAST AND PRESENT   17

Chapter 1: An End and a Beginning   19

Chapter 2: A Wild Boar Chase   31

Chapter 3: Guys, Dolls and Humbugs   47

Chapter 4: Monstrous Appetites   63

Chapter 5: Re-Rooting   88

Chapter 6: This Is Our Land   107

Chapter 7: The Boar People (Part I)   119

Chapter 8: The Boar People (Part II)   139

Chapter 9: Mad About the Boar   154

Chapter 10: The *Torc* of Galloway   178

PART TWO: FUTURES   199

Chapter 11: A *Bamboche* of Boar   201

Chapter 12: Fences of the Mind   224

Chapter 13: Losing Them Again   243

Chapter 14: The Risks of Being Alive   255

Epilogue   269

Acknowledgements   277

Further Reading   279

Index   280

This living environment is neither a finished map nor a stage, but a worlding world in constant flux.

Thomas Gieser, 'Into the meshwork of the forest: a sensory exploration of hunting landscapes in Germany'

Introduction

Below the trees and the birdsong, the bracken was still and silent. This was Great Britain, after all, and I was a human. The only wild animals big enough to stir the ferns were ones that knew to avoid me.

Or that was how it used to be, at least.

From out of nowhere a smell struck as swiftly as a flash of sunlight. It was thick, musky, almost salty. I stopped and scanned the green dimness. Hoping.

It was the summer of 2014, and I had fallen for the wild boar.

I was in the Forest of Dean in Gloucestershire. My quest was to write a dissertation from interviews with residents about what it was like to live alongside the boar: a species we had driven to extinction in Britain around seven centuries ago, and that had re-established itself in this forest over the past 15 years thanks to two illegal and rumour-clouded releases.

I didn't approach my research without care. But I was presumptuous. I imagined I would find little more than empty hysteria. That things hadn't really changed for anyone living there.

I didn't expect to find what I did.

I turned it into a dissertation that, like so many others, was marked and then filed away in a drawer somewhere. But the story I'd stumbled on wouldn't stop scratching at my mind. It felt like a miracle. I felt like shaking everyone's shoulders and pointing them towards the Dean and shouting *'Look!'*

Something was happening there that had not happened in this country for hundreds of years. A beast of myth, one that blurred the border between prey and hunter, roamed in a few of our woods again – and none of those who crossed paths with the boar could emerge from the experience unaltered. To some, the boar brought joy. To others, terror. To those who lived in proximity to them, they summoned the past into the present. Before the boar came back, no one in living memory in this country knew what it was to feel their heart beat faster in answer to the sight of an animal who could, if they chose to, kill us.

A boar looks like a creature whose maker took inspiration from bears, wolves and hyenas: stocky, shaggy-furred, all shoulders and head, with that long, long snout and teeth ready to chomp anything, and tusks that aren't always easy to see but are there.

The boar is not a predator. Yet, here in Britain, there is no other species like it. While our adders, foxes, deer, seals, whales, dolphins and sharks are all theoretically capable of injuring us, few people seriously entertain the possibility. The odd cases of a fox sneaking into a child's bedroom or someone being gored by a frightened stag are just that: odd. We know these animals. They are predictable, and they follow the rules.

We do not know the boar.

It is striking how fearful many people in Britain appear to be of wild boar, even though, proportionally, the number who have encountered them is minuscule. You only need to scroll down to the comments section of any online article about the return of the species to notice this.

'I wouldn't want my child – or anybody's child – to be ripped apart and eaten,' writes Jude Dumont below a piece from *The National* published on 23 October 2022.[1] The media plays an important part in feeding this kind of attitude, recruiting the power of words like *hostile, vicious, rampaging*.

But I also wonder if some of the blame lies with the cultural vacuum that exists around wild boar in Britain.

---

[1] https://www.thenational.scot/news/23071072.farmers-call-scottish-government-urgently-formulate-feral-pig-policy/

Portrayals of wildlife in popular culture have an undeniable impact on the connections we forge, especially when we lack our own direct experiences to call on – think books like *The Animals of Farthing Wood*, *Tarka the Otter*, *The Wind in the Willows*, *Watership Down*. Yet there are slim literary pickings when it comes to wild boar. We destroyed them long before many of our most beloved writers were born. Although the same is true of wolves, they still run and howl through our libraries, while boar are barely ghosts; as absent from our stories as they are from nearly all our woodlands today. In the fantasy novels I used to devour, including the books of Tamora Pierce's Tortall Universe, and *Game of Thrones* and its sequels, wolves serve as portents or companions or forms worthy of shapeshifting into. Wild boar, if they appear, are only ever a plot device to bump off a character or prove someone's heroism. Disney has never deigned to animate them, not even as side characters in woodland scenes. When I appealed on social media for any books, films or TV shows featuring notable boar characters whom I might have overlooked, most of the suggestions I received were limited to *Asterix* (where the boar are only nameless packets of meat) and farmed pig characters (not actually boar). My attention was piqued by a reference to the 1984 cult British fantasy novel *Mythago Wood*, which features a monstrous and powerful boar-headed being called the Urscumug; yet even then, beneath the furred head and the tusks, he is only a man. We seem incapable of letting the wild boar into our minds. Or unwilling.

In the apparent absence of positive – or at least realistic – representations of wild boar, many of us seem to have instead absorbed the bad press exported from regions like North America. Boar–pig hybrids over there have spent the last century getting bigger and hungrier. With plenty of credible accounts of injury among hunters who target these so-called 'razorbacks', their reputation for grouchiness and ferocity appears to be deserved. Meanwhile, scientific evidence that they are wreaking ecological havoc continues to mount, from eating up vulnerable native animals to dispersing the seeds and spores of invasive plants and fungi. And all this stands to reason. Wild boar are native to Asia, Europe and North Africa only while ecosystems in North America and elsewhere did not develop in concert with them. Their rise has been abetted by our own environmental damage, because an organism is more likely to become destructive – and therefore invasive – in a foreign ecosystem if we have erased the native species that might otherwise have stopped it gaining a foothold. A similar principle can surely be applied to our own knowledge and beliefs – if we have no close experience of something, it's far harder to interrogate what we hear from elsewhere.

———

Wild boar, I learned in the Forest of Dean, were so much more complex and vibrant than many assumed them to be. Yet I doubted I should be the one to tell their story, or the stories of the humans living alongside them. And while I waited for someone else to write a book about the return of boar to Britain, a new idea was setting aflame the public imagination: rewilding.

Rewilding has become many things to many people. It represents for some, including its critics, the restoration of a place to a pre-human (or at least pre-*modern*-human) state. But this is to overestimate what is still within the realm of possibility. After all, there's no way for us to know the precise workings of our ecosystems before we began to dismantle them. What we do know is that all over the world, we have reduced numbers of species, the number of individuals within many species, and the habitat they all need to survive. And those three kinds of losses continue to fuel each other in a vicious cycle, because species shape habitats and habitats support – and shape – species. Even if we could see into the past to take notes, by now we've lost too many species and their interconnections to reverse the damage. But what we *can* do is make decisions that set the stage for the revival of a host of life-making processes.

This might involve deciding not to do anything at all. Woodlands can regenerate without our intervention, if there are sources of seed close enough and animals able to ferry these.

Or we might need to physically rework the land. At the celebrated RSPB reserve of Haweswater in the Lake District, machinery was used to put wiggles back into Swindale Beck. The straightening of this stream by farmers 200 years ago had unravelled an ecological system that once underpinned a flourishing of wildlife. Now, salmon are spawning on its gravels again.

In other cases, restoration requires the re-addition of certain species. If the species is extinct, we can bring in the creature we think is most like it. For this reason, many rewilding projects in Great Britain use heritage breeds of cattle in place of their ancestor, the aurochs. As for still-living species, perhaps the most famous example of reintroduction for rewilding purposes is that of the grey wolf to Yellowstone National Park in the USA in 1995. In an online video with 44 million views called 'How Wolves Change Rivers', it's explained that by hunting and changing the movements of elk herds, the Yellowstone wolves allowed riverside trees to regrow, which encouraged beavers to return and ultimately fostered new, biodiverse wetlands. Meanwhile, by leaving carcasses lying around the place and killing their competitors the coyotes, wolves helped out a host of other carnivores including foxes, hawks, ravens and bears.

Except, this viral story is one that has been painted with the broadest of brushstrokes. Much less well known is that the reintroduction of the wolves coincided roughly with the end of a multi-year drought – which could part-explain why some tree species have resurged – and a mass release of beavers just outside the park borders – which probably had quite a bit to do with their influx into Yellowstone. Coyotes have rebounded to their pre-wolf numbers, and there is no actual evidence that wolf kills are a significant food source for Yellowstone's scavengers. 'Amid this clutter of ecology, there is not a clear link from wolves to plants, songbirds and beavers,' American biologist Arthur Middleton has concluded. It is intriguing that so many positive changes occurred around the time of the wolves' arrival. Yet the usual telling of this story leaves no room for nuance. The wolves of Yellowstone have become an ecological fairy-tale.

Similar kinds of expectations are often laid before the snouts of wild boar. Wherever boar root through the earth, we're told, we'll see volcanic eruptions of green growth, and all manner of other life will swarm and flock. Which does happen. Sometimes. The baseline of truth is that when the wild boar was in Britain before, it was a keystone species, its actions vital in helping to power the ecosystems to which it belonged.

But while the time that the boar has been gone is, in ecological terms, just an eye-blink, we have still forced much change on our landscapes in the interim. We can't be certain of what would happen if boar were allowed to return to the entire country and in significant numbers. How they might adapt their lifestyles, and how other species – many of them already nearing the brink thanks to us – might respond. There are no simple answers to the ecological simplification of our world, no IKEA-style manual for the right way to go about restoration.

That said, Great Britain is in something of a singular position. We are one of the most ecologically impoverished nations on the planet by any credible measure, including the number of species we have extirpated. According to Natural England, we've lost some 500 of them since 1800, and that's not even counting wild boar and others lost even earlier. Meanwhile, among the species left, the populations of a number of them have shrunk so much that they are in danger of becoming functionally extinct – there are too few individuals left to contribute to their ecosystems in the way they used to.

Many of the species we have lost, or are in the process of losing, are still to be found on the Continent. Yet the barriers of sea and distance deny us the luxury of waiting for them to return of their own accord where there is now suitable habitat for them. And so their reintroduction is a logical starting point.

It was George Monbiot's 2013 book, *Feral*, which blew open my mind to the possibilities of rewilding. It may well have done the same for you. And while I can't give him all the credit, it's undeniable that since Monbiot's book came out, a new momentum has swept through the conservation world. We've seen an exponential growth in rewilding projects, big and small. White-tailed eagles now roam the skies of England as well as Scotland, and wildcats look set to follow in their great shadows. Pine martens are being helped to leapfrog around the country. Beavers are poster children, unable to put a webbed foot wrong, furry brown angels come to redeem us.

But the boar is still in limbo. While the powers that be have not actively tried to exterminate existing populations – yet – the notion of legal reintroduction cannot even be whispered. Their return to a few different locations in Britain is regarded as an inconvenience or an embarrassment or just a novelty. All over the country, we are putting the easier species back in – the ones that never scare us, or always flee if they see us, or will be easy to drag back to captivity if we change our minds.

Wild boar are none of these things.

———

In late 2021, I give up waiting. I move to the Forest of Dean, an act that feels like coming home. Seven years after I first went there, I want to know what has changed and what has stayed the same. I get back in touch with many of the people I'd spoken to as a student in 2014, and I'm humbled and moved by the fact that nearly all of them give me permission to publish their quotes and experiences. Many of them have asked to remain anonymous, for reasons that will become clear. Where I give someone's first name only, it means I've used a pseudonym for them at their request. As for the nonhuman animals that appear in this book, you'll notice that where I'm not sure of sex, I use the pronouns *they*, *them*, *their*. Never *it*. *It* is no way to refer to another sentient being. If you want to know the name of someone's dog, you don't ask, 'What's its name?' (or if you do, I guarantee you have left a trail of offended owners in your wake).

While this book is about wild boar across Great Britain, much of it inevitably focuses on the Forest of Dean because there are more boar per square mile there than anywhere else in the country, and plenty of humans around to come across them. And while the Dean cannot in any way be described as a pristine ecosystem, it is still riotous with ecological connections. The boar's arrival there is thus a field experiment, one we should explore as deeply as we can to better understand how they are living with other species, and how those species are coming to live with them.

Yet the Dean doesn't have a monopoly on what happens when something like a boar comes back to somewhere like Britain. And so I head for other places where the species has regained a hoofhold, from the shores of Loch Ness to the tattered woodlands of Kent and East Sussex. I speak to people who, in their own ways, know the boar – or wish to.

And I seek out the boar themselves, to know them better. While their new history in Britain cannot be explained without humans, they are their own agents. They are idiosyncratic, intelligent, full of emotion. I was first drawn to them because they seemed so different to any other species we have in Britain. And they are. They've unnerved me, although more often, they've made me laugh or grin. Always, they leave me feeling glad to be alive in the world with such beings.

As one of the most adaptable mammals on the planet, wild boar are on the rise, both in their native range and beyond. I can't hope to encompass the entirety of their species in this book, nor their relationships with us and with others. All the same, I venture to the edges of Toulouse in France and Barcelona in Spain, for the same reason that I follow their trail up and down Britain – I want to see what the different situations I find in the present could foretell of a future in which we decide to let them come home. Because while wild boar are thriving across much of the rest of the planet, the same isn't true here. Scotland may be a different story, but in England they're already on the wane again.

We are heading for a reckoning. With climate breakdown on the horizon, this is the worst time for Britain to be missing so many species and the countless links between them. We want our wild abundance back, or at least we say we do.

But are we ready? We have walked carefree and unchallenged through our landscapes for centuries. Boar are not predators like lynx or wolves. But they require an altogether different kind of living-with compared to what we are used to. As their snouts push away earth to reveal the roots beneath, so the presence of the boar exposes our deepest beliefs about wildlife. They require us to make the kind of space in our lands and in our minds that no other British species today demands.

They are, in essence, a test.

Our desire to restore our fragmented and miniaturised ecosystems is admirable. And yet, if we baulk at restoring some of our crucial missing species, we will probably fail.

We do not know the boar, but we can.

PART ONE

PAST AND PRESENT

CHAPTER ONE

An End and a Beginning

Her hoof sinks into mud. The ground will remember her passing, for now. Behind her trot six little ones, followed by her daughter born three springs ago.

She listens to the woods on either side. Sucks the damp air in through her nostrils. Her nose flinches at a wallop of scent, from the urine sprayed onto a tree by a lynx. But she doesn't change her path. She has seen off that kind of hunter before.

She has other monsters on her mind. Ones who will overwrite her prints in the mud with their own if they detect her and her family. Prints that have four claw marks, or are long and rounded and don't fall quite so often.

Where in time is all of this?

It could be today, in an eastern European forest whose webbing of life is not quite so frayed.

It could be here in Britain, 10,000 years ago, after the end of the ice.

It could be here in Britain, in 50 years' time.

The story of the boar and the human is one that will run and run. Two species whose combined success has already changed the trajectory of life on planet Earth, and will continue to do so for unimaginable time. But first, we must travel backwards.

Our ancestors forked away from each other between 79 and 97 million years ago, after the fragmentation of the supercontinent Pangea. Then, between 3 and 4 million years ago, an animal we'd recognise as a wild boar or *Sus scrofa* emerged in South East Asia. Around 1.7 million years ago they would've begun to encounter early humans venturing into their realm. Boar and humans no doubt continued to meet as they both colonised Europe. But whereas our genus, *Homo*, was still experimenting with a variety of species at this point, wild boar had already hit on their own winning evolutionary formula. In the words of conservation writer

Benedict Macdonald, they had become – and remain to this day – 'an ecological singularity'. New species arise when new adaptations to the environment are required. Wild boar are a one-form-fits-nearly-all-places wunderkind.

It's unsurprising, then, that they crossed the bridge of Doggerland to reach Britain long before *Homo sapiens* did. Yet the ice of the Pleistocene's glacial periods was a nemesis even they could not withstand and, like us, they had to retreat south whenever the ice returned. It was a dance that lasted countless generations, at times backing European boar into the furthest corners of the continent, before they could strike northwards again.

Then came the Holocene, the epoch in which the ice never returned. In the warming climate trees basked and grew. Before Doggerland succumbed to the North Sea, across it came boar, beaver, red deer, roe deer, elk, aurochs, wolf, brown bear, lynx, human and more. A whole ecosystem on the move, pouring into a fresh new world.

The wild boar population of Britain may have been a million strong in its post-glacial heyday between 10,000 and 8,000 years ago. Wolves, lynx and bears preyed on them, and so did we. Their bones have been found among the troves of remains at sites like Thatcham and Faraday Road in Berkshire, Sanderson Uxbridge in Greater London, and midden sites on Oronsay off the west coast of Scotland. How we hunted them is uncertain, although bow and arrow may have been the preferred method, given the risks involved in attacking boar at close quarters.

But it would be reductive to dwell only on how boar were killed and eaten, instead of how humans *knew* them. Females and juveniles live in large noisy groups, and would probably have been much more active during the day, as is the case with populations in modern times that are not subject to intense human hunting. Because of this, archaeologists suggest that for Mesolithic peoples, wild boar may have been a more powerful and even sentient presence in comparison to other hoofed and more secretive creatures like deer. We would've had the time and light to watch boar being their full expressive selves. To notice what we shared in common. At sites such as Thatcham and Lydstep Haven, the bones of boar seem to have been placed deliberately in water. If this was done, as theorised, to prevent scavengers from gnawing on the bones, it may signify the respect that was accorded to boar as fellow beings. As Kate MacLachlan wrote in her study of human–boar relations in this period: 'A wild boar individual may have been viewed as a recognisable acquaintance, or perhaps a person; a being with a shared love of nuts and berries; a being who stole food from a camp; aggressive; protective of their children.'

Such ways of knowing boar would not last. Although debate rumbles on as to how forested Britain was between the end of the ice sheets and the advent of farming, no one denies that the incoming peoples of the Neolithic cleared the trees in huge numbers. Wild boar are adaptable creatures, but they still have a breaking point. Woodland was the centre of their world. As it was lost, so were they. And as we hunted them less and less, so they must have begun to fade from our collective consciousness. Ghosts at the edges of fences and fields.

The Anglo-Saxons completed the project of reshaping Britain that their Neolithic forebears had begun. By 1086 AD, according to the Domesday Book, woods and wood pasture accounted for just 15 per cent of England's land. It would've been even lower were it not for William the Conqueror's love of hunting. He established royal hunting grounds called 'forests', although the word then did not equate to trees, for as much heathland lay within these forests as woodland. Fickle refugia for Britain's last large game animals, which included red and roe deer as well as wild boar.

But boar offered unique sport. As historian Marcelle Thiébaux writes, they were wont to turn to meet their pursuers head-on, *visaige à visaige* – all the better to use their 'man-slaying tusks'. Long before we began to confine them to their last islands of woods, we were immortalising their perceived ferocity and courage in our religions, our stories, our regalia and the paraphernalia of war. In the epic *Beowulf*, figures of boar adorning warriors' helmets 'kept life-watch for fierce men'. And look again at the Sutton Hoo helmet: what forms its eyebrows?

Alfred the Great, king of the Anglo-Saxons between 871 and 899 AD, was likened to a wild boar in his defence of his kingdom against the Vikings. Yet both his enemies and his own people invoked the animal as deity, with power over fertility and war. Among the Norse gods, while Odin had his ravens and wolves, siblings Freyr and Freyja each had a boar for a companion. Even after Christianity had swallowed paganism, it was all the rage in medieval Britain to have the head of a wild boar on your heraldry, often with a long tongue jetting out. Centuries later in 2005, the coat of arms of Camilla, then Duchess of Cornwall, was revealed. On one side of it, a blue boar stands rampant and proud.

We have never quite forgotten this animal. But in the early part of the last millennia, as it thrived on coats of arms and in literature and art, the flesh-and-blood version was sputtering out in Britain. And yet there came a twist at the end of its tale. Because around 8,500 years ago, something new arrived on our shores: the pig.

Wild boar had been domesticated in the Middle East before their descendants were brought to Europe. In Britain, as elsewhere, the practice of *pannage* saw these pigs turned loose in the autumn to roam woodlands in search of acorns and other forage – the woodlands where boar still dwelled.

Cattle and horses had no hope of meeting their wild counterparts; the Eurasian wild horse (also known as the tarpan) had gone from Britain by around 7,000 years ago and the aurochs by 3,000 years ago. Wolves, who endured until the eighteenth century, probably interbred with their domesticated variants, while boar unquestionably did so. Indeed, so frequently did boar and pigs couple that, across Britain and the rest of Europe, the Middle Eastern genes of pigs ended up being overwritten by those of European wild boar. Historians note that in medieval manuscripts and art, pigs and wild boar are practically indistinguishable. Long legs, dark hides, bristles, straight tails and tusks. Even when kept apart from their wild brethren, medieval pigs showed what environmental historian Sam White has called 'an alarming propensity' to become more boar-ish in both appearance and behaviour over just a few generations.

It's as if the wild was trying to claim back its stolen children.

Most pigs in Europe today no longer carry this legacy. Beginning in the eighteenth century, new stocks were imported from China – where boar had also been domesticated thousands of years ago – and the wild was bred out for good. Yet it clings on in some heritage breeds, such as the Tamworth and the Mangalitsa. And in those pockets of Europe where pannage goes on, pigs and boar still enter illicit dalliances.

Wild boar were never erased from mainland Europe, where the remnant forests were big enough to shelter them from the rapacity of humankind. In Britain, the precise time of extinction is debated. According to records, the last great feasts of wild boar were held in the thirteenth century. Henry III served 300 in the Christmas of 1251, and then 80 in 1257. Oliver Rackham, esteemed biographer of the British countryside, suggests that the dozen boar the king ordered from the Forest of Dean in 1260 'were the last free-living wild swine in England'. If this is so, then there's a certain narrative satisfaction in the Forest of Dean having become the boar's English stronghold today. But I find it hard to chase away a vision: a male boar, hurrying through the undergrowth in an unremarked woodland somewhere else.

His heart beating faster with every distant dog bark. The stench of woodsmoke in his nose. He is old, wits gathered with the years. He knows these woods like he knows his own body. Both feel gnawed-down. He does not know that he is the last. Only that in the previous autumn, there were no sows to mount, or at least no sows who shared his petal-shaped ears and bristly back. And now, in spring, he cannot hear the mothers grunting to their babies.

He hurries on. Perhaps it's a wandering dog who brings about his end. Or perhaps he is allowed to lie down in the soft shade of an oak in the heart of the woods.

He slips away.

————

There are occasional records of wild boar being caught in Britain after the thirteenth century. But Rackham is doubtful that these came from wild populations. It's much more likely that they escaped from parks and estates. Importing animals from the Continent would have been well within the means of the hunt-loving elite. It must have rankled when, Umberto Albarella reports, a French herald on some unrecorded date in the late-seventeenth century mocked his English counterpart for the country's lack of 'fierce animals that require bravery to hunt, such as the wolf, the lynx and the wild boar'.

In 1789, the naturalist Gilbert White wrote in a letter to a friend that in Alice Holt Forest, Hampshire, one General Howe released a group of German-born wild boar, 'but the country rose upon them and destroyed them'. Dramatic language to describe what may have simply been poaching for the table. But vanquished Howe's boar were, and any others that found their way beyond fences.

Some of the genes of the British wild boar may still live on in our heritage breeds of pig. Beyond this small saving grace, that lineage is gone forever. Except for those places where pannage continued, our soils forgot the touch of snouts and the press of hooves with dew claws.

Until now.

———

Most of the last millennium was not kind to the wild boar of Europe. But they endured when so many other large animals did not, and their star is ascendant once more. Their population status is rated as 'Least Concern' by the International Union for Conservation of Nature (IUCN), which reports that the species now has one of the vastest geographical distributions of all land animals, partly thanks to humans.

And so, with hindsight, the return of wild boar to Britain was inevitable. If not intentional. There'd been mutterings among environmentalists for decades that the species should be reintroduced. But while white-tailed eagles began to fly free from 1975, and red kites received a major boost to their recovery with the release of Spanish-born individuals starting in 1989, nothing was done for wild boar.

Capitalism came to their aid instead. In 1981, a farm in Cambridgeshire started selling the meat of boar acquired as surplus from London Zoo's Whipsnade site. The market got a taste for them. More farms sprung up, buying in animals from the Continent, where they had never been extirpated and the farming of them was already long established. By the early 1990s there were 40 registered breeders in the UK.

Despite thousands of years of trying, one of the qualities that has proven most challenging to breed out of the farmed pig is escapology. Those wild boar farmers should have known, and probably did. They should have taken measures to ensure their charges didn't go wandering, which they presumably did, under the requirements of the Dangerous

Wild Animals Act of 1976. But life, as a certain fictional mathematician once said, finds a way.

Our woodlands had been waiting for nearly 700 years. Answering whatever call was sounding in their brains, wild boar began to escape from the farms. Or, in some cases, seem to have been variously helped out by storm damage, animal rights activists, hard-up owners and shooters. Each freed individual was a spark. Something new, something hot and bright with potential. Not all those sparks took. But enough did. In 1998 the Ministry of Agriculture, Fisheries and Food (MAFF) – forerunner to the Department for Agriculture, Food and Rural Affairs (Defra) – announced that two populations of wild boar had sprung up in England: one in west Dorset, and one on the border between Kent and East Sussex. In 2004, a third population joined these on the map: the Forest of Dean. Scotland followed suit when populations were officially identified in Lochaber and in Dumfries and Galloway. Most recently, boar have popped their heads up in Somerset, although whether they will be allowed to fully establish themselves there remains to be seen. As for Wales, Northern Ireland and the Republic of Ireland, their breadcrumbs of sightings over the years have yet to lead anywhere.

Escaping is the easiest part.

If we want a definitive beginning, we probably can't do better than one night in the autumn of 1989. East Sussex resident Derek Harman was enjoying a peaceful evening in front of the fire when his wife came in to say she'd seen a pig in the road. Specifically, 'A big black hairy one ... like those you see in nature books.'

He didn't believe her, so they jumped in the car and drove to the village edge. Derek was about to call off the search when a final sweep of his spotlight across a field snagged on the unmistakeable form of a wild boar.

Over the next eight years, he took part in the occasional shooting of any boar that failed to keep their presence in the woods of Kent and East Sussex discreet enough. He reserved any marvel for the weight of their corpses. This came to an end when he mistakenly shot a female who had been weeks from giving birth.

'My heart sank,' he confessed. 'For the very first time, I felt feelings of admiration for this wild creature that was re-establishing its presence despite the persecution from its human neighbours.'

Derek began to observe them instead, describing his experiences in his 2013 book *British Wild Boar*. He would put out bait and watch from a custom-built aluminium high seat that he carted around with him. His patience earned him glimpses into the way the boar were negotiating their new wild lives. Simply, they acted as if their kind had never left. They walked through the forest without a sound, never let their guard down while they fed, maintained a dominance hierarchy between different groups, and held their own against foxes and weird wolves (AKA domestic dogs).

One person who pops up regularly in Harman's narrative is 'the man from the Ministry', Martin Goulding. Goulding was a scientist sent in by MAFF to study the new populations and their potential economic impacts. He ended up publishing a book too, *Wild Boar in Britain*. In the preface, he writes that 'watching these animals below me, living freely in their ancestral habitat, is exhilarating and a privilege'.

You may have noticed a pattern beginning to emerge here.

Harman presciently subtitled his book *The Story So Far*. In the decade after his first encounter with a boar, most eyes fell and stayed fixed on Kent and East Sussex. After all, here was the largest population, and living in a human-dense region to boot.

Until the crown was taken by the Forest of Dean.

December 1999. Just north of the forest, near Ross-on-Wye, 15 wild boar suddenly found their world-defining fences gone. It isn't clear whether they broke out or were set free, although everyone seems to know someone who knows it was deliberate. It would have been at night, probably. Cold, definitely. What was it like for those individuals? Was there a tug-of-war in their minds between the memory of the human who fed them, and the call of the dark between the trees? It's said that in the early days of their freedom, they were happy to eat food out of people's hands. They were tamer than their brethren in southern England. They could've been so easily snuffed out, and some were indeed shot, by farmers and other landowners. The local Forestry Commission rangers chose not to partake in the killing, being unsure at the time of the legality of doing so. The Ross boar lived by the grace of official inaction. And yet they could still have petered out – had another 65 or so boar not appeared in November 2004 in Staunton, a village that snuggles into an auxiliary woodland to the west of the main forest. You'll usually read that these animals were, like the Ross boar, 'dumped'. Not so, according to one ex-ranger whose patch lay in the Dean.

'This is what I've been told and it's not far from the truth,' is how he opens his version of events when we speak. A shooting syndicate pooled their money to buy the boar. The plan was to drop them off in batches of 15 to 20 across the Forest of Dean and a little further beyond, to kickstart a shootable population. But the man driving the truck in the early hours of the morning got spooked when a police car came up behind him. He turned down a track and, though the police drove on, he opened the doors then and there. Some of the boar scrambled into the woods. Others found themselves in a nearby farmer's field, and they did not survive their first 24 hours of freedom. More were shot in the days after. A kind of deliverance came in the form of a sheep owner, a friend of the ex-ranger, who rounded up some of the boar with his dog. He trucked them into the heart of the forest. Whether it is only this splinter group that merged with the ones from Ross, we'll never know. Either way, they brought a new future with them in the form of fresh mates and genes.

In 2008, Defra published a management strategy for free-living wild boar in England, which remains in place today. The government's decision was to do nothing. That is, to neither persecute nor protect the boar. Instead, it was up to individual landowners to manage the animals however they saw fit. Across much of the Forest of Dean, this meant the Forestry Commission (more recently renamed Forestry England). They followed up Defra's strategy with their own, in which they committed to a policy of culling to keep the population to a certain level but not to eradicate it.

Some still lament that the Forest of Dean boar were not hunted down as soon as their presence became known. Stamped out before the sparks of them could catch.

'Wales did the right thing in our view and shot them,' said one resident to me, referring to an episode in 2014 when 40 boar were loosed by burglars in Bridgend. Some staff at Forestry England feel the same, with one admitting to PhD researcher Kieran O'Mahony that 'if we had a crystal ball on the day those 60 animals were dumped near Staunton, we would have rounded them up onto the back of the truck and sent them away or shot them.'

A crystal ball shouldn't have been necessary. The comeback of wild boar in mainland Europe has been blamed largely on the decline in human hunters and bountiful food in the form of maize and other crops. With their undiscerning diet, their large litters and their sheer adaptability, wild boar are evolved to catapult themselves towards the slightest opportunity.

Still, in 2008, the Forest of Dean population was estimated at only 100 to 150 individuals. With a spot of regular culling, the situation seemed manageable. Yet by the time I first visited in the summer of 2014, the number had risen to 800.

I was drawn to the Dean because it represented, to me, the biggest unintentional field experiment in Britain's nascent rewilding history. I knew nothing, then, of the boar who were much more quietly thriving in Scotland. And I didn't suspect that the story of the new British boar would irrevocably change the course of my own life.

But one thing I was sure of from the beginning was that their return asked a question of us, the answer to which could reshape the wildness of Britain's future.

CHAPTER TWO
A Wild Boar Chase

In the risk assessment I had to write for my dissertation, I said I wouldn't go looking for wild boar. I was, after all, going to the Forest of Dean to interview people to find out what it was like to coexist with them. For the purposes of the research, I didn't need to track down the boar themselves.

Of course, I still wanted to, the way you'd try to play it cool at a party where someone famous was in attendance. I'd already diagnosed myself with 'ecological boredom', a condition proposed by George Monbiot as the psychological side-effect of living on an island wiped clean of any remotely dangerous species. So, with plenty of hope packed along with my voice recorder, I set off for the Dean.

You're probably picturing the Forest of Dean all wrong if you haven't been before. I did. The part in *Harry Potter and the Deathly Hallows* when Harry hides there from Voldemort and the Death Eaters amuses me now because, in reality, it's a place where getting away from other people is hard. It's a cloak of forest moth-eaten with houses, fields, timber yards, picnic sites and clear-cuts, and slashed through with roads and footpaths. Forestry operations are constantly gnawing at it, creating a restless landscape for its denizens.

Yet this is also a place that saw a pair of beavers reintroduced – into an enclosure – in 2018, and pine martens the year after. Fallow, roe and muntjac deer dart across the roads, adders slink through the undergrowth, peregrines nest in the cliffs above the River Wye and goshawks stalk the air below the canopy. Driving along a winding road with a drop on one side and great old conifers looming on the other, you could be on the damp north-west coast of the USA; you can even stumble across young redwood trees, which seem to thrive here. The Dean is a new forest shifting around working quarries, abandoned quarries and just a few remnants of ancient woodland. It was ravaged for its great

sessile oaks in the seventeenth century, then flayed wholesale
in the nineteenth century for the planting of pedunculate
oaks because the foresters thought they would grow
straighter and taller (in fact, they never grew as well). The
Forestry Commission in its early years rubbed salt into the
wounds with plantings of larch, spruce, pine and fir. But still,
the Dean feels as wild as can be in today's Britain. Its borders
encompass 42 square miles of woodland. As holey as it is, it
is woven from an estimated 20 million individual trees.
Small wonder the wild boar took root here.

I came in 2014 because, in a place with the densest
concentration of boar anywhere in the country, I saw the
promise of a story that would give me enough material for
15,000 words and a good grade. Perhaps I'm being too
cynical about my 24-year-old self, but I know I went there
thinking mostly of what insights I could take.

I don't remember the moment I first read that wild boar
were roaming free in Britain once more. I don't even know
if they would've ever seized my attention if I hadn't read
Feral when it came out in 2013. Boar were one of several
species whose ecological benefits were extolled by author
George Monbiot. A few months later, I was hunting around
for dissertation topics for my master's in environmental
social science. I had no idea where to start, and I was
getting panicky.

Then I came across an intriguing series of news articles.

'Wild boars wreck Forest of Dean football club pitch' *BBC Sport*
    '"I screamed like a girl": Dog walker's shock after WILD
BOAR charges at him' *The Mirror*
    'The boar are taking over' *The Forester*

It was a case begging to be studied, and no one else had
done so yet.

The 'Forest of Dean' is the name of the wider council district, not just the actual forest. On maps, it has clear borders. But, as I discovered from the driver's seat of my car, there's another way to tell you've arrived: rootings.

Even before the road plunged into the shade of the titular forest, I could see that the verges had been ... attacked. The ground was torn open in places, dark brown amid green, with soil spilling onto the tarmac. Although I knew little about the boar at this point, from what I'd read and from what people had told me in a few initial phone calls, it was obvious who'd done this.

I soon learned it was impossible to drive anywhere in the Dean without seeing rootings, also called mootings or rootlings by some. Many creatures are good at hiding the fact that they exist from humans. Boar are not. Rooting is their main foraging technique, the ground a trove of juicy vegetal and invertebrate matter for them. If all school children had to study field signs of British wildlife – and truly they should – wild boar would make an ideal start to the curriculum.

And there was more to learn. Much, much more.

The first person to show me the woods, or at least *his* version of the woods, was Neil. It was a few days into my research trip, and I'd already done several interviews in homes and gardens. This would be the first true walking interview where, I hoped, the landscape itself would join in with the conversation.

I met Neil outside his house, which hunkered into a hillside overlooking the forest edge. He sported the camo gear and the kind of huge camera lens that defines his species: the wildlife photographer. They are abundant in the Dean.

He looked askance at the bright pink t-shirt I was wearing. But as we took a footbridge over a muttering brook, he began to chatter. 'I didn't know anything about wild boar when I started. I've been looking since 2007. I was out virtually every day looking and I'd never see them.'

It took three months for him to earn a glimpse, and another year before he saw them again. Bushwalks in Kenya had already trained him in the patient art of tracking, and back home he visited his local patch every day. Even so, after years of practice, Neil's success rate for finding boar was about one in every 10 trips.

'Round this area, find me a path, I'll tell you where it goes. This is my back garden. And so I come out here all the time. I actually know where wild boar were born last year, but that's something I won't tell anyone.'

He led us off the main dog-walking throughfare to climb deeper into the woods. The shaded air was cool, the bracken bright green and rampant on either side of us. It wasn't long before we came upon rootings. Neil stopped and crouched.

'That isn't recent, because it's wet, so that's been rained on since they've done it. See the difference in the colour of the soil? And the roots are all yellow. If there are nice white roots, the sun hasn't got to them, and they're within the last day.' All this sounded like common sense. Yet there was beauty in the precision of what Neil told me next. 'With fresh rooting, the bits of soil around the edges are more angled. Then the rain and the wind round them.'

I peered closer at the peeled-open earth. Although the dark dampness of the soil could have been taken for freshness, I could just about see the rounding he spoke of.

Rootings were already starting to fall into two distinct camps, for me. The first was what I thought of as 'exploratory rummaging', where the ground had only been turned over in a few spots, like someone opening a kitchen cupboard, shuffling packets of food around, maybe nibbling on a cracker, but feeling too uninspired by the offerings to dive in further.

In the second, a great swathe of ground had been flayed. That was the kind I was looking at now.

'You see that shape?' Neil pointed at the edge of the patch where we were crouched. 'That's where the snout's gone in.'

Yes, I could see that too, now that I knew. A hollow easily big enough to take my closed fist. A boar had made this using their *os rostri*, the disc of cartilage that, along with a complexity of muscles and the supporting strut of the prow-like prenasal bone, gives the snout its trademark shape and strength. I've since seen those fleshy discs up close – how they flex with the top rim tilting forward as the bottom rim tilts back, and vice versa in an endless see-saw.

The rootings that Neil showed me went to a depth of around 15cm, which is the rough average. Boar can, however, root all the way down to 70cm if they see fit. In the days to come, I would occasionally see what looked like miniature asteroid craters.

We rose and carried on our way. And it turned out to be like moving swiftly on in time, because the ground on either side of us was lumpy, and fuzzy green with growth. Older rootings.

Although you can easily see where boar have been, it may be months or even years after the event. For while plants are usually quick to recolonise, the ground forgets how to be flat. New roots hold it in its new form. If you were a giant and you brushed a hand across this land, once before the boar came and once after, you'd feel the difference in your fingertips. The roughness.

That day with Neil left me with a revelation: in the grand ecological scheme of things, *flat ground is not normal*. A patch of ground worked over by the boar is a metaphorical middle finger held up at the flat straight lines of the barren lawns we so love today – lawns that are a symptom of the nationwide affliction that Benedict Macdonald calls 'ecological tidiness disorder'.

In this place surrounded by the past and present tense of the boar, their presence had never felt so palpable. I told

myself the odds of seeing them here, now, were low. Hope
fluttered anyway.

'If you were tracking the boar,' I asked, 'what would you
be doing?'

'Well, I wouldn't be talking.' (Damnit.) 'And I'd be
walking very quietly.'

While I knew that Neil wasn't bothered about finding
boar today – or he wouldn't be taking me along with him
– I lapsed into silence. It gave the land a chance to keep
speaking through the man. Sure enough, it wasn't long
before we stopped again, this time for hoofprints.

'This front one is a deer, the back one is a boar. With boar,
the hooves are more splayed.'

I peered at the boar print with its two slots leaning
slightly away from each other. To my eyes, the deer slots did
the same. I couldn't see the difference. Yet.

'If this was deep mud, you'd also have a couple of
impressions there where the dew claws go in.' Neil reached
out and tapped the ground just behind the print. 'This
one's quite recent, you've got tiny little flecks of mud still
on the top ridge there which haven't been washed or
blown off yet.'

He kept looking around, saying he was searching for
baby boar prints. He couldn't see any here. With their
smaller size, they were easy to mix up with those of muntjac
and roe deer.

On we went through the woods. Although the bracken
already seemed tall and thick to me, I'd been told it would
grow even more over the coming months. Before boar were
exterminated in Britain, bracken was far less prolific than it
is in modern times. Now, in summer, it gives the boar
perfect cover. But one thing boar cannot hide is their smell.
This too was on my list of questions to put to Neil.

'The boar smell like pigs 'cos they roll around in anything
to get rid of parasites.' I nodded, though I couldn't even have
said what a pig smelled like. Another person I'd spoken to

had described boar-scent as 'ferally', which was equally unhelpful to the uninitiated.

'But especially when you've got a lone male, oh my God, it stinks. It's from the urine. Several times I've seen males turn backwards to a tree and spray. You're in no doubt whatsoever if it's fresh. It does linger for a long time but if it's fresh you don't want to be near it, it's that horrible.'

The image of a boar spraying against a tree sounded strikingly big-cat-like. And when we later came to a wire fence bent far upwards with the passage of boar, I felt another spark of awe. Even the awareness that a trace left by these creatures could kindle feeling in me brought its own fascination and pleasure.

Geographers of more-than-human relations – the field that provided the academic bedrock for my dissertation – know this well. They speak of 'affect', a phenomenon that Oxford academic Jamie Lorimer defines as the 'forces that flow between different bodies'.

I stared at that warped fence, took an impression of it into me. Perhaps that night, the boar would come back this way and smell that Neil and I had been there. They would take us into themselves.

We didn't see any boar that day. But I had met them in another way. And this experience closely followed that of people who'd already been living here when the boar first arrived. They were things sketched in the mind over months before the first face-to-face encounter. Each fresh sign formed a new pencil mark. Take the telephone poles that a woman showed me near her house. One had mud marks that went as high as my hips. Another was wrapped in an aluminium sheath that was in the process of being peeled off, loose edge crumpled as easily as kitchen foil where a succession of bodies had rubbed against it. An adult male boar can reach up to 90cm at the shoulders, measure 150cm from snout to raggedy tail and weigh up to 150kg. Females are slightly smaller, but even they are hefty with muscle. It was an alien thing, to be confronted with the sheer physical power of a wild animal.

On other walking interviews, my companions showed me the wallows the boar had carved out of the ground, and the trees where bathing boar had then rubbed themselves clean. Alone once in one of the RSPB's local reserves, I found a wallow right by a main footpath. It was filled with a luxuriant pale gloopy mud. Very fresh, very much in use. Within eyesight of it stood a fat old oak, the bark of its bole smoothed and turned grey-white by the boar. I stepped up to the tree and laid my hand on it. The coating was dry, cool and as thick and hard as plaster of Paris. Notches told of the scraping of tusks. I searched in vain for any bristles stuck to the dried mud, as if possessing one could summon its owner to me. Because, for all that they advertised themselves, the boar were leading me on a merry chase.

'You should've been here yesterday, I saw a whole bunch of them,' was the kind of quip I grew to know only too well. Like cats, the boar seemed drawn to the people who least wanted to see them. I apprenticed myself to everyone I walked and spoke with, letting them show me the signs that had become part of their personal landscapes, welcomed or not. I followed the leads I was given, heading to corners of the forest in between interviews to try and find the boar myself. There was a moment in the woods when a musky salty smell gusted by. Almost like I'd stuck my nose in a jar of Marmite. But it never came again. The nearest I got to seeing the boar was when I was leaving someone's home in the dark, deep in the woods, and from the doorstep my interviewee shouted, 'Look, there they are!' And probably they were, but my eyes couldn't find them. It didn't count. I was a visual creature. Nothing less than a shared gaze would do.

My time in the Dean ran out. I had to go back to my desk in London, to wrestle my notes and transcripts into something suitably academic in tone. I couldn't have chosen a better case study. What I'd found resonated uncannily with the existing literature on more-than-human geography. I had quotes from interviews that matched, almost word for word, what various geographers had already written about conflict and coexistence between humans and other beings. And it still turned out to be the most difficult piece of work I'd ever had to produce, because I couldn't fit in everything that I wanted, *needed*, to say.

Nor could I let the boar go.

At the end of summer, I made a final short trip. I emailed a few of the people I'd interviewed before, and one sent back what felt like a promising tip-off: a mother and her juveniles had of late been showing up at a certain spot at a certain time every evening for the last few weeks.

Following the directions I'd been given, I parked in a lay-by and walked up a flinty track. The bracken on either side reached almost to my shoulders now.

No one else was around. It seemed impossible that the boar might be, when I had already spent so much time searching in vain. And then, softly, a sound entered my awareness. One that was new to me. It was a snore, a purr, a rumble, and none of those things.

More than one animal was making it. As they foraged in the sunlit evening, they were ... communing. That was the word I found myself alighting on. *I am here. I am here. I am here.* Voices reaching for each other through the tangled vegetation.

I trod slowly along the track. The sounds grew louder. Ahead, on the right, ferns quivered. I stopped breathing, afraid to risk the noise.

Out stepped the sow. Slow, stately and measured.

She was smaller and darker than I had expected. Her ears were fluffy and pointed, like those of an elven teddy bear. Her face was grey, as if she'd plunged it into a long-cold fire. Below ridges so like human eyebrows, her eyes met mine.

I forgot all the things I'd been told about her. She simply was herself.

She stared long enough for me to take a photo. Raising the camera and looking at her through it stole something of the moment from me, but without it, I might have doubted my memory afterwards. Then she gave one loud snort. With a sound of fading thunder and the crackling of bracken, she and her kin vanished back into the woods.

It takes me nearly eight years to come back to the Forest of Dean. This time, I intend to stay. Like most of the turns in my life, I hadn't planned to move here. But if I'm to write a book about the boar, where better to be?

This place has never let me go. After the master's, I tried to forge a career in London, although nowhere felt right enough for me to put out my roots and plant myself. I was about to get on a plane to Canada on a two-year work visa when the pandemic hit. A great rock tumbling into my stream, as it was for everyone else, sending the flow on a new uncharted course. One future snuffed out, another brought to life. Just as it was for those founder wild boar, suddenly free in a strange and seemingly endless land.

When I search online for house shares in the Forest of Dean, just three rooms come up. I find myself driving to a village on the very edge that I'd never had a need to go to during my dissertation research. The room I view turns out to be smaller than it looked from the photo, and a stone of disappointment drops through me. I don't think I'd manage in here.

But the house is right below a thickly wooded ridge. It takes 50 seconds to walk from the driveway to the mouth of a holloway, a tunnel of shade and cool in the August heat. I let it carry me up into the trees. Nettles and bracken and the magenta fuzz of burdock clamour on either side. There's more green than my eyes know what to do with. I follow a desire path further up the slope. In places, the ground is damp and claggy and fresh with memories of who has passed by.

Despite being owned by Forestry England, this wood is not technically part of the main Forest of Dean; roads and villages sever the two. I hadn't been sure if wild boar would be here. But the half-baked mud can't lie. It seems that everywhere I look, I see prints of splayed hooves with the twin holes of dew claws.

I move in a month later.

The luxury of being able to get out of bed and practically fall into the woods is an astonishment that doesn't fade. Finding boar is my primary objective, yet there's plenty else to distract me. It's like becoming a child again. Following trails through the bracken on a whim, sticking my head into pot-hole-able caves, ducking under fallen trunks. I find grand old queens of beech trees, encircled by holly trees like prickly ladies-in-waiting. Small deep gorges with the look of abandoned filmsets, bedecked with hart's-tongue ferns and layers of tamarisk moss thick enough to lose my hand in. Clearings where dead trees stand growing shelves of polypore fungi, with the sacred light and air of temples. One end of the wood is formed of a larch plantation, and its trees announce the arrival of autumn by turning bright yellow. Even on the cloudiest mornings, when I see those larches, I always think for a few moments that the sun has managed to reach its way through after all.

I am spoiled for wildlife. Roe deer with their milk-moustache rumps bobbing away. A badger caught out in daylight, tumbling up the path ahead of me. Tawny owls every night – *every night*! My first lesser-spotted woodpecker (and, perhaps, my last). Buzzards that I only notice when they peel themselves from their perches like bark sprung to life.

For its all riches, the wood is bounded on all sides by footpaths, fields and roads. As soon as I feel like I'm the last person on the planet, someone comes strolling along with a dog. But the wood and I take possession of each other anyway. I am giddily free to roam here. I feel closer than ever to the boar, whose ancestors left their fences behind just as I have. If only they would show themselves to me.

I already know how evasive they can be, and according to the latest population estimate from Forestry England, there aren't many more around compared to when I was last here. There were thought to be about 800 of them in 2014. That number rose to a peak of 1,600 in 2018, but in September 2021 – the month I arrive – an updated estimate of 900 is published. Forestry England's rangers appear to have stepped up their culling game.

I walk the woods nearly every dawn and dusk. Still nothing. One of my neighbours seems to see them whenever he goes out, news that he cheerily relays when we pass each other by. In fanciful moments I suspect he is a god of boar. Just like the character Rob McKenna from the *Hitchhiker's Guide to the Galaxy* series who, unbeknownst to himself, is a rain god and always followed by rainclouds (in which case I must be a god of muntjac).

Worried that Forestry England has shot all the local boar in their never-ending cull, I check every rooting. I'm relieved if it contains roots that are bright white with the freshness of exposure. It's time for a change of strategy, I decide. It's time to go out at night.

In the first year of the pandemic, when I moved back to my parents' home in the countryside, I began to dabble in the dark. But it was only ever a brief dalliance; going for a walk when dawn was waiting in the wings anyway, or getting home five minutes after the last of the light had faded.

When I was young, I didn't walk for pleasure. Later, most of my twenties were spent in London, where walking for the sake of walking in the dark was too preposterous for me to consider.

But the wood here feels different. The peace of it gives me courage. Even so, the first time I go out with the express intention of walking in the dark, I'm aware that my mother would be horrified. It has only been a few weeks since the end of the trial for the murder of Sarah Everard.

The holloway leading into the woods is a wormhole of black. The leaves and branches feel much closer than in the light, and I keep bracing for their touch. From neighbouring fields come the dinosaurian moans of cattle. And the trees … crackle. I've never heard them make this noise before. It's like the sound of them thinking.

The path is paler than the surrounding undergrowth, making it easier to keep to than I expected. I try to breathe and tread more quietly, rolling from heel to toes. I feel subversive, and that is both joyous and discomfiting. My headtorch stays in my pocket. I don't know if this is more because I want to train my eyes or because I don't want to be noticed.

Left where the path forks. A strong stride up the steepest bit of hill. Then the crossroads marked by a holly tree. To my right, in the distance, someone's torchlight swishes through the night. Not as alone as I'd thought. I turn and walk the other way.

The light has gone by the time I glance back. I come to a stop and hold still.

A female tawny owl gives her sharp *kee-wick* call. Coming out has been worth it for that alone.

I wait. And wait. I'm thinking of giving up when the first snort comes. Unmistakeable.

They are here.

Every sound has significance now. Dead leaves crunch with heavy weight. More snorts. Each one half like a dog's bark, half like an ape's pant. My finger rests on the silicon button of my headtorch. Not yet. Not yet. I want to turn it on and see a boar before me.

Not yet.

The crunching and the snorts sound closer. *Now.*

The thin beam reveals nothing except brambles and skeletal bracken. Then comes the loudest snort yet, and hooves like a distant storm.

Autumn sheds its skin of leaves, becomes winter, and yet the temperature remains unnervingly mild. I make the best of this unwanted omen by going out on more nights.

Sometimes I hear the boar. It is a form of encounter, although I still want more. Despite the time I've already spent trying to absorb the experiences of other people, what I know is still just a candle flame – or a disembodied snort – surrounded by so much darkness.

One night, the moon burns with a fierce white glow. I follow my sharpened shadow up the path. By now I know to have a torch ready in my hand, to avoid stepping without warning into the circle of light of any dog walker out late. I find a trunk and settle among its roots. Above, the bare beech canopy is strung with fairy-lights of stars. Without their leaves, the trees are mute.

Just as my heart takes time to calm from the brisk walk, so it takes time for the wood to take me into itself. The sound and then the memory of the sound of my clumsy treading must fade. When it does, wakeful creatures resume their work. Crackling, rummaging, pawing through the leaf litter. Scratches of tiny claws on bark. It all sounds so close, even though when I turn my head by slow inches to either side, and despite the moonlight, I see nothing. But the noises go on. I have been accepted. I am part of a tree.

I close my eyes. Open them when a tawny owl begins a trilling cry. Close them again. Waiting for the boar, I am comfortable. Safe. Perhaps this absence of fear makes me the strangest creature here. I have no need to listen out for the howling of wolves or the snuffle of a bear, because long ago my own kind ripped them out of this land. Some people would still be afraid, because of the animals that are left or because of other humans. I am a woman lying against a tree in a wood at night, no child or partner needing my return, and far from any city, where I would never dare do this.

Spending hours and hours looking for something wild is no guarantee that you'll succeed. But it can tip the scales of luck just enough. Another evening, earlier this time, I'm on the final stretch of my now-familiar loop through the wood. My steps are quick. In my mind, I'm already home, senses closed to everything except the crunch of my trainers on gravel.

Until a new sound announces itself.

It isn't something I've heard before, and afterwards I'll only remember that I heard it. As if knowing it is forbidden. Yet certainty surges through me with the speed of adrenaline. Some deep part of me has made a deft calculation: it is dusk, this doesn't sound like any other animal I've heard around here before, and it's coming from more than one. Therefore: it is them.

I sink into a crouch on the edge of the path. My eyes are steeped in twilight, all colour gone to black and white. In the bracken, the boar are talking: grunts, and those short snorts that remind me so much of chimpanzees.

Ferns rustle.

Something steps out.

With my handicapped vision, what I see is the merest idea of a boar. A large anomaly of black on the pale path.

It's like watching an animation where the style has been made to look slapdash, scribbles of pencil restlessly escaping the outlines.

She – I assume this is a group of females – noses at the ribbon of grass between undergrowth and path. The only part of me that moves is my lips, stretching into an ever-wider grin. I want this moment to last forever. I am afraid. Not of her, but of her noticing me.

'Their eyesight is rubbish, their sense of smell is amazing, and their hearing is annoyingly good – bane of my life,' Neil had told me years ago.

And notice me she does. About 40 seconds after she emerges, she makes the first loud inhalation. Then a second one. And finally a long belch of a snort.

The others flee. She follows after, the bracken shivering in her wake. I, meanwhile, float home.

It's so like that moment seven years ago. But this time, I don't need to drive away. This is only the beginning.

CHAPTER THREE

Guys, Dolls and Humbugs

If this was a fairy-tale, perhaps my first reunion with the wild boar would have been the breaking of a curse. But as winter wears on, crossing paths with them remains as hard as ever. I get a trail camera for Christmas and even then, when I leave it around places where boar have been rooting, I snatch just a few glimpses of individuals sneaking by. I haven't yet found the highways or the hotspots.

I wake earlier than usual one morning so that I can have a longer walk in the wood before heading to Bristol for work. An unclouded sky gleams with pre-dawn light, and the air is honeyed with birdsong. When I hear a boar-ish noise, a sort of low grunt, I dismiss this as wishful thinking and go on.

I stop.

Three boar are standing among yet-to-bloom bluebells, their backs to me.

I sink into a crouch.

The sows begin to amble higher up the wood's slope. They're fully grown, dark-haired, very fat. Without a doubt they are all pregnant.

I move after them, placing my feet when I can in the hollows of their rootings. The soft crumbly soil receives my weight without a sound. Whenever a tree interrupts my path I pause behind it, as if the four of us are playing a game of Grandma's Footsteps.

Once, a sow pauses to nose at the ground. The one behind her gently nudges at her rump. They go on. They've given no sign that they know I'm there, except perhaps for their subtle swiftness. They climb the final bank before the wood levels out. I hang back, not wanting to give myself away in case there's a chance I haven't done so already. Then I follow.

But they're gone. I don't know how, because there isn't a twig of undergrowth in this part of the wood, and yet they have. They've vanished themselves, wizard and rabbit in one.

The memory of the sight of them remains like a bright afterglow. They looked like little bears. Or night gods answering the call of a sleepy moon.

Days later I see the Trio again. Or two of them, at least. Boarlet season is around the corner, and it may be that the third has left to give birth.

During my first time in the Dean, I never saw a baby boar. Most are born in spring. And so, since moving here, I've been counting down the days. People who have lived here for much longer heighten my anticipation with promises like 'They'll be out and about all day with the babies, you'll see them loads,' and, 'The piglets will come right up to you!'

They appear first on the Facebook group for local wildlife photographers. I know better than to ask where the images were taken, as most members closely guard the locations of their patches. One man even captures newborns, perhaps less than a day old, tumbling over each other in the nest.

Nest is a strange word to use when it comes to a species that belongs to the artiodactyls, the even-toed mammal group that includes pigs, peccaries, sheep, goats, cattle, chevrotains, deer, giraffes, pronghorns, antelopes, camels and hippos. An equally strange word is *litter*. Because all the animals I've just listed tend to bear one infant at a time. Peccaries, which look and act like pigs thanks to convergent evolution, can go up to four. But only among species of pig – including though not limited to bushpigs, warthogs and wild boar – can you find litters of up to around 10.[2]

Gestation for a wild boar lasts four months. When her time is near, a sow will leave her sounder of fellow females.

---

[2] Artificial selection by humans has led to farmed pig breeds capable of producing bigger litters.

She'll make a hollow out of materials such as bracken and grasses, and thin branches collected from the ground or bitten from the low-hanging arms of trees.

Compared to her, her newborns will be tiny, weighing between 600g and 1kg. Eyes shut tight. Nothing like the ready-to-run offspring of most artiodactyls. More like wolf pups. They are caramel-brown, streaked with horizontal stripes of darker and paler shades. The same camouflage principle as baby tapirs. They are not all softness, though. The boarlets are born with needle teeth that stick outwards in order to defend their chosen teat against their littermates.

Being unable to fight anything bigger than another boarlet, they will remain in their nest for 10 days or so, while their mother makes the briefest of departures to drink or eat. But safety is no sure thing, especially in places crawling with humans.

'It feels like a hidden kingdom,' Nick Hunt writes of the occasion when he managed to stumble upon a newborn litter in the Dean, 'A place I should not have found, and I quickly go on my way.'

For all his contrition, an undeniable thrill simmers beneath Hunt's words. I yearn to know the same, even though I also know that no boar mother would willingly yield her privacy. Humans aren't the only fear; captive wild boar kept in confined quarters have been recorded eating the newborns of their kin. Secretive nesting probably evolved in part to avert this risk.

Once the babies are strong enough for their mother to lead them out into the open, there's no question of their safety among their own kind. Care of them is the hook on which so much of boar society hangs, a society that in many ways resembles that of elephants. Females live together in sounders, and each of these is led by a matriarch. Members are drawn from her daughters, sisters or other female kin. Most females will come into season in late autumn. The synchrony means that, after each has given birth and reunited with their sounder-mates, babysitting and suckling duties can be shared, their powers as mothers multiplied.

When it comes to leadership, however, it's the matriarch they all look to. She's the one to first step out into the open to reconnoitre, and the one to stand her ground and buy time for her family to flee in the face of any threat. Inevitably, many people assume her to be male. Time and time again, I hear stories of huge boar 'fathers' guarding their offspring, even though the males play no part in childrearing. A more observant woman in my village remarks to me that the matriarch seems to always have the darkest fur. Based on those sounders I've seen so far, in person or on the trail camera, I'm inclined to agree with her.

Not that my sample size is particularly big. As spring ripens, so do my hopes, fed by all those assurances that sows with boarlets at hoof are far less fussy about being out in the day. I spend as many hours as I can stalking my wood and beyond. Finally, one morning in early April, someone on the Facebook group posts a photo of boarlets along with the name of the village where they took it. This is at about 8.30 a.m., just before I log on for work. I'll go straight after 5 p.m.. All day, as I write tweets and comms strategies, I'm gripped by FOMOH (Fear Of Missing Out on Humbugs – 'humbugs' being the local slang for boarlets, given the colour and patterning of their pelage).

At the appointed time, I jump in the car and head over. The photo's stated location wasn't specific. As I ponder where exactly to stop, a dark shape between the trees to my left catches my eye. It'll be a rotten log or stump, like it always is. I'm forever getting excited when I see an interesting shape from a distance. Things I've mistaken for boar include dogs, black bins and my neighbours.

But this time, foot on the brake pedal, it becomes clear that my first impression was correct.

I'm on an awkward stretch of road, forcing me to drive
further along before I can park. Once that's done, I rush
back towards where the boar were. I wince at the loud
crunch of dead leaves beneath my feet, although thanks to
the wood's position next to a national speed limit road, the
roaring of cars covers my approach.

The sow is still where I'd seen her, along with six others.
And, yes, *babies*, scattered all over the woodland floor, busy
exploring with a clockwork trotting. As I stand there,
seconds ticking by, I go ignored. Perhaps these sows will
allow me to watch?

One of the darkest of them flicks her head in my direction.
She snorts.

Ah. No chance.

She breaks into a run and, as if tethered to her by invisible
strings, all the boarlets follow. There are even more than I
realised, more than I can count. They surge up the hill like
a wave of sand, a coordinated furry mass – 20 at least, 25
even?

Two sows remain, close to the road. They don't seem to
have noticed that the alarm has been sounded and that
everyone else has cleared off. Two more boarlets are with
them. I take a few steps, trying to eke out the moment, to
steal a little more sight of them. But another car has braked
and is pulling over for a closer look. The boar, apparently,
can only tolerate vehicles that are rushing past. They flee.
Even so, as I head home, I'm smiling. Baby season has only
just begun, and this is surely the beginning of weeks
brimming with boar.

———

I don't see any again until the end of May. I'm near the end
of the 35-minute loop I always walk before work. It's not
unusual for me to see all three of the Dean's resident deer
species – roe, fallow and muntjac – before I'm home. I only

need a muntjac to complete today's Deer Bingo. And, lo and behold, just off the path, two of them are grazing among the bracken and the now-dying bluebells.

I stop, and frown. These muntjac are very small. And stripey.

I sink low. Higher up the slope, one of the Trio sows lifts her head to sniff at the air. Only part-hidden by the greenery, I bite my lip and wait. No belching grunt comes. Her head falls as she resumes feeding.

For the first time, I'm free to watch. One of the boarlets is just 3m away, and though he or she would only have to look up to see me, the earth is a far more pressing concern. As they dig their snout in, their entire body jerks forwards and backwards with the force of their rooting. They won't be weaned until they're at least three months old, but already they're applying themselves with single-minded purpose. Researchers have found plant matter in the stomachs of babies just two weeks old.

The humming flutter of wings catches my attention. I look up. So caught have I been by the scene at ground level that only now do I notice the blackbirds and robins that are coming to perch on the branches above. I shouldn't be surprised. I already know that birds like to forage in rootings for invertebrates or seeds – the reason why many a naturalist has remarked that robins probably follow us around when we're gardening because we are unwittingly pretending to be wild boar. And yet, to witness it myself moves me more than I'd expected. To see, in real time and as clearly as the thread of a spider's web, an ecological connection. There is a profound beauty in the way that these birds have reclaimed the knowledge that boar will break open the earth for them.

A blackbird drops to the ground near me, surrendering to impatience. One of the boarlets sees and gives chase. I have to quell the urge to laugh.

The group is gradually moving on, out of my sight. I glance over my shoulder to make sure no one is coming up the path. Then I do my best impression of a four-legged carnivore, creeping on hands and knees, avoiding twigs, quiet enough that I can't hear myself.

I remain unnoticed.

As the boarlets work, their tails make constant metronome swings. Though *tail* seems too grand a name for what looks more like a piece of string pinned to each little rump. Those tails, those rumps and everything else about them are precious. Tiny bodies, dewy eyes, big curving foreheads – they are visual sugar to us. No wonder most locals, even those who would rather see the boar gone, refer to them as a boiled sweet. In a neat parallel, Japanese people call them *uribou*, which means 'watermelon boy'.

As you might be able to guess, people from medieval times and earlier did not call them humbugs. All the same, the name feels worn-in, old. It must, Steve Cracknell writes in *The Implausible Rewilding of the Pyrenees*, 'have been twiddling its thumbs behind an oak tree for two centuries, waiting for the opportunity to catch a passing boar.'

But back to the present. My boar are starting to drift further uphill, away from the path and me. Maybe they know something isn't quite right. Even so, it's a pleasure to watch them go, to have caused them no obvious alarm.

———

One week on, the third sow returns. She's been gone far longer than mothers usually spend in the nest with their newborns. Still, she's back, with the crèche of boarlets added to – about 12 of them now, I reckon. Again I'm treated to the luxury of watching the group feed in the morning sun. Of hearing them grunt to stay in touch. Babies occasionally break off from foraging to pester each other, tottering and darting around as if springs are attached to their hooves that they sometimes lose control of.

This time, the sounder migrates towards the path. There are no trees near enough for me to hide behind. My body tenses with a weird thrill of impending discovery. The first few boarlets trot past unawares. Then the leading sow, fur so dark it looks black, steps out. She clocks me. Goes rigid. Gives a deep, dragonish breath. She takes a step forward.

'I'm sorry,' I murmur. A silly part of me hopes that a soft human voice might soothe her.

She makes the alarm call, the long deep snort-grunt that almost seems to vibrate in my own chest. The others all dash away. And true to her duty, she remains standing where she is, forbidding me, until a few more vital seconds have passed. Perhaps I feel the faintest twinge of my own fear in that long and too-short moment when the matriarch stares me down. The whisper of *what if...?* I've never felt threatened in the presence of sows with babies. No boar has ever given me reason to.

And yet, with other people, they've sometimes made other choices.

Female wild boar have long been renowned for the courage with which they defend their offspring. In the Dean, boarlet mortality is thought to be low, as evidenced by the rate at which the population has proven itself able to grow. This is likely due to a combination of mild winters and a lack of predators. Yet boar here take no chances. Their mothering instinct is dialled up high enough for foxes, wolves, lynx, and apes with blades and dogs. Some of these creatures are still around, no matter that most of the apes have swapped weapons for cameras. All the while, the high energy demands of suckling a litter means sows must spend much more time foraging in the open daylight as their babies loosely orbit them. Thus, a boar with young is a boar necessarily on high alert.

Not that her charges always make it easy for her. One woman told me about the time that a whole litter came running towards her in what seemed to be naïve curiosity. The mother responded by tossing a boarlet right up into the air with her snout and then screaming at them all. 'It was as if she was saying, "Don't do that!"'

Another of my interviewees from 2014 had once lingered too long and too close to a litter as he tried to get the perfect photo.

'I was in a woodland with lots of little trees, big lens on the tripod,' he explained. 'I'd lost track of the mother. Suddenly there was this thrashing noise and the sow came crashing through the trees towards me, and I saw the mouth open and snap shut, and she veered round. The tripod went over and, oh God, I really jumped. The truth of the matter is she could've bitten me, but she didn't. It was a warning. But it really frightened me to death.'

I haven't read or heard of anyone else experiencing this same feint, the clack of jaws. Which speaks to me of the endless flexibility and creativity of boar in their behaviour – and the efforts they make to avoid physical contact. For all that plenty of people say they've been followed or even chased after coming upon a sounder with babies, none have been caught by this animal meant to be able to run at up to 25mph.

Dogs are another matter. To wild boar, these domesticated beings must surely appear as wolves ignorant of the rules and politics of the forest. When boar escaped into Dartmoor, the papers were taken with the story of an elderly woman who used a leash to thwack a boar on the snout to reclaim her bruised dachshund, who lay shaking at their feet. In the Dean, boar seem to clash with dogs as inevitably as shards of flint tossed together in a bag; where there are boar, and dogs who are poorly controlled by their owners, there is pain on both sides. Vets have reportedly had to put down injured boarlets brought into their surgeries. As for the dogs, there is one substantiated report of a death, and plenty of accounts of bloody injuries.

A dog on a lead is much less likely to come to grief. Yet boar have sometimes appeared to launch unprovoked attacks on dogs walking along minding their own business. One possible explanation for this is that they were attacked by off-lead ones in the past. The celebrated rewilding project Knepp Wildland, which uses Tamworths as substitutes for boar, sometimes has to cull pigs who turn aggressive. The suspicion of the staff is that when this happens, it's because of previous brushes with out-of-control dogs. A pig, or a boar, might absorb the following lesson from an unasked-for meeting with a dog, or after several such meetings: next time you smell *that* animal, strike first.

Still, it's a rare occurrence. And there are other times when boar, encountering either humans or humans with dogs, seem to perform their own version of a shrug. Videos posted online by Forest of Dean locals and visitors, some of them with leashed dogs in tow, show sows who barely glance towards the camera. The one thing you can always expect of boar is the unexpected. Even old hands find themselves surprised, like Neil, the photographer who first taught me how to read prints and rootings. Before we'd parted, he'd shared a story that I still think of often, like a hand closing around a token kept in the pocket.

'I was inside a plantation, and I knew there was a clearing in the middle that the sounder used, so I buried myself in a bush next to it before they arrived. And after a while the mums knew something was there. So they walked straight towards me, sniffing. It was a moment of, "Well, what can I do? I can't go anywhere." But then the mums turned away. They went to sleep and left the babies playing in the clearing. I thought, "Oh, I'm babysitting. All right." And I was there for about three hours. It was a heavenly experience. One that I doubt I'll ever repeat.'

By now, you may be wondering what all the male boar are up to while the females are busy with motherhood. The truth is that we know much less of their lives. A group, especially with babies thrown into the mix, is far easier to find and study for stretches of time than a single individual. Males are hard enough to glimpse even in a small path-riddled place like the Forest of Dean. Only once have I met one in daylight, snoozing in a bed of dead bracken when I came stumbling by. He ran away, of course.

Radio-tracking is one way to harvest data on elusive beings. Provided you can catch and collar them first. When scientists did this in eastern Europe's Białowieża Forest, where boar are less exposed to humans than perhaps anywhere else on the Continent, they found that mature males almost never associated with each other for longer than a few days at a time. This confirms the lone-ranger reputation of male boar – although it is intriguing that a small number of males maintained 'constant companionships' over the course of the two-year study.

Things get hazier when we try to focus on the time in a male's life when he leaves his mother and the sounder he was born into. The prevailing wisdom is that this occurs from around the age of eight months, and usually by the time he is one year old. There's a mix of explanations as to what triggers this. According to some researchers, it's when his mother comes into season again, summoning suitors who will not tolerate his presence. Others say that his mother drives him out when she is about to give birth again. Both claims could be right, for different boar. Perhaps some young males even choose to go, answering the call of wanderlust.

Whatever the reason, to be suddenly alone when your life up until now has been full of other boar must be a cold shock. So it's unsurprising that some males – or maybe all of them, we don't know – form what are called 'bachelor groups'. Many a scientific paper acknowledges that these groups exist, though I've yet to find one that delves into their goings-on. Nor did I expect to ever come across some bachelors myself.

That is, until I meet the Boys.

When they first turn up one April night on my trail camera by a wallow, I assume them to be just another sounder. Females and young males can be challenging to tell apart when the footage isn't sharp or the animals are moving too fast. In males, the bulge of the prepuce – the sheath of skin that protects the penis when it's off-duty – isn't always clear amid shaggy fur, while neither the tusks nor the testicles have yet achieved their full prodigiousness.

In the earliest footage of the group, two of them size each other up, before one slams head and flank against the other. The defender retaliates. Body-blows are exchanged. A third boar jumps into the fray and, with a well-placed snout under the instigator's rump, lifts his back hooves off the ground. The three then proceed to shove each other until they're off-screen, before the biggest boar of all gallops into view and gives a loud horsey gust of breath. *Break it up!*

As I replay the footage, I remember reading in Dorothy Yamamoto's *Wild Boar* that two males competing for a female will line up alongside each other to measure their opponent, before engaging if they must. That fact, combined with this being April when most females will be either heavily pregnant or with babies already in tow, clinches it: I am looking at a bachelor group.

There are five of them. They return to the wallow often after that first sighting, though they spend far more time pushing each other around than bathing. Once, their mock competition moves onto the next stage: one of them mounts another, and begins to make gentle, ineffectual thrusts. The mount-ee simply stands there, with perhaps a look of mild bemusement. A third member of the group ambles up and starts sniffing at the couple. It's all very calm and genteel.

As the species is wont to do, the Boys keep a strict schedule, always appearing between 8.43 p.m. and 9.05 p.m. at that same spot. So, one May day, I hatch a plan. It involves dressing in dark clothing and finding myself a spot behind a bush near the wallow at 8.30 p.m. (to be on the safe side).

I've chosen a fine evening. The spruce wood is on the crest of a wide hill, and with a younger plantation to the north-west, the dying sun has a path unbroken by cloud or tree. Its molten gold light gives the millions of leaves around me an exquisite metallic sharpness.

After a long stretch of quiet: a rustling of bracken.

One by one, the Boys step out. In a close clutch they swagger, they shoulder each other. They look like lads out on the town, jacked up on adolescence. We are 15m apart.

An unexpected fear gusts through me. *Can't go back now, can you?* I think to myself as the boar come closer, the dusk sun washing their fur in amber. A memory leaps into my head of a scene from the Norwegian indie film *Trollhunter*, when the human characters find themselves trapped in a cave as a pack of trolls return for the night. Why am I afraid? Is it simply because these five are male, when the only groups I've encountered before have been composed of females?

The Boys suddenly stop in their jostling. They each start to tip their snouts up and down, scenting.

All of them look in my direction.

And faster than I can say 'Oh, shit' – they're gone.

I deflate, with some relief but more disappointment. Once again I curse the fantastical olfactory powers of boar. Then something occurs to me. I raise my hand to my nostrils. And even I can tell that I reek of chlorine.

The moral of this story? If you want to spy on boar, don't go for a swim at the local leisure centre first.

———

The Boys stay together until at least early July. The last time my camera sees them as a group is the 10th. Perhaps they've moved on; perhaps they've split up; perhaps some or all of them have fallen prey to Forestry England's cull target. Of these possibilities, my money is on the first. Because around the time of their apparent departure, four females show up at the wallow with a huge male among their company. He spends all his time sniffing bottoms, foaming at the mouth, and issuing a constant stream of short grunts, which Dorothy Yamamoto calls the 'mating chant'. Whichever female is the current object of his attention replies with a creaky squeal.

You'll often see it written, usually by male authors, that male boar keep harems. But this is to give them credit that they're just not due. Sounders go about their ways as they always do. There's no gathering-together on the male's part. If anything, they are camp followers, pitching up with a sounder when one or more of the females are on heat.

They can, however, be meddlesome; Derek Harman wrote in his book about the time he witnessed a male drive all the members of a sounder away from a bait site, except for a smaller, unmated female. This allowed her to eat her fill without being shoved aside by her larger, dominant kin, who were already pregnant. Harman suspected this to be a ploy on the male's part to bring her into season faster.

The presence of a male in his prime forbids younger boar who have not yet reached his heft. My Boys, if they still live, will become sexually mature by their second year, though they may have to wait some time for the chance to pass on their genes. Yet all is not hopeless. A female may choose to mate with more than one male during her window of fertility and, in one of many of her reproductive tricks, the babies in her litter can have different fathers.

Wild boar are what scientists call *r-strategists*, because of how many offspring they can produce in one go. This is unlike *k-strategists*, who tend to invest a great deal of time and energy in just one or a few offspring. But, true to their unusual nature, boar refuse to check many of the r-strategy boxes, such as independence at birth, limited ability to learn from elders, and minimal parenting. Boar have large litters based on the probability that some offspring will be lost. And yet, their devotion is unmistakeable.

It's a paradox that still enthrals me, many months after my meetings with the Trio. The next March rolls around. One day, in the hour before dusk, I find myself climbing an abrupt hill – a spoil heap from a long-ago mine, now reclaimed by the woods. Puffing, trainers sliding, I grab hold of the spindly trunks of young birches and pines when they offer themselves. There is no deterring me. Not when the path ahead is pocked with the hoofprints of boar.

When I reach the top, I pause to regain my breath – and then hold it in.

Cupped in the dead bracken a few metres ahead is a pile of boarlets. Six little striped rumps, three stacked on three. Breathing fast in the way of small soft beings.

Above the thump of my heartbeat, I hear the babies snuffle and squeak. One of those on the top row wriggles, then gets up and turns around. This triggers much other wriggling. Her or his eyes open, in my direction. But I have made myself as still as the trees. Their eyes close again. It's hard not to interpret a contented smile in the upward tilt of their lips.

These boarlets are so very young. They haven't yet been brought into the fold of their soon-to-be-sounder. I wonder how long it will be before their mother returns. I imagine her coming upon us and halting, the bristles of her back zinging up as she realises in electric terror that a predator is standing over her offspring. I don't want to do that to her.

And so I turn to go. But it's hard to leave. I snatch a final look at the babies, these inheritors of a tenacious dynasty. The one whose face is turned towards me opens their eyes a second time. Perhaps I'll be a shadow in their next dream, an inkling of what their future may hold.

I can hear a grunting in the distance now. I steal away, trying to be as quiet as a wild boar myself. Leaving my boot prints amid the deep cloven ones of theirs.

CHAPTER FOUR

Monstrous Appetites

In March 2015 in the Forest of Dean, a pack of wild boar hunted down and tore apart a lamb.

Or at least, that's what a local vet claimed, when she witnessed a sounder eating a lamb by the roadside and reached the conclusion that the boar were responsible for the death.

One quirk of the Dean is its free-roaming sheep. While there are far fewer than there used to be, particularly since the foot-and-mouth epidemic of 2001, drivers must still take care around some of the villages. Many don't, and so sheep are sometimes killed. By cars, that is. Yet no self-respecting boar would turn their snout up at such easy protein. Even most of the online commentators on the *Daily Mail* version of the story pointed out that the lamb had almost certainly been dead when the boar found it.

Paragraphs from the *Sunday Times* article were copied and pasted into another from Scottish outlet *Deadline News* a year later, which reported that 'hordes of escaped wild boar have been killing and eating livestock across Scotland'. In 2020, *Farmers Weekly* reported on the basis of a since-deleted tweet that a huge male boar had been shot dead after killing a succession of sheep on an undisclosed Scottish farm. And most recently, a gamekeeper from Inverness-shire says he has witnessed multiple attacks on sheep on the estate he works for. '"Once they've got them on their backs they'll use their tusks to open their stomach up and get at the soft content. We have actually seen this happening"', he is quoted as saying in the *Sunday Post* in January 2022.

I email Patrick Laurie, a Galloway farmer, writer and fellow boar fan, about the reports. My message is one big eye-roll in word form. The reports are preposterous to me. In the Forest of Dean, no one save the vet has claimed to have seen any of the free-roaming sheep – who are highly accessible to the boar – being attacked or feasted upon. And if farmers and others in Scotland have seen these attacks multiple times, why is it that no one has been able to capture it, either in person or with trail cameras left in the fields? The Scottish government wouldn't be able to ignore footage, if any emerged.

Patrick comes back with one of his typically considered replies. 'It seems unlikely that boar are killing fit and healthy sheep ... still, just because I've never seen it happening doesn't mean [they] haven't seen it or something like it. Even the worst stuff that gets blown out of all proportion often had something true at the start of it. From what I've seen of this kind of comment on everything from hen harriers to badgers, if people are feeling disempowered, they're inclined to get excited. And nothing pours fuel on the fire like when farmers and keepers are told "there is no problem".'

Looming unmentioned behind Patrick's words is the case of the white-tailed eagle. This scavenger-predator was successfully returned to Britain in one of our earliest reintroduction projects, starting in 1975. According to conservationist Hugh Webster, Scottish sheep farmers were assured that the eagles would not kill their lambs, based on experiences from Norway. Only that hasn't proved to be so over here. Most of the lamb flesh that disappears down the eagles' gullets comes from animals who have already died of other causes. But not always. The resulting arguments between farmers and those who scoff at them continue to pump venom into the rewilding debate in Scotland. So I must not dismiss out of hand what people claim to have seen the boar do.

By design the species is not, unlike the white-tailed eagle, an obligate carnivore. But we've long bestowed the wild boar with a predatory air. In woodcuts, paintings and tapestries from the Middle Ages, they often look more wolf than pig. Their frames are muscular, eyes narrowed, their fang-like tusks long and gleaming, mouths open, lips curled in silent snarls.

Even contemporary scientist Marc Bracke has remarked on the parallels between wild boar and wolves, with their scent-marking, nest-making, large litters and vulnerable newborns (there's that odd fusion of r- and k-strategies again). Meanwhile, anthropologist João Pedro Galhano Alves reports that in Montesinho Natural Park in Portugal, some locals are convinced that boar hunt and eat wolf pups.

Fears and beliefs around the bloodthirsty nature of wild boar extend to our own bodies. To an extent, this is rational. There are documented cases where people who have collapsed in pig pens after a stroke or heart attack have then been bitten and died from blood loss. During one of my 2014 interviews, a horse rider expressed her terror to me that one day a similar fate might befall her. 'I had an accident a few years ago, and I was unconscious for about an hour. If that happened now, and the boar came across me unconscious, would they eat me? Very probably. Or what if I came off the horse with a broken leg and couldn't get away from them?'

Perhaps she still held fresh in her mind a news story from Wales, just two months before. Burglars had targeted a wild boar farm. As well as killing a few youngsters by cutting their throats and bludgeoning them with hammers, the men allowed 23 adults to escape. The farmer, Greg Davies, provided an irresistible quote to the press: 'They will attack if they smell blood.'

While it's amusing to picture wild boar as furry land-sharks roving the woods of Bridgend, the way such stories are reported is damaging to attempts to calm the worries of people who live with wild boar, or could do so in the future. The British media exhibits its own kind of ecological boredom when it writes up these gleeful clickbait pieces. We don't have bears or lions or hippos, while incidences of foxes wandering into London homes are inconveniently rare. Our journalists work with what they've got and, in doing so, they help to keep the wheel of *zoophobia* – the fear of other animals – spinning.

It doesn't help that our brains are primed to notice and cling to gory details, even at the risk of misremembering. This is illustrated to me when I am out one fine January day on an organised group hike in the Cotswolds. After mentioning that I'm writing a book about wild boar, I find myself entertained and horrified in equal measure when a man asks me, 'Didn't someone get their arm torn off by one in the Forest of Dean?'

It takes me a few seconds to work out the case he is referring to: that of Clive Lilley. In 2018, Lilley was walking his Labrador off-lead in the Dean when a big boar burst from the bracken and jumped up to bite his finger. The boar then vanished as quickly as they'd appeared. Lilley felt little pain until he took his hand out of his glove – and the pad of his finger stayed inside it.

He had the pad sewn back on in hospital. A few news articles can be found that include a photo prior to surgery. For a small wound, it is impressively gory.

'Oh. Yeah, that was it,' my fellow hiker replies when I clarify that it was a finger pad, not an arm. He sounds just a tad disappointed. To be fair to him, papers including *The Independent,* the *Daily Mail* and *The Sun* had gone a bit over the top with the story, opting for headlines riffing on the theme of 'man loses whole finger'.

Add up these kinds of reports with the ones about attacks on dogs, plus accepted wisdom on the gluttony and omnivory of pigs, and it's no surprise that some people imagine our weak and unarmoured bodies pose an irresistible temptation to the boar. Yet the hard facts are these: in the 30-odd years since the return of boar to Great Britain, no photographic evidence has emerged for their hunting down other animals, and no human has found themselves being chewed on. Our wild boar have not, contrary to excitable claims, undergone an accelerated evolution into active and cooperating hunters.

But wild boar *do* eat other animals. They've been recorded eating mammals, birds, reptiles, amphibians, fish, crustaceans,

molluscs, insects, earthworms and a multitude of other
invertebrates. What concerns most people is whether and
how often these creatures may be alive when they are eaten.
And do boar put *effort* into catching them?

Researchers at the University of California think so.
They found a range of species in the stomachs of feral boar
shot in the Diablo Range in California. They suspected that
at least some animals had fallen victim when boar came
upon them on the ground – or actively hunted them down.
Over in Europe, the jury is still out as to how much of the
flesh that boar consume is carrion. It's simply impossible to
tell this from analysing stomach contents. So perhaps the
California scientists were too quick to jump to their
conclusions. But it's also possible that the dietary preferences
and behaviour of boar in North America, where they are
invasive and far more hybridised with farmed pigs, have
diverged from those of European ones. Such dramatic
changes have been witnessed in other species that have
found themselves in alien ecosystems. On Gough Island in
the South Atlantic, for example, house mice have taken to
eating albatross chicks alive. Wild boar are renowned for
their adaptability and it seems inevitable that, as they spread
across the world with our help, different groups will come
to live out their lives in different ways. At the Rewilding
Coombeshead project in Devon, the resident boar have yet
to be seen dining on the flesh-tattered bones dropped from
the sky tables laid out for raptors to feast from. Over in
Serbia, an ethnography of free-roaming pigs and their
herders reported that different herds don't always eat the
same things, nor in the same quantities. 'Some of my pigs
eat mushrooms, others don't; they learn which mushrooms
are edible from other herd members,' according to one
svinjar (the Serbian term for keeper).

That sounds like cultural preference.

Could this be the reason behind the reports of sheep-
killing in Scotland? I must allow the possibility that a few

boar there have expanded the carnivore side of their diet. Some time after my email to Patrick Laurie, I am sent the audio from the interview with the Inverness-shire gamekeeper by the author of the *Sunday Post* article, Richard Baynes. The gamekeeper describes seeing three boar attacking the ewe in the corner of the field. How he shot one of the boar, scaring the other two off into the trees. And how he had to dispatch the ewe, who was still alive.

He didn't see them flip her onto her back, and I still find myself suspecting that some illness had already struck her down when those three boar found her. But it remains an unnerving tale.

Wild boar are certainly known to take smaller animals. Peter Wohlleben, forest scientist and author of *The Hidden Life of Trees*, has observed boar in Germany quartering spring meadows in search of newborn roe deer. Research elsewhere in Europe substantiates their sometimes-predatory behaviour. In Estonia, remains of adult capercaillie have been found in wild boar droppings, and it's suspected that at least some of these were taken while they sat on their nests. In Belgium, scientists counting populations of common European adder found their original plans going out the window when boar began to encroach on their sites and eat the reptiles; within 10 years, boar triggered the drastic decline or total extinction of most adder populations in the south of the country.

In comparison to the surfeit of studies from the Continent, only one of the few conducted in Great Britain has focused on animals that the boar may be eating. Between 2009 and 2012 in East Sussex, researchers counted how many hazel dormice or dormice nests they found in the boxes they'd put out in several woods visited by boar. They concluded that the boar had a significant negative effect on dormice, perhaps by snaffling them up as they hibernated at ground level over winter. However, the team didn't seek out direct evidence of dormice being eaten, and their methodology was highly flawed. For example, most of the sites they used to provide a proxy baseline for healthy numbers of dormice were managed by the Woodland Trust or Kent Wildlife Trust, and were in the National Dormouse Monitoring Programme. This is in contrast to the boar-ish sites, which had received no such care nor protection (indeed, two of those sites were lost to clear-felling). As a result, the only thing this study can confidently tell us is that the presence of boar did not actively benefit dormice. We really do need better science than this.

Over in the Forest of Dean, anecdotes and conjecture are all we have. For some species, this place is one of their last great refuges in Britain, offering enough intact habitat to hopefully ward off inbreeding and random disasters like disease. Such is the case of the common European adder. Like all other reptiles we're lucky enough to have in this country, they go into brumation (a milder version of hibernation) during the colder months, often congregating in groups. Their torpor leaves them vulnerable to, say, an omnivorous animal who regularly ploughs the ground. Echoing the case from Belgium, a herpetologist (AKA reptile specialist) in the Dean once described visiting a hibernacula that had clearly been dug up by boar, with scattered pieces of adder left to tell the tale.

As for the ground-nesting birds in the area, there is no bloody evidence, and it isn't inevitable that they or their eggs will fall prey. On the contrary, Benedict Macdonald has noted that boar can be a boon to them, by creating the soil structures they prefer for nesting and by suppressing numbers of rodents. Local naturalist and long-time resident Ed Drewitt tells me that the nightjar, one such ground-nesting bird, continues to do well in the Dean. An enigmatic summer migrant with the colouring and patterning of leaf litter, the nightjar went into sharp decline between the 1960s and 1980s. The population has since increased in some areas, although ornithologists still monitor it nervously. Some nightjar nesting areas in the

Dean are fenced, though the birds also tend to prefer dry, acidic soils, which the boar do not. It's on a chilly June night in an unfenced area of the RSPB's Nagshead reserve in the Dean that I hear my first nightjar, that call described as 'churring'; if you quickly say *choor choor choor choor choor* in a whispery voice then you're starting to inch towards mimicking that otherworldly sound.

The nightjars return to Nagshead every year. The reserve's adder population is stable too. But the warden who leads my nightjar-listening group is glum about this bird's future in the Dean. Forestry England is shifting to a policy of 'continuous cover', meaning that most of the conifer and broadleaved plantations will from now on be thinned instead of clear-felled. Many local people detest the violent bareness of areas stripped entirely of mature trees. But in the first few years before shrubs and new trees finish taking over, these areas provide the kind of habitat that nesting nightjars and other birds like woodcock can't do without. There are a few spots in the Dean maintained as open heathland, but these alone won't be enough. Nightjars will dwindle. I predict that when this happens, some will blame the boar. They already do in the case of other declines; one resident I spoke to in 2014 and again in 2022 remains convinced that boar are eating all the hedgehogs. Data for this species' numbers in the Dean is lacking. Yet, if hedgehog numbers are dropping here, this only mirrors the freefall across the British countryside. We must be wary of correlations, especially when Britain has so many downward trends in wildlife for us to choose from.

It *is* possible that boar are helping us to speed a few creatures in the Dean towards the void. Local depletions of species are a ceaseless fact of life in any ecosystem. In those ecosystems that are healthy and unfragmented, it's usually just a case of waiting for other members of the species to come along to boost the ranks. But in Britain today, many species cannot cross the deserts we've carved out between their remaining islands of habitat. And these islands themselves are being gnawed at from both the outside and the inside by our activities – development, pesticides, water pollution, air pollution, light pollution, climate breakdown, the list goes on.

As for the Dean, the deadliest predator is not, as some would have it, the boar.

'The real predator in the forest is your untrained domestic dog. [They'll attack] sheep, ground-nesting birds, a range of animals,' Kevin Stannard, Forestry England's boss for west England, tells me. In which case, if more people keep their dogs on leads because of the risk of conflict with boar, this could have a knock-on benefit for wildlife.

Even so, an argument could be made that we should exterminate boar from the Dean and elsewhere, if we consider these locations to be arks keeping rare species safe until we get our act together. But I'm not optimistic that there is still time for some of our most threatened wildlife. And I fear that by removing a single nonhuman pressure in order to delay the loss of a few species as a result of the many human pressures on them, we would deny the potential of the boar to help a greater number of species. That their re-absence would mean less life – not more.

In a way, it seems bold to argue that although wild boar eat many other animals, they more than make up for this in other ways. To tear into flesh that may still be alive is an act whose consequences are immediate and measurable. This particular creature was here; now it isn't.

We must, however, keep in mind one important fact: in their native range, 90 per cent of the average wild boar's diet is plant- and fungi-based. To fixate on the few gory moments is to lose sight of what boar spend most of their time doing. Because, although the results are often slower and far less obvious to human eyes, what boar eat, and where and how, can together act as engines of creation.

And it all starts in the soil.

Before I meet the Trio, and well before they give birth, I see the choices they've made in their woodland foraging.

It begins in February, when the wood feels poised at the top of spring's rollercoaster. I've found so few rootings here until now that when I come across the first fresh lot of them, I take my time. The opened soil at my feet is dark and rich with moisture. When I press a hand to it and dig in my fingers, it has the consistency of butter-and-oat crumble ready to go on the apples. Left in the small craters are what must be young shoots of bluebell. Most are missing their bulbs, the ends snipped neatly off. They look like so many spent white-and-green matchsticks.

The Trio knew where to dig thanks to their sense of smell, one of the finest among mammals. They begin to hone it in the womb, their unborn brains learning to recognise from their mothers what is good to eat, just as unhatched chicks learn the sound of their parents' voices. And so the offspring of the Trio seem set to acquire quite the taste for bluebells.

Chiffchaffs and song thrushes mark the further unfurling of spring in the wood. The tips of the bluebells come poking through the earth. Walking among the latest rootings left by the Trio, I see they've switched to favouring the green lengths of the shoots instead.

Wild garlic is emerging too. The lush velvet of its dark-green leaves furnishes great swathes of the wood, more of it than I'd ever imagined would come up. I expect the boar will go wild for this other bounty. And yet, the craters always stop at the garlic border; neither leaf nor bulb is ever touched. I leave them too, but only until the day that I think the leaves are ready. I pluck one and pop it into my mouth. At first, there's only a wet crunch. Then flavour blooms and burns across my tongue. Perhaps the smell and the taste, beguiling to me with my dull, human senses, is *too much* for the boar. Indeed, the sulphurous compounds found in members of the garlic family have been shown to dissuade both insects and birds such as starlings.

Whatever the reason the Trio eschew the wild garlic, I'm grateful that I don't have to compete with them. Where I'm crouched, filling a bag with the leaves I manage not to eat straight away, I can see where the boar have foraged for bluebells in the last few nights. There's a deep satisfaction, a kinship, in knowing we have both feasted here. That the same place is nurturing all our bodies.

When the flowers of the bluebells open at last, they make a sea out of the woodland floor. Every tree is marooned. I thought the wild garlic was rampant, but this astounds me. While the Forest of Dean is known for its bluebell displays, my wood has somehow remained a secret. I still hardly ever see anyone in it. People would flock if they knew. And they might be surprised to learn how extensively the woodland floor had been rooted before the bluebells bloomed.

Some pro-boar people claim that boar don't eat bluebells at all, rather that they're attracted to the soil in which the wildflowers grow, because it tends to be less disturbed by humans and is richer with life as a result. I've even heard that bluebells are poisonous to boar. But my Trio, filling their stomachs as the next generation grows in their wombs, seem to do just fine.

Others argue that bluebells are more resilient to being eaten than we might expect. Scientists have found that uneaten bluebells and other geophytes – plants that store energy and water in an underground organ, be that a bulb, a tuber, a corm or a rhizome – can recover from the upheaval of rooting. In fact, belowground disturbance by wild boar seems able to benefit them. In studies of patches rooted by boar, the seeds of geophytes germinated more. Meanwhile, the storage organs that weren't eaten often ended up getting *bigger*, which enabled them to propagate themselves with greater success.

How geophytes respond in this way remains a mystery, although there are currently two main theories. The first is that the consumption of some plants means there are more soil nutrients left lying around for the survivors to snatch up. The second is that the geophytes are accessing nutrients that have become more abundant not because of what the boar remove but because of the rooting itself. For in the act of their foraging, boar loosen, expose and *mix* earth. Different strata of plant debris and soil, once lying on top of one another, find themselves suddenly combined. This upheaval changes the dances of nutrients and minerals within, of microbes and microinvertebrates and the webbings of mycorrhizal fungi. Although rooting can introduce so-called 'cold spots' from the deeper, less life-filled layers, folding in the rich leaf litter acts the other way. Beech trees have been found to grow better in such soil. It's little wonder, really. Boar have been rooting in their native landscapes for so long that it's inevitable that other species have learned to live with them and, in many cases, to capitalise on the changes left in their wake. The thriving of geophytes thanks to wild boar may in turn be one reason boar often return to patches that they or others of their kind have already rooted recently – not only is the food cupboard replenishing itself, but the contents may be actively multiplying.

———

During spring, and other wetter times, the damp ground yields to snouts with ease. When conditions are drier and the ground is harder, wild boar turn to grazing more on what they find above it, including the leaves and stems of grasses. Then, when autumn finally comes around, so does the feasting: fruit, mushrooms, nuts, beechmast and, of course, acorns.

For millions of years, oak and other broadleaved trees like beech have weathered the taking of their seeds, also known as mast. These trees' shared habit of producing great gluts of it every few years, in what is called a mast year, has been shaped by the desires of boar and other animals. It's a clever strategy: produce more seed than can be eaten in some years, and make the thieves go hungry in others, ensuring there are fewer of them around the next time you invest so much in your seeds. My move to the Forest of Dean is well timed to see this for myself. In autumn 2021, there are almost no acorns. The following autumn, the woods are filled with the endless erratic drumbeats of their falls.

The seeds are packed with proteins and sugars. Ideal to help a young boar grow, to restore a male after the rigours of mating, to nurture a female's growing foetuses or to enrich her milk as urgent mouths tug. Boar seem to have a hunger for acorns beyond that of any other creature, even to the point of locating and raiding the caches of others; wood mice often find themselves so robbed, another way in which boar may act to rein in their populations.

In Britain, the long-entwined history of oak and boar survived even the extirpation of the latter. During pannage, farmed pigs continued to be herded through remaining woodlands to feast on acorns. It fattened the pigs, and protected horses and cattle, to whom acorns are toxic. Boar apparently get around this problem by spitting out the skins.

Pannage has by now all but ended in our country. It held out in the Forest of Dean up to the 1970s, meaning that some of this land was bereft of porcine snouts for just 30 years. The practice continues in the New Forest, where a few hundred pigs are turned out for a few months each year. Strangely, tourism partnership Go New Forest states on their website that rings are put through the free-roaming pigs' noses as this 'stops them from rooting into the ground with their snouts[,] causing damage to the Forest'. I can only frown at the use of the word *damage* to describe something that boar have been doing in our forests for millennia. Indeed, setting the pigs loose for a few months and then removing them for another period would provide a crude version of the dynamic that our ecosystems are designed to run on; before humans turned to farming and fencing, we and many other powerful animals moved through the landscape in a restless cycle, disturbing without devastating. Like breathing on a fire to renew the flames, without blowing it out.

When I walk in the Forest of Dean, I'll sometimes find an oak seedling growing out of earth that has been rooted by boar in the not-so-distant past. In sunlight, the green of its first leaves looks angelically bright. The picture seems almost too calculated, like an advertising campaign for the benefits of boar. One perhaps engineered by a jay who thought that that friable-looking patch of soil would be the *perfect* spot for an acorn.

Yet, as narratively pleasing as it feels to see those seedlings, I can never help wondering if a boar is going to come along at some point and, given their habit of returning to certain patches, uproot the little oaks – cancelling out their original good deed.

Jays are known to pull up oak seedlings they once planted, in order to harvest the remnant acorn or the first, tender leaves. Sometimes they'll even place the seedling back into the soil afterwards. Many oaks treated in this way manage to survive, according to rewilding ecologist Frans Vera, who has found that young trees sometimes show scarring from this bird–tree rite of passage. Do jays plant acorns in the knowledge that doing so may lead to the emergence of a seedling? It seems feasible that they can put two and two together and therefore plan to leave some acorns to grow. In which case, the rooting of a boar has the potential to be meddlesome indeed.

But there's another twist in this tale. By rooting, and by dispersing seeds in their fur, hooves and droppings, boar are conjurers of bramble and other scrub. At Knepp, the flourishing of scrub thanks to the Tamworth pigs is thought to have provided new and vital landscape markers that encourage jays to plant acorns close to or within the prickly embrace of the plants. A side-effect of this is that when the seedlings emerge, they find themselves protected. Knepp's owner, Isabella Tree, reminds us in her book *Wilding* of an old forester adage: 'The thorn is the mother of the oak'. Indeed, a study into the survival of holm oak seedlings in boar hotspots in Spain found that those planted under scrub fared far better than those in the open or under other trees. Yet the possibility that some of this scrub came about thanks in part to the boar went unmentioned by the researchers.

———

Even if plants are slow to return to a particular rooted patch, or a boar returns for another feast, bare ground itself can help to kindle life too. It's easy to see how the birds benefit. But so do insects. British conservationists sometimes clear foliage to create habitat for ground-nesting bees and wasps. In other words, they're pretending to be boar. Bared earth offers space and building material. It also heats up more than the surrounding vegetation, generating microclimates. Researchers in Italy investigated the importance of boar rootings to an endangered butterfly called the Italian Festoon. The host plants of this butterfly are pioneers that thrive where boar have been. Yet having bare ground alongside them is, it turns out, necessary too; the empty space helps the weak-flying Italian Festoon reach the plants to lay her eggs. It also lets the sun in, whose tender warmth nurtures those eggs and the larvae that hatch from them.

Isabella Tree writes of the chain reactions she observed after Tamworth pigs were brought to Knepp. Among the pigs' rootings in damp areas, sallow grew thick. Being the most important food plant of the caterpillars of purple emperor butterflies, the tree's flourishing triggered an eruption of the butterflies that still shows no sign of petering out. Meanwhile, in Knepp's drier places, ants used the bared and loosened clods to build new anthills, which provided basking spots for the small copper butterfly and the common lizard, sheltered the eggs of grasshoppers, and nurtured fungi, lichens, mosses and other plants that could never have thrived on the surrounding acid grassland. Who knows what other connections there might so far have gone unnoticed?

Go to the Forest of Dean in warmer months, and the first animal you see may well be a dor beetle scuttling across the path. Or 20 of them at a time. Coated in a shiny black that reveals a secret iridescence from certain angles, and big enough to have a face that human eyes can study at leisure, dor beetles are no less magnificent for the sheer abundance of their kind. They also lack the indifference that many insects seem to have towards us; stop to peer down at a dor, and often they will stop and stare back at you.

They are a species of dung beetle. They love droppings and in the Dean seem to go particularly mad for boar poo. I've never seen them tackling horse or sheep poo. When in more curious moods, I find it satisfying to take a twig and flip over a moist-looking pile of boar droppings. No matter how fresh they look, there'll always be at least a few boreholes visible on the undersides: the calling cards of insects primed to set upon dung as soon as it has landed.

My prize find to date remains a scatter of droppings of stupendous size, surrounded by a crew of minotaur beetles busily carving them up and digging deep burrows beside them. I didn't actually know the name of the species until I looked online for 'big black dung beetle three horns' afterwards. I learned from the same search that the burrows may have gone down as far as a metre.

With their three sharp forward-facing horns, minotaur beetles are the triceratops of the insect world. Although found across England and Wales, they're considered to be scarce. Boar droppings are a windfall for them, while they and other dung beetles are in turn a windfall for birds and bats. The tunnels they dig allow more air, nutrients and water to penetrate down through the soil. And by hurrying the droppings into the soil along with their eggs, the beetles ensure that the contents of those droppings are delivered more quickly and effectively than if they'd been left sitting aboveground.

But what, I hear you ask, are those contents?

What goes into the mouths of boar is the subject of intense scrutiny and debate. But what comes out of their bottoms has been very much neglected. I myself am guilty of this. At least, I was until early 2021. I was studying for a second master's degree, this time in wildlife conservation, and I once again had need of a dissertation topic.

My conversation with one of the professors on the course went something like this:

'Mark,' I said, 'I really, really want to do something around wild boar. A field project. Not a desk-based project. Do you have any suggestions?'

Mark replied, 'Well, one of the things that interests me most about boar is what they're dispersing in their droppings. But I know investigating that isn't everyone's idea of a good time—'

'SAY NO MORE.'

Mark went on to explain that it might be worth looking for mycorrhizal fungal spores and oribatid mites in the droppings. I was familiar with mycorrhizal fungi. These organisms are essential to the thriving of 90 per cent of plants on Earth, including trees; by sending out the threads of their mycelia through the soil to bind with roots, mycorrhizal fungi weave entire underground networks that connect a multitude of individual plants. Trees require these partnerships to obtain otherwise unobtainable nutrients from the earth, and perhaps to exchange vital information and resources with other trees.[3]

But I'd never heard of oribatid mites.

If you find yourself walking over healthy soil, then beneath every step you take, an unnoticed community of creatures are hatching, moulting, foraging, hunting, breeding, dying. A square mile of Serengeti within every boot print. This community is formed of an incomprehensible variety of microarthropods, from springtails to soil mites. And oribatid mites, many of which are nearly or completely impossible to spot with the naked human eye, are the most abundant of all the soil mites. Across the world, countless numbers of them are chomping their way through fungi and dead plant matter, playing a crucial role in the creation and enrichment of soil. Our lives would be very different without them – if we could still exist at all.

But oribatids, like many other mites, are slow, slow things. Which means it's likely that they use other species to taxi them to pastures new. They rely on *phoresy* – the beautiful name given for when one organism (inadvertently) provides a dispersal service to another. Dispersal is essential to the survival of species, and part of what makes ecosystems tick. It enables a species to colonise or recolonise more places, and to swap genes to increase genetic diversity – all of which reduce the risk of extinction.

It's already well established that wild boar can disperse organisms on their bodies. Seeds can become temporarily wedged between their hooves, while their shaggy and

---

[3] I say 'perhaps' because in February 2023, the journal *Nature Ecology and Evolution* published a critique of the widely popularised hypothesis that trees deliberately help each other out via their fungal networks.

bristled pelage acts almost like Velcro. When scientists on the Continent have brushed seeds off boar and deer shot during hunts, boar have emerged as clear winners when it comes to the number and diversity of plant species represented. Simply, no other British animal has fur like theirs.[4]

It is also already known that the guts of boar present an alternative means of travel to seeds and fungal spores. So my professor's suggestion to include the spores in my own project was mainly to give me a positive finding to crow about if the real goal turned out to be a dud: could oribatid mites, as animals rather than fungi, pass through the digestive tract of a wild boar and come out the other end alive to tell the tale?

No one had investigated it yet, for terrestrial organisms at least. The sheer abundance of oribatids relative to other soil mites meant it made sense to focus on them; if mites were making it through the boar, I could reasonably expect most of these to be oribatids. With my study design planned out, all that was left for me to do was to go out into the Forest of Dean and collect lots of fresh boar droppings. Simple!

Reader, it was not simple.

First, my supervisor and I had to convince the university's health and safety people that I was not going to kill myself or anyone else through close contact with the poo and the hellscape of diseases and parasites it might contain. After a prolonged tennis match of emails and risk assessment amendments, I got the all-clear. But the length of the permission process had eaten into the slice of time I'd put aside for my fieldwork, leaving me with just a week and a half to hare around the forest.

At this point, I hadn't moved there yet. It was the first time I'd been back since 2014. I shouldn't have left it so long,

---

[4] Hygiene habits also play a part; roe deer have a cat-like urge to groom regularly, combing themselves down with their teeth. This means seeds have much less chance of hitching a long-distance lift.

and now I didn't even have time to appreciate it, because my one and only goal in life at that moment was to find boar poo. Each morning I woke at the crack of dawn to drive from Bristol to one of my earmarked locations. With it being high summer, the Dean was packed with people, but I rarely saw anyone else. I was too busy plunging down trails pocked with boar prints, pushing through bracken and into young conifer plantations where a traffic of hooves had left clear roads through carpets of moss. My eyes stayed fixed on the ground; even if I'd passed an actual boar, I probably would've missed them.

I became an apprentice of what naturalist Polly Pullar calls 'turdology'. Before they dry and fall apart, fresh boar droppings can be of prodigious size, with an almost brain-like texturing of folds. There's no mistaking them for the smaller pellets left by fallow, roe or muntjac deer, which I often found sprinkled around the boar droppings.

The trouble was that most of what I found was too dry and old. Any live and mobile mites would've already escaped from these. They were useless to me.

'You don't tend to see a huge amount of boar poo around the forest because the dung beetles are so good at getting rid of it,' Ed Drewitt will later remark to me when I reminisce about my struggle. And indeed, I had to steal one of the few fresh samples that I did collect from right under the scrabbling legs of a dor beetle. Despite the guilt, I was consoled by the knowledge that they would have a much easier time than I would of tracking down more droppings.

In fact, dung beetles love boar poo so much that they don't necessarily care if it has been pickled in alcohol. I discovered this during the control part of my study. This involved putting a portion cut from each sample into a life-killing 70 per cent ethanol bath, then taking it back to its collection site and putting it on the ground for an hour. The idea was that if I found any mites in the control samples afterwards, it meant they could have burrowed into the poo instead of already being inside it when it exited the boar.

Each time, I sat on the forest floor near the sample, and read a book. On one occasion, sticking close turned out to be a good decision, because it wasn't long before two dor beetles arrived out of nowhere and descended upon the precious poo. I had to keep nudging them away with twigs.

In the end, I only found a total of six fresh-enough samples. At the university lab after each collection, every new technician greeted me with, '*Oh*, you're Boar Poo Girl!'

To extract the tiny spores of mycorrhizal fungi, I shook a portion of each sample in water, then passed the resulting solution through a series of ultra-fine meshes. When the captured detritus went under the microscope, I could count the spores. Unsurprisingly, there were plenty.

The same extraction process wouldn't work for the soil mite part of my study, because the point was to determine whether any such animals in the droppings could *survive* passing through a boar. I needed to make them come out of the droppings under their own steam. Taking a method more commonly used for coaxing microarthropods out of soil, I placed a light bulb above each of my samples. The idea is that the growing heat and dryness forces any animal capable of movement to flee downwards until it plops into a flask of ethanol waiting below.

My first sample yielded … nothing. No need to panic, yet. I suspected I'd used too much poo, over too short a timescale, giving little chance for anything to escape. And a few days later, when I eyeballed the beaker of ethanol beneath the second, smaller sample, *something* was visible. No more than 2mm across. The microscope fully revealed it.

Bathed in light, the creature looked as if made of hammered bronze. Even in death, long and many-jointed legs curled with predatory poise. They were not an oribatid. They were a hunter of them instead, from the Mesostigmata order of soil mites. Those spidery legs were one mark of their killing trade; how easy it was to imagine this beast chasing down prey in the jungle realm between leaf litter and soil. An emissary from a world that I was glad to have learned of.

When I move to the Dean a few months later, doubts keep niggling at me that there's an alternative explanation for the Mesostigmata mite I found, as well as the several other mites and springtails that turned up in later samples. What if there'd been fragments of soil stuck to the dung that I hadn't noticed, and the microarthropods had come out of that instead?

And so I repeat the experiment at home.[5] Getting the kit together is easy: a fine-meshed flat kitchen sieve, a bottle of 70 per cent ethanol from a specialist website, and a desk lamp. The wild boar poo is, of course, free. By now I know all the best places to gather it. Also, since it's winter, I'm no longer in competition with the dung beetles.

I give my long-suffering housemate firm instructions not to disturb my apparatus, and construct a cardboard barrier to prevent meddling by his two cats. Then I wait.

This time … still no oribatid mites. But I find other soil mites, including a kind I haven't seen before, possibly from the Astigmatina order. And the crucial point is that I took care to shave off all the edges of the dung before it went under the lightbulb.

These animals were swallowed by wild boar, and intact enough after the travails of a mammalian digestive tract to crawl away afterwards. To say they impress me is an understatement.

---

[5] You have no power here, university health and safety people!

I didn't have enough confidence in the findings from my dissertation to try submitting a paper to a scientific journal. And so you can only take my word for all this. However, recall earlier that I said no one had determined whether *terrestrial* organisms could be dispersed by boar via internal means. In a study described in the peer-reviewed journal *Freshwater Biology* in 2008, scientists investigated whether boar were capable of dispersing aquatic organisms. The research was done in the Camargue, where aquatic plants likely form a substantial share of the local wild boar diet, meaning the boar could be engulfing a variety of creatures living around those plants. The scientists collected dung and dropped it into tanks of water to see what hatched. Quite a lot did, as it turned out, including rotifers and copepods. It was only half as much as what hatched out of the mud rubbed onto trees by boar in the same area, but even so – the eggs of a variety of species made it through the mammals. It's logical to assume that the eggs of soil mites and other land-based creatures might also survive this journey. There would be no way to find this out using my extraction method, however, because eggs don't have legs.

From a short-term point of view, boar are bad news for soil microarthropods and mycorrhizal fungi (and perhaps those aquatic critters in the Camargue). Rooting can trigger drops in local mite populations. As for the fungi, boar devour their fruiting bodies, while the ploughing of the soil can macerate plant roots and fungal filaments alike.

But the changes that can occur in the soil after rooting by boar may, in the longer term, benefit its animal denizens as well as its plant ones. A study carried out in Poland into the soil impacts of badgers – who can act something like mini-boar in their digging – found that oribatid mite populations recovered after several years. What's more, some of the sites that had been disturbed five years earlier were even richer in mite species than completely undisturbed sites. Provided the soil is allowed to lie fallow for long enough, boar rooting could surely lead to similar results.

And there is the other ecological pay-off, in the form of phoresy. The fact that some mycorrhizal fungi appear to deliberately lure boar with the scent of their fruiting bodies is hint enough that being eaten can be a good thing. Some plant seeds need to journey through an animal's digestive tract in order to germinate. Likewise, some fungal spores find their infectivity – their ability to bond with the root of a plant – much improved if they pass through a boar first. When I extracted spores from the droppings during my master's project, I put a few under a more powerful compound microscope. Their walls were bumpier and thinner than you'd normally expect to see with such spores, but this chimed with a study from Italy in which truffles were fed to a pig, and the spores later taken from the droppings to be closely analysed. Their surfaces were found to have become thinner and rougher in structure. Most importantly, far more of them went on to germinate and generate connections with plants than the control spores that hadn't been eaten.

Wild boar (or Uber boar, if you will) aren't the only animals in Great Britain able to provide a taxi service to smaller organisms. But what's unique about them is how far they can go – and where. Over a day or a night they might travel up to 7km, or much further in certain cases. They also tend to be less discriminating than other species about the places they pass through or in which they feed or rest. This might include habitat that ecologists would call degraded, such as exhausted farmland, or forest clear-cuts. But it might also include places where other species have wiped the slate clean, such as beaver meadows, which are abandoned beaver pools that have dried up and filled with soil. These habitats aren't degraded in the same way as places we've chosen to devastate, but they may share a similar lack of mycorrhizal fungi and mites. And with this absence of key soil organisms, the recovery or succession of plantlife aboveground may be achingly slow.

Unless there are boar about. Wherever they go, I imagine they leave sounds in their wake that only the smallest of creatures can detect: a rain of seeds from wiry coats, and a manna of droppings that hold new promises of life.

Wild boar are bringers of ends and beginnings. In feeding themselves, they feed others – or create necessary conditions for others to live. A deft composition of death and renewal, though one that we are now overwriting. Boar can be a burden in ecosystems we are stripping away, in part because it is now so much harder for species to move between places and keep the flames of their existence burning in each. Yet it also seems likely that our returned boar are ferrying a host of life-making organisms across distances they could never go on their own. And in doing so, the boar may be helping to restitch connections we never even noticed we had cut.

CHAPTER FIVE

Re-Rooting

There is nothing else like a boar among British fauna.

Badgers are perhaps the closest thing, purveyors of their own brand of rooting. But they rarely peel open sprawling patches in the way that boar do, and they don't go as deep. Nor do they roam nearly so far, curtailing their ability to disperse other organisms.

And so, given all we know about the ways in which wild boar help to alter the destinies of other species and of entire ecosystems, it's no wonder that rewilders are slotting pigs as boar substitutes into landscape restoration projects up and down the country. Heritage breeds of pig like the ginger, short-haired Tamworth or the sheepy Mangalitsa can be worthy understudies. And I will go to see their work for myself. But for my first forays out of the Dean to see what wild boar can do for rewilding, it's the boar themselves that I want.

Hence I find myself boarding a bus in Inverness one chilly wet February morning in 2022. We pull free of the city's traffic lights and turn left to follow the shoreline of Loch Ness. Long black lines sometimes appear on its calm surface, as if sinewy beasts slink just beneath. Beyond the loch, low clouds have skimmed off the tops of the hills.

I disembark in Drumnadrochit, a village crammed with shops and cafes all displaying images of the Loch Ness Monster in its various reptilian forms. Most places are shut for the off-season and the village has a ghost-town air.

In a car park I locate Scott Hendry, one of the rangers at the nearby Bunloit Estate. Bought by a company called Highlands Rewilding in 2020, and formerly worked for forestry and game shooting, the 513-hectare estate has now embarked on a new journey. I found out about it through a blog post of Scott's celebrating the boar, who have been resident here for 15 years already. Their presence makes

Bunloit most unusual among British rewilding projects, which normally start with a boar-shaped hole and fill it with a pig. Bunloit turned out to have no need for this.

Scott drives us out of Drumnadrochit and up a steep hill. We pass a hand-painted sign saying, 'SLOW DOWN FOR FOX SAKE'. A Highlands native in his early 30s, Scott speaks with a strong burr as he tells me more about the birth of Bunloit and its ethos. Before anything was done to the land, Highlands Rewilding conducted a 12-month consultation with the local community and other stakeholders. 'We wanted to be above board and open about the project,' Scott tells me. 'Local engagement's been a big part of it.'

Bunloit's previous owner had ringed the estate with fences, which Scott suspects was done to block public access. The owner had cared only about shooting deer, employing fewer people than Highlands Rewilding does now. One of the first jobs for Scott and his colleagues has been to remove the fences, with 8km of it given away to local farmers so far. 'It's an important part of rewilding, taking those manmade barriers away. Not just for the wildlife but for promoting public access. We don't want to keep people off the land. The more people that can use the countryside, as long as they're doing it in a responsible manner, the better.'

We emerge onto a plateau of scrub, birch and heather. Scott parks in a lay-by and we get out into the damp cold. Much of what lies around us is peatland. But the careless planting of conifers has degraded it, so much so that scientists have calculated that it is responsible for a net loss of carbon dioxide from Bunloit. If it was healthy, it would be absorbing and locking away the gas. Therefore, restoring the peatland is a priority. Another is the addition to the site of landscape-sculpting animals, be they farmed or wild, Scott explains as we walk further in.

'I've really got my heart set on getting beavers.' He points out a spot along the nearby river that would suit the rodents just fine. 'I'll be most disappointed if we don't.'

Having worked before as a countryside ranger in the Great Glen while studying environmental science, Scott is part of the first generation of land managers who've learned their trade amid growing enthusiasm for rewilding. His deep-seated love for wildlife has brought him here, and he relishes the animals already present as well as those he hopes for; as we walk towards a grassland that looks out over Loch Ness, a fox flashes orange through the gorse on the hill below. 'Fantastic,' Scott grins. The fox reappears further down and pauses on a rock to glance back at us. 'You very rarely see them out in the open.'

As we stand there in appreciation of the fox, a horned head pops up behind what I'd assumed to be another rock. But, no, it is the back of a pale Highland cow. I laugh. Now I see the gorse is filled with them, adults and calves alike, a cattle rainbow of black, orange and gold-yellow. I'm used to photos of Highland cattle standing stoic on windswept plains devoid of scrub and trees. It occurs to me only now that they might not wish to be in such places.

We walk on until we reach a spot that boar have recently swept through. This is obvious from a glance. Although I'm still surprised that rather than one semi-continuous patch of flayed earth, as is often seen in the Dean, the boar here have taken a scattershot approach, with lots of little patches all over the place like inverted mole hills. I mention the difference. Scott replies that he sometimes sees bigger patches worked over in the woodland. Perhaps it's something to do with the condition of the grassland or the particular foraging preferences of these boar. The outcome remains the same, however.

'They're opening the seedbank,' Scott says as we walk among the rootings. 'You can't see it this time of year but in the spring and the summer, in the areas that have been rooted up, they've allowed the wildflowers to take hold. Mostly foxgloves and ragwort. Not everyone's a fan of ragwort, but it's an important species for invertebrates.'

Geophytes like bluebells are only one among many plants that readily leap upon the opportunities offered by wild boar. In fact, *they open the seedbank* tends to be the first item on any list about the benefits of boar. In a weird way, noting it feels pedestrian. But it shouldn't because the vast majority of the British landscape is lacking in animals with this superpower.

Scott is still establishing his own baseline for how the mini biomes of Bunloit – grassland, woodland and peatland – currently look and function. Although the rooting of the boar here looks promising, he needs more time to understand the changes this may be conjuring. Meanwhile, walking the land and reviewing trail camera footage has allowed him to observe interactions between Bunloit's various denizens.

'With the cowpats, the boar have come and rooted around in what's left. They've made almost a perfect circle where the cowpat is. Maybe they're looking for dung beetle larvae.' And as the Highland cattle help the boar, the boar help others in turn. 'What I've been noticing is that some of the areas of disturbance seem to be attracting species like pine marten and badgers, and they're defecating in those areas. So I imagine that would result in more seed dispersal, depending on what they've been eating.'

While I haven't seen pine marten or badger poo in any of the boar rootings back home (yet), I have seen that of birds. It's a lovely loop: boar expose the soil, attracting birds and beasts, who leave behind nutrients and perhaps seeds or spores, thus quickening the germination of plants and fungi.

It isn't always so simple. A diverse ecosystem is a webby tangle, more interconnected than we'll ever know. But sometimes, in shining moments, single threads may be illuminated.

I'm pulled from my reverie as we enter an oak wood and the slope, slippery with moss and leaf litter, gets steeper.

Much steeper. The next few minutes, and indeed the next few hours, end up feeling more like a boot camp than an interview. As Scott talks about Bunloit's woodlands, I say 'Hmm' at appropriate moments and try to keep my feet under me.

'This is semi-ancient oak woodland.' A jay flies by, punctuating Scott's words. 'We're hoping that the boar activity here will open up space for undergrowth to take hold. One of the things that seems to be missing from a lot of the woodland is understorey. In a lot of areas we've just got trees. No level of scrub cover. Hopefully as the years progress, the presence of the wild boar will allow for more scrubby species to appear.'

We come to a stream that has sliced its way down through the fern-bedecked rock. Scott lends me a hand to help me vault the miniature chasm. After the stream and the oaks is a dark and silent tract of Sitka spruce. Elsewhere on the estate are lodgepole pines and Douglas firs, and the days of all these non-native conifers are numbered. Bunloit's team is steadily chopping them down to let the peat and the woodland soils breathe. Some of the timber will be used to build wildlife hides. I'm getting a sneak preview of the estate while it's rough and not yet ready.

After the spruce plantation, we're suddenly back in native woodland, this time birch and hazel. Sodden brown heaps of last year's bracken smothers the ground around them. I note aloud how much of it there is.

'Yeah. The bracken grows to seven feet high here. And in the areas that the boar have disturbed? No bracken. It's incredible. If we could just manoeuvre them about the place, that would be great,' Scott jokes.

He has touched on another step in the boar recipe for enriching plant diversity, in addition to stirring the soil and its seedbanks: breaking up mats of vegetation formed of a single dominant species. In another word, a monoculture. And in Britain, it's often bracken that does the dominating.

Able to grow higher than 1.5m, this native fern is a ubiquitous hallmark of landscapes that have been overgrazed or skinned of their trees. Green scar tissue. Once enthroned, it hampers the return of other plants. Even where trees manage to re-grow, bracken swarms the spaces around them. Its rhizomes – underground stems with an eldritch-black colour – are poisonous to most animals. But boar can tolerate them, to a point.

Scott's observations at Bunloit echo those of the charity Trees for Life. They experimented with keeping a sounder on a section of its Dundreggan estate for a few years from 2009. The boar did a thorough job of clearing bracken, with birch, bird cherry and Scots pine seedlings all rushing to claim the space. Ecological consultant Alison Strange has suggested to me that boar like to root where bracken grows as the soil there is more friable, a quality that would surely aid the establishment of new trees if given the space.

Yet even in the Forest of Dean with its high density of boar, bracken still rules much of the undergrowth. It's also quick to return given the chance. Trees for Life found this to be so a year after they'd moved their boar to a different area. They ended up stopping the experiment when two of the animals were diagnosed with tumours; bracken was suspected to be the reason, given that the fronds and possibly the spores can cause cancer. When it comes to restoring wrecked woodland, there's no just-add-boar recipe – emphasis on *just*. Boar can't do it alone. But they make a vital difference.

I'm reminded of that a few months before my trip to Bunloit, on an evening in late autumn when I go walking with the local naturalist Ed Drewitt. He takes me to a damp clearing near his home where tracts have been opened through the bracken. And in those openings grow the broad plump leaves of foxgloves. This species of plant works to a two-year plan, producing leaves in the first year, and an impossibly long stalk festooned with pink-purple bells of flowers in the second.

'Because of the boar, all these foxgloves have just come up in the last year,' Ed says as we crouch to boar eye-level. He should know, given he's out here almost every day. 'The diversity of wildflowers is quite low in the forest, so these foxgloves are a welcome treat for bumblebees and others.'

I don't see any boar that evening with Ed. Nor do I expect to as I stand beside Scott, peering at some fresh-ish rooting among the birches and hazels. As for the ranger himself, it is only some time after my visit that he glimpses the Bunloit boar in the flesh. Mostly he relies on trail cameras to see them. He has several batches of fresh footage waiting to be reviewed, so we climb back uphill and stop for lunch in a draughty cottage being renovated as a holiday home. A squall of rain blows through just as we get inside. On a recalcitrant laptop, we manage to go through some of the videos. They feature the same family each time, who are easy to identify thanks to two among their newest members: boarlets who are shaped exactly like wild boar and act exactly like wild boar but, instead of being brown and stripey, are pale and *spotty*. I am enchanted.

'It's obviously a call-back to the domestic stock,' Scott remarks. Not that he cares. We both grin and chuckle as the spotty boarlets, their littermates and the adult females jump around and shove at each other.

The sounder has 11 members altogether, although one of Scott's colleagues thinks another sounder has started to come in. Wandering males occasionally turn up too. The population is far smaller than the Dean one, although Scott isn't too worried about inbreeding. 'They found their way naturally here, from well away, so they have the ability to disperse,' he says. 'They're not penned in here. They can go up and down the glen. It's heavily wooded, down to Fort William.'

What does concern him is the opinion of the stalker employed by Bunloit to keep Sika deer numbers down, a man who thinks the boar should be 'managed' – that is, shot if they wander in. 'I understand the point of needing to manage, but from my perspective on this project, there's not a massive population of them. They've been here for 10, 15 years, maybe longer in fact. They've not caused any problems, so I don't see why we as a rewilding project need to manage them. Not only that, but everyone around us shoots the wild boar. I don't see why we need to shoot them as well. I don't see why we should have to follow the status quo.'

The *everyone* includes Forestry and Land Scotland (the Scottish equivalent of Forestry England), which owns some of the surrounding land. The Scottish government may not have published an official plan for managing wild boar yet, but some of its employees have been discreetly taking their own action for some time already.

When the rain eases off, Scott packs up the laptop and leads me higher up the estate. We enter a different, colder world, whose border is marked by a blanket of crystalline snow. Planted conifers give way to a mosaic of moorland and forest of Scots pine, birch, rowan and aspen, their trunks and branches adorned with curls of lichen. The crackling and dripping of wet is everywhere. As our boots splash through bog and crunch through snow, Scott shares his hopes for this woodland. All the living Scots pines here are old. The previous owner's approach to management led to high numbers of Sika and other deer, and their grazing meant few tree seedlings survived. Now that more of the deer are being culled, the forest is being freed to pursue alternative destinies.

Scott remarks that the boar rarely come here, though we both keep our eyes open for signs anyway. It's clear how much richer his daily life is because of them. And yet, when I ask him if he always feels a thrill to encounter boar – whether seeing or hearing them – he doesn't wax lyrical about the curing of his ecological boredom, as I'm prone to do when someone asks me anything similar. 'It's just always nice to see or hear any wildlife. I get excited to see them, just like we saw that fox, a very common animal. There's no fear, it's just lovely. From my perspective, they're here now, they're part of the ecology.'

I'm surprised that he lumps boar in with foxes. But as I think about his answer, it begins to make sense. The more a place brims with life, and the more you expect this of a place, the less the boar will stand out.

And that is as it should be.

The boar have carried out plenty of hardcore gardening at Bunloit. But there is something that I don't see during my visit there: a wallow.

A wallow is always a satisfying thing to find. No two are the same. Big or small, shallow or deep, clay-pale or 70 per cent cocoa-black. Edges pitted with hoofprints, and sometimes clawed pawprints where a dog has taken an illicit paddle. Boar may create them from scratch, or enlarge the ruts of forestry vehicle tracks or the hollows left beneath the vast root-plates of fallen trees. In beaver-inhabited parts of Europe, boar can grant old beaver pools a second life.

On my woodland forays through the Forest of Dean, I keep an eye out for wallows. I save each one I come across in Google Maps, forming a constellation of blue pins. Still, it's a few months before I discover the most spectacular one yet, hidden in a pocket of Norway spruce. Along the trails that lead to it, ferns and brambles have been daubed an off-white where muddy bodies have brushed past countless times. Around the wallow itself, three of the thickest spruce trunks bear a mudline up to about a metre, with roots polished to a beeswax-shine. Livid amber gouges speak of tusks and other teeth, bleeding resin that has hardened into glittery quartzlike veins. Male and female boar alike bite and notch bark in this way to leave their saliva as olfactory calling cards. It has also been suggested that they select conifers to make use of the anti-microbial properties of the resin.

Wallows are an essential fixture in every boar's schedule. They act as social hubs, as anchor-points to which disparate groups and individuals all gravitate. When I start to leave my trail camera at the spruce wallow, my reward is a series of glimpses of boar lowering their guard and – to all appearances – *relishing* being alive with each other. They grunt and squeal. They shove or nudge or chase each other. They touch noses. They sit on their haunches and shake their heads with the same slappy sound and motion of dogs drying off. They sniff the rubbing trees for flavours of who has already been by. They use the buttress-like roots to scratch their rumps, sometimes so vigorously it makes a noise like wood being sawed.

They dive into the mud, usually snout-first like a piggy torpedo. Wallowing helps them to keep insects away, and by rubbing against trees afterwards they rid themselves of parasites. The mud also helps them to cool down. Boar can't sweat, so on a hot day there must be a deep pleasure in sinking their haunches into the soft slick. Indeed, wallowing has been called a 'luxury behaviour' by Marc Bracke of Wageningen University, because most other similar-sized ungulate species don't dare to make themselves so vulnerable, nor spend precious time doing so. There is a fearlessness in it. Wallowing may have a sexual function too, as males appear to do it much more than females during the main mating season in autumn. After he captured footage of a male in the Dean weeing in a wallow and then having a good splash, a friend of mine wondered if males alone do this to scent-mark – although my own camera has on a few occasions caught females squatting and weeing. The act always looks deliberate, considered.

None of the boar behaviour I've just described makes wallows sound particularly appealing. The water these hollows hold is dirty, opaque and sometimes anointed with urine. But that's a human way of looking at it. Wallows, like rootings, create dramatic new structures in a landscape. And over countless millenia, other species have inevitably learned to use them. Many a time my camera catches animals like foxes, deer and even owls coming to drink.

But it's only when I meet a few boar-loving ecologists that I truly begin to appreciate the life that wallows make possible.

On a rainy November day a few months before Bunloit, I arrive at Coombeshead, the Devonshire farm of infamous rewilder Derek Gow. White geese mill around the gravel driveway, honking and eyeing me like forbidding parking wardens. Rather than the man himself, I'm here to speak with Gow's protégé, Peter Cooper. Peter is a conservationist with a sprawling portfolio, which in addition to his work for Gow includes spoofy conservation videos and the tender raising of glow-worm larvae for reintroduction projects.

After cups of tea, we walk through the farm towards the reserve where the herbivores – and the boar – roam. We pass a barn full of water voles scurrying up and down in their tanks, white storks standing with dignity in the wet, dens hiding wildcats, and a trio of lynx prowling the perimeter of their enclosure. A menagerie of species like a book of spells waiting to be cast upon the land.

In the top field are two of the wild boar I've come to see. One is female. The other has huge testicles that draw the eyes like magnets. He grunts at our approach and trots up to the wire.

'Hello, pigs!' Peter replies, raising his voice to the kind of excited pitch that I use for greeting cats and dogs. The male is named Gerard, Peter tells me.

I am invited to pet Gerard. With my glimpses of boar at home always so fleeting or low-lit, it's a pleasure to feast my eyes on him, and to sink my hand through the steel-wool toughness of the hairs behind his head. He is an undulation of mud colours, from the pale clay of his nose to the peaty ring around his muzzle, to the tannin-dark of his ears. Behind the rigid disc of the nose, the skin is wrinkled like the back of an old man's neck. The white tips of his tusks poke out from below the wedge of his snout. But they're not as big and long as I might've imagined from their appellation.

Gerard shows no reaction to the pressure of my hand on him. It bears making clear that he is an extremely tame individual, and that I would never dare to get so close to a *wild* wild boar. If I ever tried to, it might well put their life at far more risk than my own, given our default response of putting down 'problem' animals.

As I admire Gerard, Peter fills me in on the boar they have at Coombeshead. As well as these two, there's a pair of young males, and a female who currently has a litter of juveniles in tow. At least, I think this is what Peter says, because Gerard's squealy grunts will be all that I can hear at this point when I listen back to the interview. (When I remark on this to Peter by email, he replies: 'He's just trying to contribute, listen hard and you can hear some serious reflections on soil health amongst his wheezing.')

Peter moves towards the gate. 'If you have any apples on you, chuck them away now. He'll know instantly and he'll knock you down for them.'

It's nice to know that Gerard and I have the same favourite fruit.

Once we're on the same side of the fence as the two boar, they sniff at us but otherwise give us our space. This is

unsurprising. One of their jobs is to be ambassadors for
Gow's rewilding work. I'm tempted to leave a review online:
Very polite and welcoming front-of-house staff.

They are, however, very messy staff. Which is the point.
Much of the field is a churn of mud, which conspires with
the rain to suck at my boots. We tread past a gathering of
nonchalant Exmoor ponies, who alone wouldn't be able to
achieve the regeneration that Gow wants in these seven and
a half hectares.

'Arable fields regenerate quite quickly. But with pasture
there's heavy nitrification over time from so much dung,
urine and manure, and there's over-trampling and erosion. If
you let it go wild you just get lots of the same grass species,'
Peter explains amid the squelching. 'The boar have been
here for about two years now, steadily diversifying things.
They refresh the seed base, turn over the soil, and in the
wallows we're starting to see chickweed and scarlet
pimpernel. The idea is to kickstart this pasture. If you are
doing rewilding of an area, I think pigs or boar are the most
important herbivore you can have at the start.'

We head downhill into lichenous wood pasture. The boar
have left their marks here too, in the form of flattened areas
scooped into brambles and old hedges that serve both as
windbreaks and places to sleep.

Then we come to a wallow. It's shallow and surrounded
by a beach of hoof-mashed earth. Some of the hoofprints
are far too big to belong to boar. They've been left instead
by Derek Gow's five Asian water buffalo, who've been
brought in to assist the boar with reshaping the land. Their
relative and ancestor of farmed cattle, the aurochs, would've
played such a role before its extinction from Britain and
later the rest of Europe.

One species missing from the coterie here is the red deer,
which also wallows, especially stags during the rut. Given
that Derek Gow's boar and buffalo seem not to mind
sharing, it seems likely that red deer would've also

collaborated in pocking the landscape with muddy pools when they existed in significant numbers all across Britain. This may well be happening in Scotland again where boar and red deer ranges overlap. Not so in England and Wales, where there are only a few red deer herds, and in locations where boar are not known to be. And unlike boar, red deer have sweat glands. This means that wallowing is perhaps less of a biological imperative, especially when predators like humans are about. Whatever happens in the future, in the places where they've returned, our boar are creating opportunities that British ecosystems have been missing out on for centuries.

'I think there's many little relationships we've yet to dig into,' Peter says as we walk on. 'I remember doing wildlife surveys in Romania, found a boar wallow, set up a camera, and got a stone marten coming for a drink and a Ural owl coming for a bath on the same night. So even the larger fauna still really benefit from these tiny pools.'

It so happens that during the same week I visit Peter in Devon, I go on separate walks in the Dean with two local ecologists who are raising their families there: the aforementioned Ed Drewitt, and a friend of his, Jim Swanson. They both have much to say on the matter of wallows.

'There's this perception that a pond's got to be lovely, clear water. But not all ponds are like that,' Jim tells me as we amble down a path through a heathland-ish reserve called Edgehills Bog, which is managed by Gloucestershire Wildlife Trust. 'Some of the rarest organisms are found in those temporary ponds, or muddy ponds, or ponds that are in dense woodland. They don't look attractive but they're very, very important because they're scarce, they're not common in the landscape anymore.'

These ponds offer stepping stones between the Dean's larger bodies of water, allowing different populations to connect and exchange genes. They also act as refuges, because they lack predatory fish. Jim talks of finding dragonflies, pond skaters, water boatmen, newts, frogs and tadpoles in wallows. These species haven't wasted any time in once again using the works of the boar to their advantage.

Peter's mind falls on amphibians too. As we leave the boar–buffalo wallow behind us, he speculates that the now extremely rare natterjack toad might've often used wallows to breed, when both this species and boar could be found all over the country. 'As soon as you get a fully developed pond, the more competitive amphibians push natterjacks out.' Which means that boar, if we ever allow them to, could be instrumental in the toad's recovery. The same logic can be applied to a creature I've never heard of until Peter tells me about it: triops, or the tadpole shrimp. When I research it later, I'll find that it looks like an earwig hiding unsuccessfully under a tiny horseshoe crab.

'It's quite common all across Europe in established or ephemeral pools, but in the UK it's only found in two ponds: one in the New Forest and one on the west coast of Scotland,' Peter elaborates. 'And yet it's a species that has been unchanged since before the dinosaurs. It's got an incredible life cycle where the eggs can dry for years on end until they hit water and hatch again. So it seems quite bizarre that such a resilient species can be so reduced in the UK and still common in Europe.'

To Peter, the loss of boar is a stark reason for this. They create homes for triops, and may do even more than that.

'Think of how thick the bristles on Gerard are. It keeps in all the mud.' He mentions the study from the Camargue which found that aquatic invertebrates can hatch from the mud rubbed onto trees by boar. 'So the idea is that a boar goes into one wallow containing some tadpole shrimp eggs, picks up the eggs in the mud, trots along and goes to the next wallow, deposits them, and boom.'

Yet when it comes to wallows, more is at stake than the fate of a few individual species like triops or the natterjack toad. Soon after my visit to Coombeshead, I walk with Ed

Drewitt through his local woods on a cold yet glowing amber evening. On the side of his work as a naturalist, Ed takes people on safaris in the Dean to look for boar and other animals. We sometimes pause and fall silent, waiting to see if any boar will emerge into the open. In between these moments, Ed shares his thoughts on how the ecosystem of the Dean is changing, and the threats it faces. 'Part of why some butterfly species here are declining is because water is draining down the old mines. It's being taken away from the surface, into deep holes.'

'Really?' I exclaim, much louder and higher-pitched than I'd meant to be, betraying my presence to any boar in earshot.

The Dean's history of mining goes all the way back to Roman times. Beneath its pelt of forest and earth lies a honeycomb of natural tunnels that humans have expanded over the last two millennia. A few of the coal mines are still in action, worked by a rare and dying breed of freeminers. But there are countless shafts and entrances no longer used. I hadn't considered that they might be gulping down the forest's precious water.

'Yep,' Ed replies. 'And the forest is becoming much drier.'

This is bad news on top of bad news, given how patterns of rainfall in the UK are warping in step with planetary climate breakdown. As a whole, the country is expected to receive much less rain in summer and more in winter. Every drop of water the land can catch and hold will matter. Boar wallows are a way to do this.

When it comes to water conservation, there is of course another species that Britain will need ever more in the future. I hope to meet it in the flesh for the first time when I explore Coombeshead with Peter.

'Walking through here does make you feel like a Mesolithic hunter,' he remarks as we follow a trail tramped down by boar and buffalo. The mud begins to thin to a delta of little streams, and a clearing opens ahead of us.

Water is leaking into my cracked old hiking boots. I don't care. Because I'm looking at my very first beaver dam.

It's huge. A Jenga of sharp-ended branches that together go 3m high.

'We've been camera trapping here and you see the boar walking across the dams, along with other wildlife. We've had badgers, otters, polecats, roe deer, foxes.' Peter leads me across, in the footsteps of those other animals. He describes how part of the complex of pools we're entering was once a drainage system dating from Victorian times. It has become a collaboration between past humans, present humans and present beavers.

From the way that Peter talks about both beavers and boar, he seems to love them equally. 'They're two lost species you probably don't see together anywhere else in the UK.'

It is in beavers that rewilders' hopes lie for rewetting our increasingly parched landscapes. Progress in seeding them across Britain is picking up, although it still feels slow. The one family of beavers in the Dean remains confined to an enclosure. Their positive impact is strait-jacketed. The Dean boar are at least carving out new wet spots, in places where beavers cannot go.

But perhaps boar need beavers too. Or, rather, perhaps a woodland with boar will do better with beavers added into the mix. I've learned from Forestry England's Kevin Stannard that recent surveys of brooks in the Dean have found higher-than-expected loads of sediment. While investigations are ongoing, Kevin thinks that rooting by the boar is to blame. It's concerning because too much sediment can sicken a watercourse. Prey becomes harder for predators to find, or predators are harder for prey to see, while the settling of the sediment can rewrite the flow of the water in ways much less hospitable to life. If more of it is washing into the Dean's brooks, this suggests that there are more boar around than the area can bear.

But equally, it throws a light on the life that remains absent. A study in west Devon found that the dams of a single beaver family trapped over 100 tonnes of sediment lost from the surrounding intensively farmed grassland. If beavers had the same freedom of the Forest of Dean that boar have, their dams could surely catch at least some of that dislodged earth. The roles and effects of any species can never be considered in isolation from those of others: none of us is an island, though humans try to make it so.

In everything they do, boar help to show us that nature's true state is motion, not stillness. Fresh rootings have a battlefield quality to them, torn ends of white roots poking through with the bleached colour of old bone. And yet they promise life.

As for wallows, once one ceases to be used, its destiny is to dry out. My favourite from my first visit to the Dean in 2014 turns out to be gone without a trace when I return in 2021. But there is time for a wallow to hold many stories before its end. At one end of my wood is a shallow pool that looks to have been sculpted by the boar, though it seems not to be in use by them anymore. Its clear water bears an emerald veil of pond water-starwort. One day the water will be gone, but by then there will probably be another pool nearby, and pond water-starwort growing there instead.

I come back to Coombeshead the summer after my first visit for the inaugural Wilderfest, a micro festival for rewilding. I am very much looking forward to seeing Gerard again.

But I learn from Peter that he has died.

One morning, he didn't appear at the fence for breakfast, so Peter and a colleague went looking for him. They found his body in the woods, resting on a bed of dried leaves he'd plumped up before he lay down for the last time.

Most captive boar in this country are destined for slaughter. Gerard was allowed a far more peaceful end. He may have spent all his life within the grip of fences. But in that life, he helped to give an inkling of what could happen if we were to offer wild boar and other missing creatures the wrecked canvas of our countryside and say, 'Do what you were born to do.'

CHAPTER SIX

This Is Our Land

When I move to the Dean, falling in love with my new wood is inevitable. And the wild boar are part of this. Seeing their rootings, old and new; the hoofprints which each come with a pair of stiletto points; the places where in nights and days gone by I've heard or glimpsed them. I'm not alone in the feeling. I have walked and spoken with other residents of the Dean who, like me, rarely meet the boar, but welcome the wildness that they are helping to reinfuse this place with. We're glad to see the breaking-open of verges, rides and woodland floors, and the messy fuzz of new plantlife.

I'm still caught in the heady state of can't-believe-all-this-is-outside-my-front-door when, one late-autumn day, I notice orange spray-paint marks on some of the beeches and oaks. I know what they mean, and it's hard not to see them as modern versions of red crosses daubed on the doors of plague houses. A few weeks later, just before Christmas, laminated signs from Forestry England appear on the local stiles and gates. They declare, 'Essential forest operations will be taking place in this area over the coming weeks. Some paths may be closed whilst the trees next to them are felled.'

I head south to spend the holiday with my parents. By the time I return after New Year, the work has begun. The wood rings with the shrieking of chainsaws. Chopped trunks lie among the leaves that were only just dropped as the trees planned for the year to come. Their stumps are left raw and bleeding with a smell whose appeal belies its wrongness. My usual paths have been overwritten by deep vehicle tracks that are ridged like fish flesh after the bones have been pulled away. Everywhere that isn't a thoroughfare for the foresters' machinery seems smothered by heaps of discarded branches that try to trip me with each step. Huge trucks armed with mechanical claws begin to stack logs along the edge of the wood, blocking off the trails I used to take to get out onto the road. In a final warning, signs have appeared bearing black hand icons and the word 'STOP!'

Forestry England isn't clear-felling my wood. They are instead 'thinning' them, which means removing some trees to give others more space to grow, and to let more light reach the ground to coax up a richer undergrowth. I hope it works here, especially given the amount of existing undergrowth that has been lost as the foresters' vehicles reclaim old tracks. Yet it seems unlikely, when there are so many muntjac, roe and fallow deer around, ever-ready to nibble away at any young trees or scrub they find.

I'm not prepared for the dislocation and bitterness I feel at this rearranging of my adopted landscape. Although I know the shockwaves of climate and biodiversity breakdown are on their way, I hadn't expected these pangs to come so soon. It's my first true taste of *solastalgia*, a condition named by philosopher Glenn Albrecht for the emotional pain in having your sense of place violated. I don't doubt that those animals who are hefted to this wood, dependent on it in a way that I am not, feel it even more.

Solastalgia must have visited the people of the Forest of Dean repeatedly over the centuries: when William the Conqueror closed off great tracts of it for his own pleasure; when the sessile oaks were torn out; when the conifers sprouted; or when mines and other hubs of industry began to close. And, for some now living there, when the boar returned.

In 2014, it was easy to find people in the Dean who didn't want the boar around. Richard was one. To meet him at his house, I parked near a church and walked past a wide verge that had clearly received much attention from the boar.

Among patches of bare earth furry with dead roots, newly formed lumps were being fixed into place by plants like dock, daisy, dandelion and creeping cinquefoil.

A man in his late 60s, Richard was a long-time activist with both Greenpeace and Friends of the Earth. Although he'd moved into the area after the boar did, he spoke of it as if he'd been here far longer. He pointed to the verge I'd passed and recounted with warmth how people used to have picnics on it, or else sheep wandered over to graze it. Now it was fit for neither man nor beast – except the boar.

Richard's garden looked out towards the hazy ridges of the Cotswolds. On the other side of the house, a shimmering green copse of young oaks ate up the noise of the nearby road. The little church was the icing on the cake of this quintessential English village. On a hot blue June day like this, it was hard to imagine wanting to be anywhere else. I could understand Richard's already-deep sense of ownership. So when a lone male boar started coming at night to root up the verge and the other patches of grass nearby, he felt compelled to act.

First, he would try to repair the damage done. 'If I saw it in the morning I would set to as quickly as possible before the soil dried out, to get the sods back in position as closely as I could. If you don't do it straight away and it happens again you've got no chance of getting rid of the undulations, and then you can't mow it.'

As we stood on the drive outside his house, Richard mimicked himself pushing at soil with his foot in a practised motion. 'But it's not easy to do. You're dealing with quite fragile pieces of soil that just about hang together. And once it's been disturbed it can flow away in the next rain, so the drains at the end there get blocked with grass and soil from the digging. The council was out again trying to empty the drains yesterday, but they only succeeded on one.'

Although pro-boar people often rolled their eyes at complaints around the rooting of verges, the blocking of drains in the middle of a village posed a practical worry. Still, the way Richard had mentioned it almost as an afterthought suggested that this alone hadn't been the impetus for what then evolved into his one-man nocturnal crusade.

'By the middle of October I was getting fed up of repairing the verges, and they were getting less resilient even with the repairs, so I felt that I needed some plan for repelling the boar.'

This meant getting up around 1 a.m. each night to walk up and down the lane that led to the verge and the church. At the sight of Richard and the walking stick and torch that he brandished, the male would always run away. But he would always come back.

The sleep deprivation was unsustainable, so Richard next installed a passive infrared sensor system designed to detect human burglars. He scattered the individual sensors around the far boundaries of his property, as well as hanging one from a tree in the copse, weaving an invisible web. The main alarm had a display that told him when a particular sensor was triggered, so once he had shoes on and went out the door, he knew in which direction to go. When a sounder of females started coming with their youngsters to plough the rich ground in the village, he chased them off too. If he felt any nervousness at marching out in the dark to shoo the boar away, it had clearly been steamrollered by his affront at their nerve.

When I get back in touch with Richard in early 2022, I expect to hear that he has retired his surveillance strategy. It had sounded far too wearying for anyone to maintain. On the contrary: he has upgraded and fine-tuned the system instead. He gets holidays sometimes, because the boar visit in what – even after eight years – feels like random cycles. But he still considers himself and his neighbours to be badly affected by the boar. One day in the spring, I conduct a slow drive-by through the village. The main grass verge, the land that Richard tried to defend, has succumbed to nettles. It isn't quite the rapture of diversity I'd been hoping to see. This is not surprising, when people must be regularly fertilising it with the poo and piss of their dogs, and the woods are too far away to provide a good bank of seeds.

Even in a place with 'Forest' in the name, one simply does not expect one's village with its church greens, asphalt roads and cottages to be invaded by shaggy creatures with tusks. Richard's actions, while extreme, were and remain understandable. Perhaps he fears the boar will one day graduate to desecrating the churchyard itself, as has happened elsewhere in the area. Gravestones notwithstanding, the green spaces we've carved out of the land for human use – paddocks, garden lawns, parks and playing fields – are basically boar ready-meals, just a thin film of grass over a smorgasbord of earth. A well-designed fence can keep boar out. At a cost of perhaps thousands of pounds.

Still, for residents, coexisting with boar would be easier if it were simply a case of keeping them out of a few specific places. But this isn't a conflict whose boundary lines are as sharply drawn as a pavement edge, nor one that ends at the pavement.

I'm unsurprised when Viv tells me that, rather than being frightened of the boar, 'Normally they're frightened of me!'

Behind glasses with bright blue plastic frames is a formidable older woman, armed with an uncarved walking stick plucked from the woods. The latest Covid variant, Omicron, is still raging, so Viv will not risk social niceties such as a cup of tea in the kitchen first. But I suspect that even in normal times she would've been too eager to get going to hang around for that. After my arrival at the front, she takes me straight through the garden to a back gate fortified with a heavy chain. The land beyond belongs to Forestry England, at least on paper.

I see beech trees, beech roots, leaf litter and soil. Viv sees memories of a different nature: mists of bluebells hanging over carpets of moss. Although we're only at the beginning of February, I learn that the mists and the moss will not be returning even as this year wears on.

'The boar have absolutely decimated the bluebell woods. This area, on an April or May evening, the smell was just intoxicating. The bluebells are constantly trying to regenerate but they just don't have the chance, the boar keep coming back.' Viv pokes at the broken ground with her handy stick, finding an upended bluebell shoot with a small wan-coloured bulb on the end of it. 'That's the size of the bluebell bulbs we now have. You know what bluebell bulbs should be? Nice fat bulbs ready for spring. Now they're little spindly things.'

To wild boar, bluebells are food. To some humans, they are the supreme symbol of spring in Britain. In this country, we're so starved of abundances of flora and fauna that a woodland floor covered in bluebells is a salve for the soul. I think it's down to more than just their beauty. Perhaps the reliable thriving of bluebells is taken as a sign of the living world's forgiveness. Which makes it unsurprising that bluebells have become a totem among people who want the boar gone.

'This has been happening since 2005,' Viv goes on. 'The boar made a beeline. I remember one of the rangers telling me, "You want to be careful, Viv, they have a penchant for bluebells". Forestry activity could be damaging them too, there may be more light, but I think the main culprit is boar.'

The bluebells aren't the only thing in this wood to have suffered. Pointing at the thick beech roots near our feet, Viv tells me I shouldn't be able to see them. They've been exposed by the rearranging of the soil. 'You can see the roots are starting to rot. Squirrels are chewing them. These main big anchor roots will be lost, and in a storm they'll blow over.'

If trees do sometimes fall because of boar exposing their roots, then this is another power to add to their arsenal. A fallen tree feeds other life. It's little consolation, however, if you feel the boar have already taken too much.

As we walk downhill, a drizzle starts up. I watch my footing, which is easier said than done while holding out my phone to record the conversation.

'You used to be able to walk really easily along this because it was all covered in moss.' Viv gestures around her. 'All this horrible mud, it's really slippery. Local people used to walk in these woods, on this bank. They don't come anymore.'

She moved here in 1980, just missing the last free-roaming pigs, but well before the boar came. Her academic background is in social history and photography rather than ecology, yet her observations of the wood around her come across as deep and precise. 'There were orchids down at the bottom, bee orchids. They've all long gone.'

In fact, throughout our time together, her dialogue follows a recurring motif in which she describes something that used to be here but is no more – because of the boar. Fungi of the Russula genus, better known as brittlegills, which used to make rainbows of colour across the woodland floor. Moss. Great-crested newts. Mice. Voles. Tawny owls, whose prey has all been eaten. Woodcock and tree pipits, whose ground nests have all been ransacked. The list of species that Viv believes have been consumed or driven out by the boar is astonishingly long.

Viv pauses at one point to pick an old beech husk out of the thick leaf litter. 'Look at this. Something I've noticed is, last year in particular in this beech wood, the leaves and the beech husks didn't break down. Normally over the winter they disintegrate and are taken back into the soil to feed the trees. I think the whole of the understorey and the sub-soil here are damaged. You rootle around the leaf litter, do you see any signs of mycelium? There should be some underneath these dead leaves, some sort of evidence of threads of stuff.'

With this final indictment, the impact of the boar borders on the apocalyptic. No mycelia means no mycorrhizae, those physical networks that bind fungi and plantlife and enable forests to flourish.

While I can accept that a place can have too many boar, I cannot accept that the beech wood I am standing in has been stripped of its mycelia. After all, I find my feet crunching through fallen leaves anywhere in the Dean where broadleaved trees grow. But if Viv really has seen a slowdown in decomposition and fewer mushrooms, what else might be causing these changes?

After meeting Viv, with the help of the British Mycological Society I get in touch with an expert. On Zoom, Thorunn Helgason, head of the School of Biological Sciences at the University of Edinburgh, seizes the question I've put to her with the keenness of a squirrel at a hazelnut.

'I suspect drought,' she says off the bat. 'A lot of mushrooms fruit in autumn because of the moisture. What time of year it rains matters. We've had some really dry springs and then you get it absolutely chucking it down, which isn't what we're used to in Britain. Because it normally rains all the time.'

When Viv holds the beechmast husk out to me, we're still a few months away from the official drought of the summer of 2022. But Thorunn, sitting nearly 300 miles to my north, is talking about multi-year trends in rainfall.

'It's certainly going to reduce decomposition, and I'd be really surprised if that doesn't affect some species of fungi.'

She uses the example of a Scottish study into a rare species of fungus that appeared to have significantly declined over several years, only for genetic analysis of soil samples to show that it was still thriving; it just hadn't been sending up mushrooms, perhaps because of drier conditions. 'How people perceive fungal communities is through their fruiting bodies. That to me is like trying to estimate community abundance or diversity based on the number of acorns and apples on the ground.'

As for Viv's charge that the boar have wiped out the mycelia, Thorunn thinks this unlikely. 'If the mycelia are broken, I think they just re-join up and recolonise. If the boar are coming through and disturbing a lot, you will see the difference, but that might just be because they've changed the *composition* of the community. They might not be disturbing the mycorrhizal function belowground at all.' Thorunn adds that some mycorrhizal fungi create fruiting bodies invisible to the human eye, and that different species live at different depths in the soil, so may be affected by the rooting of boar to different degrees depending on the depth or the extent of that rooting. Near the end of our conversation, she chuckles ruefully. 'I feel like I've just made it a lot more complicated!'

Complicated indeed. How to know for sure whether, and by how much, the boar may be playing a part in the losses that Viv perceives? Her powers of observation are surely not at fault, for she manages to open my eyes further to the changes authored by the boar. During our time in the beech wood, she points out several rotting tree stumps that are dark and mossy all over, except for raw, orange-coloured wounds where chunks have been freshly pried off.

'This area used to be noted for yellow-necked mice. They nested in these rotted stumps,' Viv explains. 'What boar then do is break open these old stumps and eat all the mice.'

A few days later, I'm ducking and shouldering my way through a young Norway spruce plantation in search of boar. Most of the trees have been planted close enough to each other that their many spindly branches all merge into a brown and forbidding mist of spikes. But there are always passageways to be found through these plantations, the ground upholstered with springy cushions of moss. And, often, there are signs of boar: patches where the moss has been peeled away, and scatters of droppings. This time though, I find a third sign. It's an old, greened stump torn open on one flank. Shards are spilling away. While I peer at it, a familiar snort sounds through the trees. I look up in time to see a flicker of movement as the culprits take flight.

In the same way that you can't seem to stop seeing an unusual word after you've learned about it (Baader-Meinhof Phenomenon, if you want to know its name), I find many more ravaged tree stumps in the weeks after, all over the forest. If not mice, there must be *something* the boar are after, to do it so frequently. Grubs, perhaps. Regardless, the action must be speeding along the rotting of those individual stumps. Just one more way in which wild boar help to shape the rivers of energy that flow, unstoppable, between all living things.

———

At the end of April, as the bluebells in my own wood run riot, I return to Viv's beech wood. She hadn't exaggerated about the change to her flowers. Had she not described how it used to look, I wouldn't have ever considered this to be a 'bluebell woodland'. The plants I'm looking at stand in small patches, or as lone individuals, islanded by leaf litter and bare dry patches of soil.

This place is part of the heart of the forest, so it stands to reason that it would be visited by boar more often than mine. One of the studies that found that bluebell bulbs can grow bigger in response to rooting was carried out in Kent and East Sussex, where the boar have always been few and spread thin between the woodlands; perhaps this explains why Viv's bluebell bulbs seem to have shrunk. In her experience, the boar here come in waves too powerful and too frequent for the bluebells to regroup.

But should they? Bluebells are the only spring woodland flower for which we hold such great expectations. We don't bemoan the lack of primrose carpets or wood anemone carpets. These two are common plants, beloved plants in their own way, but we're used to seeing them as small parts of a vaster tapestry. A violet-blue mist of bluebells is, arguably, a mirror to the yellow of a field of oilseed rape – just another monoculture. And one that we may be equally responsible for, if it exists because of the absence of animals like boar. Perhaps to a Mesolithic person, a bluebell woodland would look miraculous. Or freaky.

I wonder also if bluebells seem to be a delicacy to British boar in part *because* of their present abundance. Where they grow thick, they offer a sprawling food source that requires the bare minimum of effort to forage. As George Monbiot suggests, 'Wild boar and bluebells live happily together, but perhaps not wild boar and only bluebells.'

Despite all this logic, I can't help my stirrings of joy when I see how bluebells dominate my own wood. Their bloc beauty makes me a hypocrite. Even so, casting my eyes over the woodland floor beside Viv's house, I see other things growing: new bracken shoots, bramble leaves and beech seedlings. In fact, there are far more seedlings and saplings here than in my wood, or indeed other parts of the forest. Are they thriving with the help of the boar? The possibility can't be discounted.

Viv's bluebells are no longer the perfumed sea of violet-blue they once were. The ones that remain are still beautiful, yet she can only compare it to the place she knew and loved before. Environmental change often approaches with insidious stealth. It's like trying to catch the moment that twilight becomes night. This bluebell patch is a rare exception. Viv has watched it be whittled down over just a few years, because of the boar. Is it any wonder, then, that she attributes all her other losses to the boar too? Compared to the invisible yet growing shadow of climate breakdown and the gnawing effects of other human impacts, boar are ready scapegoats.

Yet Viv is a reminder not to pigeonhole people who consider themselves anti-boar. When I mention the reintroduced pine martens, her eyes light up and she grins.

She's equally delighted at the mention of wolves and lynx. She would very much like these two species to return, and not just because they might help manage the boar. Her fear, it seems, is all for her landscape, not herself, although landscape and body are not always separate beings.

The land beyond a garden is not also garden. But for some, it feels otherwise. Home extends far beyond their own fences, past the verges, reaching along the tracks and deep into the woods. And the would-be owners want to keep it exactly as it is. When people complain that boar have made a 'mess' of the forest, both within and beyond the woodlands, it's tempting to roll the eyes. 'The grass verge issue, that just drives me nuts. It's a grass verge, so what?' one photographer asks in exasperation.

And yet. When you are used to having the freedom of a place, of making and walking the same paths as if your feet are both stitch and needle, binding and re-binding you, the boundaries of home grow hazy. When the boar churn up the earth in the woods and eat the bluebell bulbs, it's personal. The boar are taking and remaking places that have, until now, been yours alone.

CHAPTER SEVEN

The Boar People (Part I)

Curious things happen on islands. Among them: if a species arrives and finds no predators or parasites waiting, evolution cracks its knuckles and starts to disassemble the parts that once provided vital defence. Anything that costs a great deal of energy to develop or maintain, and can no longer justify itself, may end up discarded, from armour to wings. Instincts, too, can be shed through lack of use. The organism becomes naïve, as if fresh out of the Garden of Eden.

A parallel is to be found with humans in places like Great Britain. We stripped out the aurochs, bear, boar and wolf – species that could've harmed us in fury or self-defence even if they weren't our predators. And after the loss of most big animals, we proceeded to steadily eliminate other wildlife from our lives. Already on an island, we made an island of ourselves.

This evisceration of worldly experience is evident in news stories of people dismayed to find themselves suddenly sharing their spaces with other animals. My anti-favourites include 'Vicious badger roams Scots school grounds as farmer warns parents' (*Daily Record*), 'Man calls 999 because he's scared of a hedgehog' (*ITV News*), and 'Rewilding of Horsham Park a "mad idea" amid fears long grass could house "lots of insects"' (*Sussex Express*).

Our national zoophobia is a symptom of our isolation. Knowledge and familiarity are forms of protection.

If a species that has become naïve suddenly finds itself in the company of an antagonist again, it may be able to revert in time. Moose in the United States did so within a single generation as bears and wolves began to return in the twentieth century. Howler monkeys on Barro Colorado Island in the Panama Canal learned how to stay safe when they heard harpy eagle calls, even though the reintroduced eagles had been away for at least 50 years.

But the time it can take to progress from clash to coexistence is a tumultuous one. Compared to the hundreds of years that boar have been absent from Britain, the decades they've been back for have been mere moments. Culturally, we're still caught in the first few rapid heartbeats, adrenaline riding the rush of our blood in the face of the unknown.

In churning up the physical substance of the British landscape, wild boar have dramatically changed how places feel to some of the humans who live there too. And why should this stop with the land?

How have the boar changed the very substance of *us*?

When I browsed news articles in 2014 ahead of my first research trip to the Forest of Dean, their claims of boar-related chaos seemed outlandish. My only frame of reference was the media-stoked hysteria whenever a London fox strolled into someone's house.

The doubt was wiped away by the very first interview I did. Fresh off the M4, I arrived beside a horse paddock, delivered from the confines of my car into bright clean country air. But I was here to listen to a story of blood and tears. It was one experienced by Liz's husband, Dan, though he didn't have the time to meet me. By the end of my meeting with Liz, I wondered if he had also not wanted to relive it.

As we stood in the sun, Liz's account of her husband's memories came out in jagged pieces, toing and froing between different points of the attack. He'd been walking with their two little terriers Honey and Howie on a path he knew well. Liz had already told him she didn't like him going there, because she'd heard about a big male boar who'd been hanging around and chasing off other people's dogs.

A blow came from behind without warning. Dan caught himself, though not before he grazed his chin on the ground.

He looked up to see a boar bowling Howie over and biting him. At Dan's shout, the boar ran away, but Honey – ever-protective of her brother – gave chase. Dan plunged into the undergrowth in pursuit. He heard Honey squealing. He began to weep. As he was searching, the boar circled back to him. He swore and shouted to keep him at bay.

Finally, Dan found Honey in the bracken. She was bleeding from a tusk wound to her back leg. As Dan gathered her up in his jacket and carried her away, Howie came limping up, fur soaked in blood too. Dan added him to his arms. After rushing the mile back to the car, he rang Liz to tell her what had happened. At first, she thought he was joking.

Both dogs made a full physical recovery. But they, and their owners, became far more nervous about going into the woods.

———

The love we may hold for other animals, *chosen* animals, can make us vulnerable in ways we wouldn't be otherwise. There is the threat of actual injury when a human finds themselves between their dog and a boar. And there is the anguish of a companion's pain, even death.

Horses and their riders can find themselves so entangled too. A survey of Dean residents by University of Worcester researchers in 2015 found that 58 respondents, or 11 per cent of the sample, had experienced their horses spooking after seeming to sense boar. Two horses reacted so violently that they hurt themselves. Even if only those people who felt most strongly about the issue bothered to answer the survey – a perennial curse in social science – it's still unnerving to imagine 58 different riders dotted about the Forest, trying to control panicked horses.

A year before that survey, it hadn't been hard for me to find riders to interview for my dissertation. Horses had stopped dead and refused to go further, or had reared or bucked. Liz's once bolted. Some people had stopped riding in the woods or been forced to sell nervy horses.

It is commonly known that many horses are afraid of any kind of pig. There remains no definitive answer for why. Going by discussions on hobby forums, riders are very much divided in terms of whether it's boar themselves that horses fear, or specifically their smell, or simply their strangeness. No animal behaviourist seems to have investigated the question, a research void that is begging to be filled.

Lydia, one rider I spoke to, had more unusual circumstances than most in the Dean: she was partially deaf. She no longer took her hearing dog into the woods in case he ran off after boar. Yet, in a way, she felt *less* vulnerable than other riders. She couldn't hear the boar – their grunts and snorts, the rustling of undergrowth – and this lessened the risk that she might otherwise transmit her fear to her horse.

'If you're sat on your horse and tensing up, the horse gets more nervous because they feel what you're doing,' Lydia explained. This made sense. A human physically binds themselves to their horse when they mount; the motions of their body, and therefore their mind, cannot be hidden.

Despite her suspicion that fear made things worse, Lydia couldn't help feeling it whenever she rode. Perhaps that fear is part of the reason for the problems that riders still have with boar in the Dean, and why the horses never get a chance to accept them. A horse becomes nervous when it senses boar; the rider remembers; when the rider next sees boar, the worry in their stiffening body infects the horse beneath them. A circular flow of senses between two different animals. Scientists in the field of more-than-human geography call this kind of experience *becoming* – the changes, however ephemeral or lasting, that humans and nonhumans undergo through their encounters with each other. When we feel the force of another's existence through the senses of our body, we are remade. And so: a rider is in the process of becoming-horse. A ridden horse is in the process of becoming-human.

And to meet a boar means, even if for a fleeting moment, becoming-boar.

———

Rose was another member of the anti-boar contingent. She was both a dog owner and a horse rider. Yet it was the encounters she'd had on foot that refused to loosen their grip on her.

The first had been unremarkable. She'd seen one small boar in the distance and had felt curiosity. Nothing more. The second time, she found a huge individual standing on the path ahead, barring her way. Backtracking would've cost her extra miles, so she cut into the trees. Whereupon she walked into the midst of an entire sounder.

'I was panic-stricken, that horrible adrenaline-rush feeling, real fear,' Rose spoke quickly as we sat in her kitchen. She kept switching between past and present tenses, the memory throbbing. 'I don't know what to do, I can't go back that way because the other boar's there. So I just got out of that area as quickly as I could, and they didn't come for me that day, they didn't seem that aware of me. I think that's the time I've been most frightened, and I felt that awful adrenaline rush until I got home, which took about a mile and a half. The whole way home I was absolutely panic-stricken.'

To me, there was a deep and almost unnerving intimacy in learning of the movement of muscle and blood and hormone in another's body. Dismay crept in, too, that my boar – or the boar as they lived in my own mind – were the cause.

Despite that terror-drenched meeting, Rose continued to go out walking alone. Why wouldn't she? She'd done so for years. But now, it came with a price. On another day, a summer's evening around 8 p.m., she came across a sounder with boarlets. According to Rose, a huge male was with them, although this was almost certainly the matriarch. Regardless, Rose shouted, which had made the boar run away in the past.

'But not that night,' she said, voice dropping. 'The male came for me, and I just stood there, kept still, shouted "Go away!" And he kept on coming at a trot. So I slowly edged away and went behind a tree because I'd heard that their sight isn't very good. He seemed to lose me, and he went back to them.'

Hiding behind a tree spoke of calm logic, a more pacifist approach than throwing stones as someone else told me they'd done. Rose hadn't been so ruled by fear that time that she simply ran away. This didn't surprise me. She was a woman in her early 60s, living alone on the edge of the woods, keeping horses. I sensed a core as strong as an oak. But the boar were a storm of an intensity she had never encountered before. 'From then on,' she continued, 'I couldn't go where I wanted to because I knew they were there.'

Rose's words rang in tune with so many other voices that I've heard in the Dean.

I cannot go where I used to go.

There are people who ride or walk, alone or with dogs or children, who now avoid certain paths. Or certain areas altogether. Who go only in daylight, never near dusk, and never in the night. Only with a companion. Only at the times of year when the bracken is low enough that the boar can be sighted. Or the times of year when fewer boarlets and protective mothers are around.

The shock of fear that first pulsed through their bodies when they came face to face with a boar, or when a boar chased off their dog, or when their horse took fright, has crystallised, taken on a permanency. As you learn something new, neurons in your brain change their connections with each other. Experiences rewire you. They prime you to process future experiences in a particular way. Fear can beget more fear, a circle becoming harder and harder to break.

I cannot go where I used to go.

It isn't only the people themselves who have changed. They can no longer go to the places they used to go to because those places no longer exist, not as they knew them. Landscapes have become haunted, both by memories and by trails, prints, dung, bent wire, mud on trees, tooth-scores, rootings, wallows. The boar have made the forest *theirs* instead.

Even when these people do go into the woods now, they consciously modify their behaviour. They don't take their children with them, or they keep their dog on the lead all the time, or they sing or talk loudly when they find themselves passing through a place that feels boar-ish.

This is another power of the boar, then: to conjure fear in certain people that can dictate where they go and what they do there. Though it is a power that depends on how we choose to respond.

Ecologists speak of something called the *landscape of fear*, which describes the space-and-time map that an animal holds in their mind of the movements of other animals they perceive to be dangerous; the peril and safety that marks each place they know. Rarely do you read or hear an explicit reference to humans' landscapes of fear. But we do talk about them. Some of us know them all too well. *I don't go down that path, I wouldn't go there at night, I only go with a friend* – these things could be said by anyone who has felt the rawness of being vulnerable in the human world.

The people I've met who have described experiencing the most extreme reactions to the boar have all been women. What to make of this? Many of them insisted to me that they weren't wimps, and I believe them. Like Rose, the woods had called to each of them. Only later did the register of its voice change to one of hostility.

After I move to the Dean, a new neighbour tells me in a half-joking tone that she's never met a boar, and hopes she never will in case it attacks her. Does the awareness of our physical vulnerability – in comparison to most men – make it easier for us to imagine other beings exploiting that? I'm lucky; when I lived in London I rarely felt unsafe. But on the occasions when that undercurrent of fear came alive in me – one that I know many others carry with them all the time – my map was rewritten.

I never feel afraid in the woods. There are places in London that, now a little wiser, I would never dare pass through alone in the dark. But night in the woods is somewhere I can go with a torch in my pocket and the freedom to wander. To curl up against a tree and listen. Drift away into half-dreams, if the air is warm enough and the bole is the right shape to cup my back. When I hear the snort or the dragonish exhalation of a boar, or my torchlight snags on a great dark form, the spike in my chest is glee. Not terror.

I'm not alone. Plenty of other women in the Dean are unafraid. Viv, who blames the boar for ruining her beech wood, seems to hold too much anger towards them to have any space left for fear. I think also of Angela, owner of the Pygmy Pinetum garden centre, who wears an impish smile as she recalls shooing away a young male boar who had broken in to pilfer her stock of bird food.

Many of those women who particularly fear the boar are horse riders, while I have yet to come across a male rider in the Dean. Perhaps for these women, fear for their own bodies is knotted up with fear for their animals. Or maybe they and others have simply been more open with me. Nearly all the men I've spoken to who want the boar to be better controlled or eradicated have only ever given financial, aesthetic or ecological reasons – ones that on the surface feel cool and emotionless. In an unguarded moment, perhaps they might admit to more.

Landscapes of fear would be lighter psychological burdens if the zones of safety and danger within them remained static. But they don't. They shift. Contract. Expand.

'You tend to take note of where you've seen the boar and you avoid that area for a bit. Then you think after a while that they've probably moved on. So I have a mental map for them now.' Rose's voice grew firm with anger. 'And when the bracken's up, you're watching for it to move, which could be anything in there … but you're constantly, you never just … I used to just shut my eyes when I was riding through the forest, knowing the horse wouldn't bump into anything. But I'd never do that now. I'm frightened every time I go out. I'm apprehensive. You just don't know.'

You just don't know.

I know there are boar in my woods, and I always hope to see them, and yet they always surprise me. Sounders can be vocal affairs, sometimes. Sometimes not. I've heard several accounts where the teller was walking through bracken, only to realise they'd placed themselves in the centre of a sounder. Imagine a chorus of boar heads lifting in unison above the ferns to look at you.

There's another country in Europe that, although it is no island, offers something of a parallel to the British case: Sweden. Wild boar returned there in the 1970s, and wolves in the 1980s. In a 2010 survey about attitudes towards these species and others, one third of respondents said they were afraid of meeting boar – a *higher* number than those who feared wolves. This is presumably because boar are far more populous. Yet, while Sweden has more boar than Britain does, the density is far lower; not only is the country bigger, but more than 70 per cent of it is forested, compared to our paltry 13 per cent. The boar have far more space to spread out and to avoid humans. Of Great Britain's wild boar, only in the Dean do they seem to be packed in enough to achieve a kind of neurological critical mass. The things that people living there have told me have never been echoed elsewhere in England or in Scotland.

If you can't know exactly where boar are, then you have to assume they could be anywhere within your chosen perimeter. That they are everywhere. Nowhere in the woods or around its edges can be trusted. This becomes the case even more over spring and summer as the bracken grows and better hides the boar, whether they mean for this or not. When the woods should be at their most joyful, a riot of green life, they become full of dark promise instead.

And when you do meet a boar, you can't know what they'll do.

Late May. I am walking through a wedge of scrubland with houses on either side. The sun has set, though a few scattered clouds hold the dregs of its light. No one else is around, and being here already feels like a wasted exercise. I'd heard a rumour that there's a sounder often to be found in this place. I can't believe it, certain that the rangers would've shot any boar comfortable enough to be here.

A rustling. On my left, 15m away, stands a huge sweet chestnut tree. Its lowest branches reach to the ground, and they are shaking. The noise coming from the space hidden behind them is too much to be a badger or the like.

I can't get any closer thanks to a wall of brambles. For the next few minutes, I make do with peering through the thorns as the branches keep shaking and leaf litter crunches.

A snort. Then the ridge of a long dark shape flowing through the undergrowth. I crouch and tuck myself into an alcove of the bramble wall, feeling it catch on my clothes. I hear the boar emerge on my side, onto the path. Her head, and then the rest of her body, draws into view.

She is now 4m away.

I can't tell if she smells or sees me first. I've forgotten to change out of my blue hoodie, and I must be bright against the dark green. She inhales with that deep hissing sound, lifting and dropping her snout. Then she begins to do something I've never seen before: she turns her body to face me side-on, before taking a step forward so that her head is pointing at me again, before taking a step back to show me her flank again.

She repeats these motions over and over. And at last, I recognise this strange dance.

'They come towards you and once they get close enough they'll stop, head up in the air, really deep breaths, and then they'll turn sideways, which is their way of saying, "Look how big I am",' Neil the wildlife photographer had said to me years ago. 'And they'll stand there for what seems like forever, though it's probably a couple of seconds, and then they just go.'

But she is not going.

I've never been so close, for so long, to a *wild* wild boar before. There's enough light left for me to see the many different shades of her face. The bristles of her crest have risen, running from the back of her head to halfway along her spine. Highest at the shoulders, it lends her the proud profile of a hyena.

I want this moment to last for as long as it possibly can. And yet, another part of me is thinking: *don't take the risk*. Every other time I've come across boar, once my presence has been detected, they've bolted. My lack of fear has only ever been reinforced – but in this moment, caution curls its fingers around me, and I yield.

'Okay, okay,' I murmur, rising slowly. She takes a few steps back. But doesn't run.

I begin to walk back the way I'd come. Every time I glance over my shoulder, she's still standing there. There's a question written in her body, but who is asking it: her or me?

I don't know what would've happened if I'd waited longer. I don't know why she chose not to run.

For as long as the boar have been learning how to be here again, and learning us, we've been trying to learn them. *Trying* is very much the operative word here. That this book so often draws on examples from other countries is testament to our lack of home-grown knowledge. And it isn't only that we broke a chain of understanding when we destroyed our boar population centuries ago. Over time, and especially over the last century, our capacity to watch and work out the ways of wild things has diminished in step with those wild things. And into this void of unknowing pour all of our assumptions and fears, fuel ready for a match.

The sow in the scrubland showed me no aggression. But plenty of people in the Dean say that they or someone they know has been charged. It has even happened to cyclists, I hear. In each incident, the person escaped unharmed.

'If a boar was actually charging you, they run faster than Usain Bolt so you wouldn't have a hope in hell of getting away from them,' Neil said when I asked for his perspective. 'They're very short-sighted, so if I'm a boar and I've seen you and I can't smell or hear you, how am I going to work out what you are? I'll come towards you. I'll put my head up, sniffing the air, and I'll walk quite fast. And that's when people say, "I was charged".'

Neil acted out the scene as he narrated, shifting into boar-mode. He moved at what was meant to be a boar trot, telling me as he did that sometimes it might be that a boar is trying to establish your identity as quickly as possible. Check the threat out, then get out.

Yet, as logical as all this sounded, it didn't match up with every account. The man who once found himself confronted by the jaw-clacking sow defending her boarlets had, another time, had a nervy brush with a male.

'A big tusker suddenly came out from the ferns. I could tell instantly he was going to go for me. And he absolutely *careered* at me. I managed to get inside the garden gate just in time. Pro-boar people will say, "Oh, that's just a mock charge". Well, fair enough, it might be, but I will challenge anybody to stay still and let it happen.'

Given the number of people with a story about being charged, and the fact that the person escaped in every single case, it's reasonable to be sceptical that the boar in question was out to get them. But something *is* happening for people to believe it, to experience it, to lay down memories and be changed in the process.

Perhaps the problem begins with deer. They are, after all, the only point of reference that people in Britain have for large wild land animals. This, as well as their ubiquity, has left us with a rigid belief of what behaviours in such animals are 'normal'. Of what is natural. And by not always instantly running away like a deer does, the boar are *ab*normal. *Un*natural. They have the audacity to challenge what we were once certain of: that every other being on this island is terrified of us. Boar are the breaker of taboos and uprooters of our entire world-view.

And so, faced with a creature that is choosing not to run but instead to step towards you, perhaps a human might get a little panicked. Your brain clutches for any kind of information it can use. You may have heard stories from other people about being charged; from these, an expectation has been quietly sketching itself, and is now given life by this boar that is, *oh Christ*, coming closer. No time to gauge speed. Any rational thought is overridden by a klaxon yelling at you to get the hell out of there. And even once you are safe from the danger that the creature might pose, your body is still singing with it, writing the memory of it. A memory that you'll probably speak of to others.

'Humans recognise what they see not from the optical information supplied by their eyes, but based on knowledge and experience,' comments Satoshi Kikuchi, a professor of cognitive psychology at Shinshu University, in response to what comes to be labelled a 'phantom bear panic' on the Japanese island of Hokkaido between April and May 2022. He adds, 'If you had received information that bears had appeared in residential areas, then you will see bears.'

Perhaps big cat sightings spring from the same well. As in various other parts of the UK, the Forest of Dean is apparently home to a healthy population of so-called panthers (as in, melanistic leopards or jaguars). Most recently, several residents insist they've seen a lone wolf. You can probably tell that I place these sightings in the same category as the Loch Ness Monster.

When I conducted interviews for my dissertation in 2014, out of pure curiosity I often asked people if they thought the reports of big cats were credible. A surprising number of them did, which would seem to disprove George Monbiot's theory that it is the absence of dangerous wildlife that causes our brains to superimpose them onto housecats and muntjacs. However, my research into this wasn't exactly rigorous, and one might retort that the boar are not dangerous *enough* to satiate us. But I digress. My point is, if some 2,000 or so people per year in the UK believe they have glimpsed a very big cat instead of a very small cat, it doesn't seem beyond the realms of possibility that some of us will mistake a curious trotting boar for a furious running one.

And yet, while a charge may not actually be a charge, we still can't know for sure what a boar intends. Nor how to anticipate their actions. It stands to reason that, when faced with a creature such as ourselves – a creature that is unpredictable, that may run or stand there or throw stones or have a wolf at heel – boar will call on their intelligence to tailor their response. A deer won't usually take a chance, but a boar may decide that they can risk continuing to forage. Or that a human is worth a closer look. Or that a determined trot will be enough to make you leave her and her babies alone. Hence, one of the commonest words people use to describe the boar is *random*. No matter that the encounter will almost certainly end without harm. Out in the woods, between the trees, amid the bracken, in the moment when you meet a species that is willing to hold your gaze, cool logic can fall away.

The horse rider Lydia said something to me that, perhaps more than any other statement I've heard, embodies what the boar mean for people who fear them.

'I don't know that I'm safe.'

After Rose had shared her own story, it was strange to emerge from the cool dimness of her kitchen to a cloudless blue day. She needed to feed the horses, and we both needed to stretch our legs, so I walked with her down to the paddock. Her house snuggled into the side of a hill, and her land stretched to the bottom of the vale. Buzzards cried above. The warm air smelled grassy with hay, while insects danced in tree-cut sunbeams.

I turned Rose's experiences over in my mind, but they felt distant. As if told to me in a language of which I only knew a few words. I just didn't know what it was to come face to face with another animal and feel terror. And to be so ruled by that terror that it could make a den inside me and change how I lived.

As I stood in the field, distracted, one of the horses turned and put its back to me. It probably didn't care that I was standing there. But after a second, panic jolted through me as my own adrenal glands opened their floodgates and I jumped out of the way.

From as early as I could remember, my parents had impressed in me the rule that you must never, ever go behind a horse. Because it might kick and kill you. I'd spent little time around horses in adulthood, yet it turned out that the lesson hadn't faded. I might not be afraid of wild animals, but apparently my bravery had limits.

Remembering that moment in the paddock makes me wonder if some of the children growing up in the Dean have come to fear boar because of their own parents' fear.

Rose didn't grow up in a place with boar. And she hadn't heard frightening stories from other locals before her own experiences. Or at least, they hadn't mattered enough to her to mention them to me. Was the terror of seeing that boar on the path the waking cry of some ancestral memory, or the result of an unconscious absorption of culture from abroad?

And, just as important to ask: why are some people *unafraid* of the boar?

———

Another kitchen, another cup of milky tea, another woman. Anne had a bright smile and a birdlike delicateness. If Rose was an oak, she was a wren. She and her family had been here since 1997, drawn partly by the beauty of the area. All you could see from her house was hillside and trees plump with summer.

When Anne first saw rootings, she didn't know what had caused them. After she learned that boar had arrived, over months she observed the rootings creeping closer and closer to her local woods. She waited in hope. When she met one at last, she wasn't disappointed.

'The neighbour rushed in to say, "There's a boar walking down the road!" So of course we all ran out. We followed it for quite a long way, and it wasn't disturbed by that. I think it was a male on its own. It was pretty big, and I was quite amazed at the size.'

Anne began to see boar often, alone or in sounders, with her mild-mannered Labrador at heel. 'It always makes me sort of jump in fright when I see one. Sometimes they can look absolutely huge and terrifying. And on lots of occasions the dog and I have been followed. I've always just turned and walked slowly away and they've sometimes walked after me. Which is fine. Although sometimes you start looking round to see if there are trees that you could climb if it came to it, and there never are! And anyway the dog can't climb trees.' Anne laughed at herself, as she often did through our conversation. As if this could reconcile the apparent contradiction between the words she used – *fright, terrifying* – and the delight with which she said them.

'I love seeing the boar. I love watching them. But sometimes it's the scariest ones that are the best.' She began describing an encounter that had happened just the week before. 'If I see them, I don't pursue them. But I also try not to change where I'm going to go. With this one, it was coming up the path towards me, and it was relatively close at that point, so I veered off the path, and it veered off the path too, and I thought *Oh*. I veered off some more and it veered off again. So at that point – and I've hardly ever done it – I made a noise to scare it. I went *"Wuh!"* and raised my arms, and it just turned tail. And then I saw all the babies. So that's why it was more aggressive.'

Anne's experience made a memory of my own stir. I'd been out snorkelling on a Maldivian reef when a black-tip reef shark came gliding towards me. Black-tips aren't brave around humans. Normally. Up until then, I'd barely seen more than the flick of a tail as they slunk away into the depths. But this one – this one approached, and circled. In the memory, there is nothing except that eye, a grey globe split by a long black slit. Looking at – no – into me. Holding my two-eyed gaze. I knew in a cool, back-of-the-brain kind of way that it wouldn't attack. But for a few seconds, I believed it would. Fear surged through my body with the elegance of a slow-motion lightning strike. Then the shark turned and swam away, and the essence of my fear tipped into something else.

Thrill.

Anne didn't use that word, but others have. The joy of not being in control, of finding yourself somewhere new where human laws don't hold sway. Of not knowing what will happen and, instead of rejecting this, revelling in it.

Nan Shepherd, beloved author of *The Living Mountain*, wrote about standing in a cold tarn in the Cairngorms with her feet at the edge of a great depth. 'That first glance down had shocked me to a heightened power of myself, in which even fear became a rare exhilaration: not that it ceased to be fear, but fear itself, so impersonal, so keenly apprehended, enlarged rather than constricted the spirit.'

A fear that makes us more, rather than less.

Those who embrace the fear of boar may do so partly for the delicious uncertainty of these encounters. But, like me, they don't feel totally adrift from the possibility of knowing boar. They insist that the animals' body language can be read, that encounters can be guided.

'If their tails are up, they're much more likely to be bothered,' Anne said authoritatively. Another woman had noticed that boar tended to lean slightly backwards with tail raised if they were readying to approach her. She always heeded the warning. And if the boar followed anyway, well, they weren't trying to attack. They were no keener than her to risk injury.

But there is always that little *what if*, the key ingredient in the joyful fear of boar.

'I can't help being conscious that they are very big, and I know that they can move very fast and if it actually came to it…' Anne laughed again, 'I think they'd win.'

As I listened, I buzzed with a silent pleasure at recognising that she shared with me the same complex thrill of being in the presence of a creature with unknown intentions.

When I asked Anne if she'd made any adjustments in her daily life for the boar, she answered, 'I'm usually more conscious of it. So there's a couple of paths that are quite overgrown where they quite often seem to be, and I do think twice before I go there. But I still go.'

There was an important reason for this: she stayed attentive to the body language of her dog.

'If there's boar, she just stops, and she stares in the direction. And then I stop and I'm really trying to hear and sometimes it can take ages, but I put her on the lead at that point. And then wait till something happens. Sometimes nothing happens. But usually, she's right.'

Other people said similar things. Dogs' ears pricking up, the posture stiffening, or a suddenly intent gaze – these are all signals that it's time to shorten the lead or to change direction and go down a different path. It's a tuning-in that harks back to the days long ago when we used the senses of dogs, and our ability to translate these, to help us hunt down prey. And there is, I think, a beauty in this. A becoming-dog-boar – or, if the owner notices the boar first, a becoming-human-boar for the dog. It's a mirror to the loop of fear that seems to emerge between some horses and riders.

It is evidence of adaptation.

Some of those who wish the boar weren't here have changed their behaviour, and hate the animals themselves for this. Those who embrace the boar have often done the same, but don't begrudge this. They don't mind keeping their dogs on leads, or tying falconry bells to collars to broadcast a jangling warning, or switching direction to cede their path to a boar. To experience the fear of boar as something good is not to abandon the animal common sense that is always in us, even if buried. The wild boar are respected as beings in possession of both consciousness and physical power. The risk of them is weighed, and found lighter than joy. In Britain, the idea of shifting habits or adopting new ones to accommodate a wild animal is, in a way, unimaginable. But there are already people showing us that it can be done.

'I want to see the forest become more wild,' Anne told me. To her, the boar had initiated a process. They weren't an endpoint in themselves – they were a gateway. But to what?

Since the loss of wolves, no human in Britain has had to pause before they step outside and think *what if...?* about a wild animal. For centuries, no human here has carried the awareness of wild animals that is the natural condition of all other species and, indeed, of many other humans.

And perhaps there's no better word for this than *rewilding*. A rewilding of ourselves.

CHAPTER EIGHT

The Boar People (Part II)

The first group of boar to return to the Dean were dumped by a down-and-out-farmer. The second were let loose so that hunters could have their sport.

Even if both these stories are true, we'll never know the full truth of the heritage of the Dean boar. We can, however, make several assumptions about both them and their brethren roaming elsewhere in the country.

Every one of the founders of our populations in Britain was born on a farm. Long chains of their ancestors would've been born in captivity too. Perhaps the odd wild male might've come along to break down a fence and add himself to the family tree. But we know for sure from DNA analysis that there are also farmed pig genes in at least some of our boar.

The founders' genomes – the full library of genes in each body – may even have been curated by captivity itself. Conservation-minded zoos often face an uphill struggle against the inadvertent selection for 'captive-friendly' traits in their animals, which further down the genetic line could reduce an individual's chances of survival and reproduction in the wild were they to be released. It also seems logical to assume that farmers would've culled or sterilised the wildest of boar from among the stock destined to go free in Britain. Or that some of these individuals made their escape, thus removing their genes from those particular pools anyway.

Even if the founders had been genetically 'pure', the fact remains that they grew up on farms. Their food was given to them by humans. They were used to being near us. Their worlds stank of us. The Dartmoor boar who hit headlines in 2007 for their run-in with an elderly lady's dachshund were reported to have been attracted another time by the sound of a quad bike, which was taken to mean that they were well accustomed to being fed by a farmer.

And yet, when the Dean boar found themselves free again, despite their heritage and despite everything they'd ever known, they flowed into the woods with the determination of roots finding cracks in stone.

Not every new tribe of wild boar in Britain has survived the crucible of our modern countryside. But those that have feel like a miracle. What might have gone through their minds during the upheaval of their homecoming? And, if their being here has changed us, how exactly has it changed *them*?

Pigs are smart, supposedly more so than dogs and three-year-old humans. This is accepted wisdom. Logically, therefore, boar should also be smart. I had this assumption in mind when I asked photographer Neil if the ones he tracked ever came to recognise him. I wanted him to give me a straight yes. I was especially keen to know if wild boar were capable of recognising members of another species as individuals, that is, inclined to behave in different ways to each other.

Neil let me down, because he couldn't say if any had come to recognise him beyond his membership of the human race. However, the question did get him talking about one young female who'd etched a deep impression in him the summer before. 'She was blacker than her siblings. They start out brown and go blacker when they get older. But she was very black, and smaller than the others.'

She'd stayed in her natal sounder to raise her first litter, mother to three out of a summer crop of 25 boarlets. Neil could only tell how many belonged to her because he'd spotted her with them before they'd joined up with the sounder.

'She was curious, and protective. With the other females, they'd look up for a moment like they were thinking, "Oh, I can't see anything, never mind". But this one would stand up, and she'd walk about 50 yards away to get the wind blowing through me to her. She was always, always doing it. She'd suddenly be over there and I'd be thinking, "Any second now you're going to snort, aren't you?" And once she did, they were gone.'

Now as I read back over Neil's interview transcript, my curiosity is piqued anew, because I'd normally expect that kind of surveillance behaviour from the matriarch. The black-haired female's mother was, according to Neil, huge and clearly the leader of the sounder. Yet the daughter took it upon herself to become a nuisance to a human whose particular scent she may or may not have come to remember from previous times.

Equally as intriguing as the personality at play was the way in which Neil described the sounder fleeing each time: 'They all seem to know what direction to go in. It's not a scatter-all-over.'

Other people have said similar things: sounders seem to coordinate their escape, often going in unexpected directions before regrouping and vanishing out of sight altogether.

'I wish I could understand their snorts,' Neil added. He didn't expand further, although I thought I knew what he was really saying: what if those snorts contained instructions? The word *snort* doesn't do justice to the alarm call that boar make. It needs a few more letters in it at least, to better match the long, low belching sound that seems to resonate all the way from the belly. It's a sound that surely has the space for a map route. Then again, boar make it even when they appear to be alone. We just don't know.

We know far more about farmed pigs, who in studies demonstrate a range of cognitive aptitudes (at least by human standards). Among these, pigs understand that certain gestures and sounds can represent objects; they show 'Theory of Mind', whereby an individual is able to imagine the perspective of another individual; and, yes, they can – at least in some contexts – tell different humans apart. They are no doubt supported in such endeavours by their prefrontal cortex, a part of the brain vital to 'higher-level' cognition, and one that in pigs is proportionally similar in size to that of primates.

The performance of pigs in labs is perhaps even more impressive when we consider that their brains are overall smaller than wild boar ones. One of the unavoidable prices of domestication is a smaller brain, and out of all the farmed creatures in the world today, pigs' brains have shrunk the most. This doesn't automatically mean that wild boar are smarter than their domesticated brethren. Much of the loss is thought to be down to the lack of olfactory stimulation in the lives of farmed pigs, given that they no longer have need of their superpowered smelling sense with all the accompanying brain-software. Regardless, it's plausible that, after us, wild boar are the most intelligent of all land animals native to Britain.

Even the already-respectable degree of intelligence that scientists have assigned to pigs may itself be an underestimate. Henry Mance of the *Financial Times* points out that cognition studies tend to focus on animals that favour eyesight. Yet for any pig, including wild boar, the world is largely felt, learned and known through their nose.

Despite the lack of research into wild boar brainpower, tantalising hints exist. As reported in an article in the *Guardian* in 2019, one researcher from Vienna who'd been trapping wild boar noted that they had taken to disappearing upon his arrival in their woods. He wondered if his physical appearance or his car or some other identifying feature might be giving him away.

In Basel Zoo in Switzerland, keepers noticed that a group of boar had taken to carrying their apples to a creek to wash sand off. They continued to do so even when intrigued scientists kept them hungry, thus showing themselves capable of delayed gratification. Humans tend not to manage this until they're at least five years old. What's more, the Basel Zoo boar had been transferred from several other zoos and, while none washed their food at their previous homes, some brought with them a habit of standing in water while they ate – a behaviour that the scientists suggested might be 'a group tradition'. In their new home, these boar seem to have taught each other a new way of doing things. You could call this culture.

You could also call water, in the context of food-washing, a tool. Tool-use is one of the hallowed markers of the kind of intelligence that humans venerate, a touchstone for thinking about how other animals think ever since Jane Goodall watched chimps bending twigs and stripping their leaves off to turn them into termite fishing rods. Consider, then, the case at a zoo in Paris of a group of Visayan warty pigs. Close relatives of wild boar, the warty pigs decided to start digging nests using sticks clasped between their teeth. The behaviour was puzzling, because the sticks didn't appear to make the digging process more efficient. Indeed, when scientists decided to offer them spatulas, these were shunned. Perhaps it was simply a quirk that caught on, in the same way that orcas off the west coast of North America took to wearing dead salmon on their heads in 1987 but had all grown bored of the practice by the following summer.

Play is another behaviour that in adult animals we associate with intelligence. In 2021 in the Italian city of Genoa, a passer-by filmed a wild boar pushing a football around with their snout with apparent delight. It's hard not to smile at the footage. Earlier in the year, another boar, or perhaps the same one, had been spotted with a football in a nearby playground.

I suspect that wild boar across the world have plenty more surprises in store for us which, in retrospect, won't feel surprising at all. But it will take work and time to uncover them, not least because so much boar social life takes place at night. Trail cameras are one answer to this, as illustrated by a case in a Czech Republic nature reserve in 2020. Researchers had been catching and collaring boar there, placing a camera in front of each baited trap. While the cameras were set to only take a photo every two minutes, that proved enough to record an unexpected event.

One night, two young boar were trapped. Hours later, the rest of their sounder arrived, led by a single adult female. In the first image of her, she sniffs at the thick logs holding the trap door in place. She looks interested, her ears held high.

In the next two images, she is transformed: the hair of her shoulders and back has bristled into a great crest, her ears are flat against her skull, and in the infra-red her single visible eye gleams bright white. The camera has frozen her in the act of charging the log. She arches, mustering her strength. She looks like a forest god.

In the final few images, neither she nor the other free boar are in sight. But the two logs keeping the trap shut have been pushed out of place and one door is ajar.

29 minutes after the adult female was first photographed charging the trap; the two captive juveniles have vanished.

The researchers considered this to be a clear case of intentional rescue, noting that the female had risked injury in attacking the trap. It may not even have been the first time she'd done it; before they started to use cameras, on two separate occasions the researchers had received an electronic alert that a trap had been triggered, only to find it empty when they arrived.

The female didn't need to rescue those two juveniles. The images show she was accompanied by at least four other young boar, probably her own offspring. She had fallbacks to carry forth her genetic legacy. Arguably, she put all their

THE BOAR PEOPLE (PART II)   145

lives at risk by making so much noise and remaining at the
cage for so long. Her action was not rational. *29 minutes*: that
length of time speaks of single-minded purpose. Of an
intense emotional pulling. It's as if she simply couldn't ignore
the terror of her children.

My own trail camera hasn't captured any such obvious
demonstrations of altruism. But in the early spring, I watch
something that makes me wonder.

I'm reviewing a new batch of clips from the spruce
wallow. In my haste, I start them from newest to oldest
instead of the other way around. Over the course of several,
recorded in the early hours of one morning, a sounder of
adults and last year's boarlets spend all their time sniffing the
same patch of ground. Just one of the females is doing
something different: she's staring out into the woods, her
stance erect. Vigilant.

Only when I watch the footage from the morning before
do I grasp the reason for the group's obsession. The camera
has captured a Forestry England ranger standing over a
dead boar, one they've clearly shot. The body is a deflated
heap of fur and legs, and it lies exactly where the sounder
will sniff. Over the next few clips, the ranger attaches a
cable while an idling vehicle grumbles out of sight. With a
whining from the winch, the body starts shifting along the
ground. Its progress halts just before the edge of the frame.
The camera doesn't trigger again until dark, when the
sounder comes.

The previous night, a large lone boar had meandered
past the wallow. They might've been a male, or a female
whose sounder didn't cross the camera's field of vision. It's
possible that they were the one who died the next morning.
Did those boar who gathered around the scent attend to it
with recognition, even distress? Were they detecting death
or simply a presence that would soon weather away to
nothing?

And did they connect it with the other scents that must have been there – those of humans?

———

Some of our wild boar populations began with a slow smoulder that escaped the notice of most. Not so in the Forest of Dean. The first group in 1999 seems to have been, shall we say, a little more naïve. They were reportedly rounded up once; how easily their story might have ended there. Even after the second group arrived, a stubborn streak of tameness remained, as clear as the rips that some had in their ears from removed farm tags. A few made such names for themselves that locals still talk about them. Gerald would trot through one village at 6.30 every evening to check out the bin pickings and beg for bread at people's doorsteps. He once got into someone's kitchen and had to be lured out with the rattling of a packet of crisps.

The Pygmy Boar were so-called because they liked to hang out on the grass outside the Pygmy Pinetum garden centre, which sits at a crossroads near the heart of the Dean. The Pygmy Boar were a litter whose mother had been poached, and tourists were only too happy to feed them in exchange for photos. They grew so popular it started to cause traffic.

The Beechenhurst Six took to grubbing for food at the picnic tables outside Forestry England's popular Beechenhurst Lodge. Again, they'd lost their mother, although not before she'd taught them their begging trade. When one of the boar realised that the food always came out of the cafe first, they decided to cut out the middleman (that is, the cafe patrons) and found their way inside the building. After that, Forestry England put up boar-proof fencing all around the site.

And then there was Boris: a boar so tame, he let people come up and scratch him. You've probably seen his face already. Being so mild mannered and amiable, he was beloved of photographers, and lives on in many a stock photo. David Slater took perhaps the most famous image of him, in which he stands just a metre away from an old lady with a walking stick. Although she's side-on, her face looking away from the camera, her smile is just about visible. She isn't afraid, and neither is Boris. His posture holds more curiosity than wariness. He and the lady look like neighbours going different ways who have paused to exchange pleasantries.

All these boar ended up being shot. Forestry England killed some of them, and poachers took care of the rest. They were easy pickings.

By the time I first came to the Dean, there were no more such legendary boar, and it was something of a lucky dip whether you'd meet individuals who seemed comfortable going about their business in full sight of humans. While I did not, plenty of other people continued to do so, based on what I was told in interviews and all the amateur footage I could find online.

Four years later in 2018, naturalist and author Nick Gates posted a video about his own meeting with the boar. It begins with him in the car on the way to the Dean, explaining that he hopes to see them for the first time. He pulls up in the middle of the forest and, hey presto, there's a sounder rooting by the road. They're working at the grassy ground, ignoring the humans gathering to watch. At one point they permit Nick to crouch just two or so metres away.

I cannot imagine this happening now. Indeed, it seems impossible to find footage like Nick's these days. Wildlife photographers and others who have put in countless hours honing their tracking skills all now say the same thing: the boar have become far warier.

It may be that the tithing of the least-wary boar has driven a population-wide personality shift at the genetic level. Yet this alone seems unlikely. Because all over the world, wild boar have shown themselves able to adapt rapidly to threats of the human kind – particularly hunting.

When a hunting season opens, within the space of a week or so an entire population may alter its lifestyle. Boar keep strictly nocturnal hours, avoid places with less cover even if it means finding less food, and relocate beyond their usual home grounds. They even seem able to realise when certain individuals are being targeted over others, because males turn especially secretive if it's only they who are being shot; a change that's even more striking considering the males are more solitary and thus surely less likely to witness others being shot. And once the hunting ends, boar may return to their old haunts within days.

Compared to driven hunts with their big clamorous groups of humans and dogs, the practice of stalking appears to effect less dramatic behavioural changes in boar. This type of hunting involves just one or a few people, and it's far quieter. Dogs aren't used, except perhaps to locate a boar once shot. A single stalker can slip into the skin of a forest's awareness like a splinter instead of a knife blade. Even then, the boar learn. They respond. The Forest of Dean's rangers, who often cull boar by stalking and have targets to meet, know this all too well.

'The boar will move on and find somewhere else if they learn it is risky … they are clever animals. So we have to rotate where we go,' one of them told PhD researcher Kieran O'Mahony.

When the second group were loosed in 2004, they were bereft of any sense of danger. My ex-ranger contact shot one in daylight a few weeks after they arrived. He recalled how another member of the sounder came trotting up to investigate the body, so he shot that one too.

It was never as easy again.

In the summer of 2022, photos pop up on Facebook of a gang of juveniles with half-faded stripes and gingery brown fur. No adults are with them. According to the photographer, they've been hanging around on the edge of Cannop Ponds, a popular picnic site with plenty of tourists to beg from. They show no fear of humans.

By the time I can get over to Cannop a few days later, it's too late. They've vanished. Or have been vanished. Most of the people commenting on the photos believe they were orphaned by Forestry England rangers, even though the agency's policy is to avoid shooting sows with dependent young at hoof. Poachers may have been responsible instead. The rangers might, however, have stepped in to shoot the orphans afterwards – because begging youngsters will turn into begging adults, and that is felt to pose too much risk to the public.

It's no coincidence that those juveniles took so swiftly to the same lifestyle as the Beechenhurst Six and the Pygmy Boar. As quickly as boar learn to fear us, they can just as quickly unlearn this, especially if food is involved. We can become a resource to them. Local naturalist Ed Drewitt tells me that some individuals have started pushing over his and his neighbours' black bins to get at the rubbish bags within. This anecdote is rather amusing, on one level. On another, it's nothing less than a reboot of the story of the boar's original transformation into the pig 9,000 years ago. A story that is probably more like those of dogs and cats than of chicken, cattle, sheep, goats or horses. While there is inevitably a degree of disagreement among academics, the domestication process for pigs probably involved boar being attracted to settlements by crops and refuse. The bolder boar, who took more risks and obtained more calories as a result, would have produced more offspring, offspring who were then in even better condition for producing lots of young. Sows living closer to humans would have been easier to take newborn boarlets from, and the social nature of their species would have made them easier to hand-rear.

Eventually, we placed fences around them.

Domestication of any species is never a one-way affair. It is always a collaboration. And wild boar are very much feisty co-authors in our shared history. As one lifelong resident phrased it in the Dean's unique dialect, 'They be their own bosses.'

Boar once chose, and still sometimes choose, to come closer to us. But they are always ready to draw back.

A few weeks after the Cannop orphans appear and disappear, another group turns up in my own wood. It's early morning and I'm walking home when, further up the path, dark bulky animals come ambling into sight. One, two, three, four.

Someone has a lot of Labradors, I think, and then, *Oh*.

I practically dive into the bracken. More boar file across the track: five, six, seven, eight, nine. Nine! The last one is slightly smaller, and redder. From where I crouch about 20m away, I can just about discern a hint of striping along their flank.

The group disappears into the greenery on the other side of the track. I stand and step forward. Too soon, as it turns out – with a cacophony of snorts, the juveniles flee in a whirlwind of shaking bracken.

At first, I wonder if they're the offspring of the Trio, whom I haven't seen in many weeks. They're a little too old for that, though. But I'm sure I would've come across them before if they and their mothers were regulars in the area. Just how far have they wandered?

I next see them on my camera at the spruce wallow. That's about two miles from our first meeting place, as the boar trots. Their choice is unsurprising. The first heatwave of 2022 has peaked, but July's end still holds the land in a searing grip. Water and mud are valuable resources. The wallow seems rarely left alone for a minute by the many groups of boar who orbit it. The Orphan Nine grab as much time there as they can. My notes on the first few video clips of them, on 28 July, go:

10.53 a.m.: *They're practically acting/looking like hyenas. Lots of raised manes.*
10.54 a.m.: *They're hyper. One does a little spin.*
10.55 a.m.: *They seem hyper aggressive/tetchy. One rubs itself on the camera tree with a sawing sound (image shakes).*
10.58 a.m.: *Intense fighting, one pretty much gets tossed in the air.*
10.59 a.m.: *Dance of the crazy fighting boar.*

They appear at the wallow throughout August. I count them every time. Nine, nine, still nine. They must be finding enough food to be spending so much energy frolicking and fighting each other. They remind me a little of the Boys, but there's something less purposeful about them. Something manic. They're a mix of males and females, but they're all too young to have left their mothers or been driven away already — of this I'm certain.

On a few occasions, the Orphan Nine's slot at the wallow is cut short by the arrival of a complete sounder of sows and boarlets. Although the orphans far outnumber the adults, they need no persuasion to run away. Once, though, one of them turns back and steps towards a sow. And it's hard not to read some kind of hope, or longing, in that act.

I never see the orphans in the flesh again. The last time they appear on my trail camera in 2022 is in September, back in my own wood.

Then, in February 2023, a group of eight adult boar appear at the wallow. I can't be 100 per cent sure it's the orphans. But eight is a big number even for a sounder. These are fairly small-looking adults and, much more intriguingly, they're a mix of females and males. This is not the usual way of wild boar. Over many minutes of footage, the apparent-brothers try to mount their apparent-sisters, who scream at them or tuck themselves down into the mud of the wallow. It's troubling to watch.

Yet the fact that the group has apparently chosen to stick together after losing their mother (or mothers) points again to the flexibility, and perhaps the emotional needs, of their kind.

I wish them well.

———

Our boar are in a constant flux of rewilding and dewilding, borne on the currents of their ability to interrogate and manipulate our shared world. A place is left in no doubt when it finds itself inhabited by boar. Their prints, trails, wallows, rubbings and rootings are everywhere. The landscape has come to belong to them, and they to it. *Hefted* is a word born of the practice of bonding upland sheep to their hills so well that the sheep keep safe over generations the knowledge of where their flock belongs. But this word can be carried beyond its original borders. Our boar have hefted themselves. Each matriarchal sounder collects and passes on knowledge that can only be undone if every one of its adult members is slain. Knowledge of where to hide, to rest, to bathe, to rub, to medicate, to drink, to eat (or beg). Knowledge that males might absorb before they leave, and share with other young exiles. Knowledge that can be lost and, if so, must be gathered again.

There is no reason the remaining members of the Orphan Nine will not survive. Thrive, even. My brush with them showed them to be fearful enough. I hope they stay that way.

Our wild boar have remoulded themselves. They are always remoulding in response to the world – and bringing us along for the ride.

CHAPTER NINE

Mad About the Boar

Wherever boar have regained a hoofhold in Britain, they've made it known with the markers they leave. Not just the rootings, the wallows, the trails and the mud rubs, but also the ones they nudge us to make. In the Woodland Trust reserves of Kent and East Sussex where the boar – or recent memories of them – cling on, colourful information boards suggest keeping an eye out for them. The annual Wild Boar Week festival in Rye, originally founded to celebrate the history of pannage in the High Weald, was only too happy to promote the presence of living wild boar once they returned.

In the Forest of Dean, though you may not see boar, you may see the laminated A4 sheets with Forestry England branding that have been stuck to trees and gateposts, warning you not to feed them. The independent cider brewery Jolter Press does a line called Forest Beasts, with bottles featuring a boar in a dapper suit. If cider isn't to your taste, you can sample locally distilled gin at the Drunken Boar Mobile Bar. Cyclists can take part in the Wild Boar Chase, an annual mountain bike ride through the area featuring various routes including the 'The Hog' (38 miles) and 'The Full Boar' (45 miles); children can ride in the Humbug Chase. In my village's churchyard, far from the boundary of the woods, signs inform visitors that the gates are locked at night to keep wild boar out. On the Forest of Dean notice board on Facebook, any mention of the animals can be expected to receive an emoji mix of likes, hearts and angry faces.

These are all everyday signs of how the wild boar are weaving themselves into local cultural consciousness in the places they have visibly returned to. But in the Dean, the story runs deeper and hotter than they alone can tell. For in the wake of the boar, altogether more human conflicts have emerged.

In late 2021, I am surprised to be granted an interview with Kevin Stannard, whose formal title is West District Forest Management Director and Deputy Surveyor for the Forest of Dean. I'd expected him to turn down my request. When it comes to wild boar, no matter what Forestry England does, they are pilloried.

I meet Kevin at the West England headquarters in Coleford. It's the same place I interviewed a ranger in 2014, and my conversation with Kevin has more than a hint of déjà vu, given how the challenges around the boar seem no smaller than before.

'I love them, don't get me wrong,' is the first thing Kevin says once we've sat down in a draughty meeting room. 'I think the wild boar are like any part of our native flora and fauna. They just fit.'

Despite the sector he works in, Kevin has the air of someone who spends almost all his time in the office. And as the local boss for Forestry England, he probably does. Yet he fondly calls the Dean, his home for the last 11 years, a 'particular beast'. It's clear that he treasures the moments he does get outdoors. When I ask him what his favourite one with the boar has been, he offers this: watching humbugs play on a sunlit bank, with his daughter at his side. 'That's nature at its best, isn't it?'

But he's unequivocal about what needs to be done. 'We have too many boar. There is no doubt that at low densities, boar provide very valuable ecological services in disturbing static ecosystems. The problem is that with a high density of boar, the repeated disturbance of the same piece of ground prevents species from establishing. So if we can get the number down to around 400, then we should get the ecological benefits, and fewer negative interactions with people.'

400: the wild boar population size desired by Forestry England.

90: Forestry England's original population target.

819: the estimated population size when I first came in 2014.

1,635: the estimated population size in 2018, the highest it has ever reached.

937: the estimated population size at the time of my conversation with Kevin in 2021.

600: the estimated population size given to me by someone who wants the boar to stay.

6,000: the estimated population size given to me by someone who wants the boar gone.

These numbers make their own strange poetry. They speak of uncertainty, and belief.

The target of 400, Kevin tells me with confident frankness, has 'No scientific basis for it. There has always been a target of 800 deer here, back to the year 1668. So 400 boar is simply half that number. It's part historical, it's part convenience, and it's part us going, "Well, when we thought we had 400, we didn't have a major problem". It's no more a credible target than that, really. The reason we had to have an actual target is that we were coming under extreme pressure from the animal rights groups, who mistakenly believed we wanted to exterminate the boar. That was never the policy, so naming a figure was equally as much to reassure them that it wasn't zero.'

When we thought we had 400.

For all our human ingenuity, counting pigs in a small British forest appears to remain a crude science. The annual census is done at night over the course of a month and 80km^2 of land, with the rangers counting individuals through thermal imaging cameras. The numbers are then extrapolated via a standard scientific method to arrive at a figure for the whole forest. However, it's impossible to be sure how close that figure is to the reality. In the 2021 census, the given margin of error means there could be as many as 1,400 boar or as few as 600.

Kevin points out that records for boar killed in road traffic accidents correlate roughly with the census, as does the level of support for culling – the more boar, the more people who find themselves wanting more management. Even so, much dissatisfaction remains with Forestry England's survey method. I've consistently found that people who welcome the boar think there are fewer than officially stated, while those who want the boar much reduced or exterminated think there are far more.

'It's just them standing on the back of a truck with a camera,' Richard, the man I'd previously interviewed about his anti-boar alarm system and nightly patrols, emails. 'People I chat to locally and deeper into the forest aren't seeing any difference in boar numbers.'

Richard is the one who believes there are 6,000 boar. Other people – including myself – find this figure impossible to believe, given how hard the boar are becoming to find. Yet Lydia, the partially deaf horse rider, seems to be having the opposite experience to me. She hadn't known that annual censuses for the boar are published online, but she scoffs to hear that the population is reported to have fallen from its 2018 high.

'I can't really feel there has been any difference,' she emails. 'The boar are closer to my house than ever before, they're mooting just outside my gate, which didn't happen until last year.'

Yet the boar don't distribute themselves evenly around the forest. Many of them will visit the same area if it offers enough bounty. While sounders may chase each other off on occasion, particularly at hunters' bait stations, they don't hold territories in the way that other species like wolves do. Residents who envision great hordes of them may simply have the misfortune to be living in boar honeypots, or may be overestimating the numbers based on the amount of rooting around, even though a single boar can be prodigious in their ploughing. Fear may play a part too. If you guard against the risk of meeting a boar by assuming they're everywhere, surely this will bleed into your numerical guesswork.

To muddy the waters more, Forestry England only counts boar on their own sites. Thousands of individual landowners occupy the gaps, and while they only hold an average of 0.5km^2 each, it's likely that some boar are avoiding the thermal cameras. Because of this, Kevin himself thinks there are more than the census indicates. However, both within and around the forest, many farms and estates have a shoot-on-sight policy for the boar. And that's if they don't set out bait to draw them in for the killing, like the farmer does on the other side of my wood. He plants maize for the boar, a neighbour has told me; if so, he's a bit of a black sheep, for most crop farmers around the Dean wish to keep the boar well away. I've been told there are 10 landowners gunning for the boar along the southern edge of the Dean alone. What might we get for the whole perimeter of the forest if we were to extrapolate *that* number?

For the boar, the Dean is a mosaic of peril and refuge. Only a fence may separate the two states. And even these boundaries lose their meaning when poachers come at night.

The one thing that is easy to count is how many boar are being shot by Forestry England. In the early years of the cull, the agency never came close to its targets. But between 2019 and 2021, they shot about 1,460 individuals, a significant improvement in their terms.[6] Drop the stats from their website into a graph, and you can watch the two lines that represent the estimated population and the number killed closing in on each other.

In the last few years, Forestry England has received funding for extra manpower. This may explain the increasing

---

[6] Boar killed in road traffic accidents are also included in the annual cull figure, but remain a small proportion of the total.

effectiveness of the cull. Yet my friend Ed Drewitt speculates that the rangers have grown to know their patches, and the boar, better. That over time they've reacquired the knowledge needed to kill, even if the weapons now are rifles, rather than spears and arrows.

Kevin's comments chime with this. 'They know the pattern of behaviour of boar in their locations. On any given day they will position themselves in the most likely place to be able to do their jobs. I don't know how they make those decisions. I just know they're very effective in what they do.'

For all that we are talking about killing, there's something fascinating in his choice of words. As if, through their time in the woods hunting boar, his rangers have become different, more unknowable creatures.

I get a glimpse of their craft from Dennis, the ex-ranger. We talk in his back garden, from where we can see the house in which he was born. He knows every track and patch of wood in this place. His hunting experience is matched by his enthusiasm for living boar, his dialogue when he speaks of them decorated with descriptors like *beautiful, fantastic, lovely*.

When Dennis stalked boar, the weather and the seasons guided him. Yew trees gave good shelter to deer and boar on rainy days. In autumn, he focused on beech and oak stands where the mast lay thick. In years when the berries of the hedgerows were plump, he might have found boar feeding on these instead.

He would walk as slowly and silently as he could, looking, listening. Rifle out of its slip and under or over his shoulder. 'Then you might see a leg, a tail, and the next thing you've got to make sure of is that it's safe. With the rifle I used, the .308, they're very lethal weapons, potentially a three-mile bullet if the shot is 45 degrees. Anyone can miss. You want to stop that bullet. If you've got some big oak trees or a hillside, a bit of a bank, you know you're safe.'

Even with a bullseye, a bullet can go straight through an animal. The responsibility is huge – to the individual being killed and to the humans walking around the forest. Given the number of hunting accidents that happen on the Continent, it surprises me that we don't hear of such things in the UK. It's also a testament to the care taken by the rangers.

But they have not always been left to their work.

The cull has long had its critics. A group called the Forest of Dean Wild Boar Cull Saboteurs – among its members a number of activists already battle-hardened from the badger cull in Gloucestershire – ramped up its efforts in 2014. Those efforts included relocating bait, pushing over shooting towers and, at night, sitting in front of those towers containing the armed rangers.

Online, the rangers were subject to death threats. Two resigned. Those remaining now take video equipment, trackers and emergency alarms with them on their outings for their safety.

'We as a group would never consider death threats or threats of physical harm a viable tactic. We have removed people from the group who have posted details or threats towards rangers or Mr Stannard,' Drew Pratten, a Saboteur who has been regularly quoted in local and national media press, emails back when I get in touch.

These days, press reports about the Saboteurs have dried up. Drew assures me that the group remains very much active. His email comes with a photo: the head of a boar, eyes half-closed, nailed to a tree. I've seen it before. The story was widely covered when it occurred in September 2015. The head appeared 'on a popular family trail, where people walk dogs, and take their children for walks in the woods,' according to a statement posted by the Saboteurs.

What they didn't add, and I learn from Drew now, is that the tree was on a track right next to his house. 'I've received death threats and threats against my family and animals,' he goes on. With the nailed boar's head, 'Things started to escalate and no one else wanted their name public because of this. My family asked that if I carried on could I step back from publicity, and I could hardly say no.'

The Saboteurs blamed the act on poachers. Given that the Saboteurs devote some of their time to trying to foil poachers instead of rangers, this is logical. And yet it seems illogical to draw attention to your own illegal activities. And there were, and still are, plenty of other people in the Dean wanting the cull to proceed unimpeded.

One such collective was Hogwatch,[7] who formed around the same time as the Saboteurs. Forgive my dramatic segue, for I don't wish to imply that anyone from Hogwatch sawed the boar's head off and nailed it to the tree. Their activities were entirely paper-based, with members collecting signatures for petitions, writing to officials and running a website aiming to counter what they considered to be over-positive attitudes towards the boar. Yet there was nothing genteel about the reaction they received from some quarters.

'When we first started our little group, we were bombarded with insults,' Olive, one of Hogwatch's founders, told me in 2014. 'They accused us of being wildlife haters. But I belong to all the animal groups and support the RSPB and Gloucestershire Wildlife Trust. I care for an animal if I find it injured. I don't hate nature or wildlife at all. I hate the boar now, and I hate the people who support them, and I never felt that way before.'

After my departure in 2014, boar numbers kept rising, generating ever more frictions. Kieran O'Mahony arrived in 2017 to research a PhD that would delve deep into the

---

[7] Not to be confused with the Zoological Society of London's hedgehog monitoring scheme of the same name.

political entanglements of boar and humans in the Dean, and he couldn't have timed it better. 'When I began fieldwork in autumn, boar geographies were at their broadest and human tensions were high,' reads Kieran's thesis. 'Newsworthy events – digging in cemeteries, gardens, verges, amenity and sports space – were commonplace. The topic of conversation in pubs and shops was often boar-related as people discussed overnight digging or nearby sightings.' To him, the boar were redefining the relations that people held with their friends, neighbours and other acquaintances. They were breaking, forging and remaking human connections. Some people were even driven to move away.

The Forest of Dean was already fecund ground for conflict by the time the boar arrived. Because so much of it is owned by Forestry England, and this land is threaded through with villages and houses, the agency's decisions and actions have a palpable impact on many people's daily lives. It's like living under the remit of a second local council, but one you haven't had any chance to vote for or against. When the boar began to make themselves known, among both their champions and haters they became a touchstone for wider discontent with Forestry England.

And yet, when I walk with Kieran through the forest in late 2021, he tells me he has sensed an easing around the matter of the boar. He has settled here; the Dean sent its roots into him during the course of his research and did not release him. Others who've lived here longer, including Kevin, agree with Kieran's perception. I'm unsurprised. The number of articles in local and national papers has dropped off in sync with the boar population. As if the rangers' bullets have, in piercing the bodies of boar, released the pressure.

'The Boaring Truth now seem to be the most visible group talking about boar,' Kieran says as fresh falls of leaves crunch beneath our feet. 'I think perhaps they're trying to be more diplomatic than some past boar advocacy groups were, and it's softened the politics slightly.'

The arrival of the boar ushered in a mini-ecosystem of action groups, which competed with, cooperated with or opposed each other. Most are gone now, including the UK Wild Boar Trust and britishwildboar.org. The Boaring Truth endures. A group of volunteers with a well-turned-out logo and website, they describe themselves as 'wildlife lovers and conservationists, based in the Forest of Dean, who simply want to see wild boar given a fair chance at earning their place back in the wilds of the UK'. On their Facebook page, their updates are mildly worded.

But wounding memories are hard to bury.

'The boar have made me an activist,' Olive had told me before, her words hinting at how the boar have written themselves into her identity. It has proved a thorny path to walk, as I am reminded when I write to her to see how things have panned out since we last spoke. I learn that Hogwatch has also disbanded. 'The hatred towards us was unbelievable, incitement to damage our homes etcetera, from the animal rights activists. No one was allowed to say anything about the boar. There was no middle ground, no discussion.'

Lydia, who was also involved in Hogwatch, feels the same. 'The animal rights people and hunt sabs are really aggressive and frightening if you voice any opinion that hints you don't like the boar or would like to get rid of them.'

Another landscape of fear to add to the map.

———

Despite what appears to be a growing calm, the desire to keep the boar down remains strong. In 2019, Forestry England launched Our Shared Forest, a project to develop a land management plan to guide what the area 'will look like, feel like and be like in 100 years' time'. The plan lumps the boar in with 'invasive species' including muntjac, grey squirrels, Himalayan balsam, giant hogweed and Japanese knotweed, although it does add that 'the presence of these species at low densities may be beneficial'. When the plan went to public consultation, 84 respondents provided comments in support of the boar cull. Just 12 comments supported the deer cull. While the consultation results may not necessarily be representative of the community as a whole, they echo the things I've heard – and *haven't* heard – with my own ears. Most people who want more culling fear, or at least claim to fear, that the boar are seriously damaging the Dean's environment. At the same time, few of them mention the negative impacts of the current concentration of deer. Others acknowledge the issue and still brush it aside.

'The deer population is large, of course they do damage trees. Personally I love the deer,' Viv tells me with barely a pause between the two sentences, just after she's described at length the despoilment of her beech wood by boar.

There are thought to be around two million deer in the UK, comprising red, roe, fallow, muntjac, Sika and Chinese water deer. Only red and roe deer are native.[8] Deer numbers are likely to have gone up even more thanks to a venison market stunted first by Covid and then by Brexit. Shooting has also become more difficult in places since the Covid-induced puppy boom, which has resulted in many more people heading outdoors with often poorly trained dogs.

It is indisputable that our remaining woodland, and places where trees could otherwise return, are under siege from hungry cervine mouths. Deer eat leaves, shoots and bark from seedlings and mature trees, and bushier plants that

---

[8] The story of the roe deer in Britain bears traces of the boar's, because they became extinct in England around the eighteenth century, and many of southern England's roe deer today descend from animals from the Continent.

might otherwise have formed a rich undergrowth. A wood with too many deer can see its abundance of birds fall by 50 per cent, according to Paul Dolman at the University of East Anglia. The British Association for Conservation and Shooting calls the damage 'the carbon hoof print'.

My own beech wood is cavernous. There's a majesty to the tall trees and the airy spaces between them – like a sylvan Mines of Moria – but it's a majesty that the future will pay for. There are so few young trees. This is not how a wood is meant to be.

All that said, it's important to be aware that this is not a simple case of 'too many deer'. Like boar, and like any other member of an ecosystem, our native deer species play important ecological roles. It's rather that we have removed so much woodland that deer are currently crowded into what remains. And those remnants lack the predatory forces needed to keep deer on the move and their numbers in check.

Why is it that people in the Dean find it hard to recognise the destructiveness of having too many deer there? Perhaps it's partly their meekness, and the grace and delicateness of their bodies set against the low dark hulks of boar. Historian Marcelle Thiébaux notes that in medieval bestiaries, the stag is associated with Christ, and the boar with Satan.

But I think it's more than this. Wild boar are *present* in a way that we are unused to. They reshape our landscape in real observable time. The changes are right in our faces. To see the scale of the deer's damage requires far more effort. We have to stop to peer at seedlings and saplings to notice the ends of twiggy branches that have been bitten off. And we have to stand back, look at the woods, and see the trees that are not there at all.

When I raise this contradiction with Kevin in 2021, he nods. 'It's a statement about how little people know about the management of the countryside, because deer are one of the biggest threats to our native flora. And yet people don't talk about deer culling in the same way they talk about boar culling. There is a Bambi factor to it. People like to see deer.'

Yet he's equally scornful about the people who take action to defend the boar. 'Even at the height of the animal rights activism, it was all about the boar. It was almost as if they couldn't give a monkey's about the deer.'

There's certainly a novelty factor at play when it comes to boar. Boar are usually at the top of the list for clients going on the Forest of Dean wildlife safaris run by Ed Drewitt. The safaris are a key part of his income. But more and more, the people he takes out are leaving with their hopes dashed.

'Compared to a couple of years ago when I started the safaris, it's definitely been harder this year to find boar,' Ed remarks when we go walking, a week before my meeting with Kevin Stannard. 'As someone who's out all the time, both showing people the boar but also just out and about generally as a naturalist, I've got my ears and eyes out for them, and my feeling is that numbers are lower than the Forestry England estimate. And interestingly I've been seeing deer more easily. My feeling is that they've been focusing on shooting boar, and I presume they've been shooting fewer deer as a result.'

There's no way to prove or disprove Ed's suspicion, because Forestry England doesn't provide data on the Dean's deer cull. They do provide graphs estimating numbers for each species of deer, which show there has been a drop since 2018, yet little change between 2021 and 2022. This isn't enough to go on.

One boar may have more ecological impact than one deer. But with 1,360 of the latter in the beleaguered ecosystem of the Dean, including a growing contingent of the cute but non-native muntjac, neglecting control of the deer in favour of control of the boar strikes me as a perilous strategy.

Ed and I come to a crossroads. Here we stop to see if anything will rustle out from the undergrowth. It's dusk, the golden hour when boar emerge from cover and enough light remains to see them. As we continue to discuss the cull in low voices, a shiny dark Forestry England jeep comes trundling along the track.

'He'll be looking for boar,' Ed murmurs.

The jeep's window is down. Through it, a sunglasses-clad ranger raises his hand in a wave as he passes. There's a stiffness in the motion, a reluctance. He probably recognises Ed, who is obliged to keep Forestry England informed of when and where he is doing his safaris. Between the ranger and us is an awkward knowing: we are looking for boar to watch, he is looking for the same boar to kill.

'Forestry England is in an unfortunate position where they're having to be knee-jerk reactive,' Ed says as the jeep recedes into the distance again. He's a soft-spoken man, gentle in voice and movement, and yet his frustration is palpable. 'They're too quick sometimes to do something when people say there's a problem, and I think it's time now they stand up. They could be braver about the boar. I'm not necessarily against their numbers being controlled. But I think we need to be more precautionary. If you're doing a periodic survey, how do you know when you've reached 400? I just don't want them to kill too many.'

Forestry England has more to juggle than just varying public opinions, however. For there is a thundercloud on Britain's horizon. Its name is African Swine Fever.

Called ASF for short, African Swine Fever has been around since the early twentieth century. Yet a ferocious outbreak began in 2007 that has been devastating farmed pig populations across the world ever since. Though it is harmless to humans, Dirk Pfeiffer, a veterinary epidemiologist at City University of Hong Kong, has called it 'the biggest animal disease outbreak we've ever had on the planet.'

In addition to all the animals who've died of the disease, many have been culled in a bid to contain the spread. In Fujian Province in China, pigs were filmed being buried alive.

The disease has, of course, become a plague because of how we produce pork today. And even though scientists have traced some outbreaks to pigs eating virus-riddled pork carelessly fed to them, wild boar haven't escaped blame for the spread of ASF. In an eerie parallel to the fence built by Hungary in 2015 to try and keep migrating people out, hundreds of kilometres' worth of fencing has been erected by Bulgaria, France and Germany to block flows of wild boar. Needless to say, such barriers affect all kinds of wildlife, while scientists question whether they have any impact on ASF's spread.

En-masse culling is the other weapon being deployed against ASF in wild boar. Yet this may end up deepening the harm, beyond that wreaked among wild boar populations by the virus itself. In a 2019 article for *The Conversation*, Marianna Szczygielska of the Max Planck Institute for the History of Science pointed out that the Polish government's directive to hunters to slash its boar population by 90 per cent could lead to hunters ferrying the virus around the region via blood on their clothing and cars. It has also been found that if all the adults in a sounder are killed, any surviving juveniles may flee a great distance. Radio tracking has shown orphaned boar roaming up to 30 miles in the aftermath of their loss. The world has become new to them all over again; they have no one to guide them. Just like my Orphan Nine.

Poland continues to report periodic outbreaks of ASF among wild boar and farmed pigs. By contrast, when the disease made its presence known in Belgium in 2018, the response included bans on recreational hunting of boar. Belgium was declared ASF-free in 2020 and has remained so.

The UK's pork industry is nervously watching developments from across the Channel. I ask Kieran while we're out walking if he thinks the disease will reach us. He replies that it's a matter of when; that it may well have arrived by the time this book is published.

His prediction seems increasingly sound. Brexit saw the loss of border checks on fresh food, checks that at the time of writing are still waiting to be replaced. Newspaper *The i* reported that new safety checks would not be implemented until the end of 2023 – assuming no further delays. It's as if the government *wants* ASF to reach us.

The disease will probably establish itself in the UK when a person working at a farm eats some infected pork imported from abroad and, by touch, passes the virus on to a pig. Still, this hasn't stopped the National Pig Association (NPA) from making repeated claims that the wild boar population in the Forest of Dean must be controlled to avert the threat of British pigs contracting ASF. The National Farmers Union (NFU) in Scotland has recently begun to say the same of boar populations up there.

All this hand-wringing is to me like fretting over a leaky tap while floodwaters rise around your feet. As of 2022, there were 3.4 million pigs across Britain. Most of those pigs spend most of their lives indoors, where the risk of contracting ASF from roaming wild boar should be far lower – but where the risk of yet another disease arising is far greater. The NPA and Defra also appear to have disregarded research by the Animal and Plant Health Agency, itself an arm of Defra, suggesting that even if boar in the Dean do contract ASF, the disease 'is likely to spontaneously disappear, limiting the duration of the risk this produces to commercial pig production'. It's also the case that there are very few pigs around for the boar to fraternise with; there are just two commercial units within 2km of the Forest of Dean boundaries, plus a few smallholdings.

All this seems to reassure Forestry England not one bit. If a dead boar is ever found that has not clearly been hit by a car, the body is taken to be tested. The agency is always primed to pick up the phone to Defra.

Despite ASF's current monopoly on everyone's attention, there are plenty of other pig-borne diseases to add to public health and farming worries. After ASF, at the top of a long list are trichinellosis, brucellosis, hepatitis E, tuberculosis and leptospirosis. For the last two years, I've had an alert set up on Google Scholar so that every few days, it sends me a list of all the latest scientific papers published in relation to wild boar. Nearly all of these focus on the pathogens that wild boar may carry in their bodies. There's far more money in such research than in exploring how wild boar live, and how they affect ecosystems.

Back in the Dean, while ASF may preoccupy Forestry England, people like Ed hold other, more pressing fears for the boar. Among these is the risk of creating a so-called bottleneck. This refers to when a population is reduced to a fraction of its former size, and the inevitable stripping-away of genetic diversity that happens as a result. Bearing in mind what I've learned from ex-ranger Dennis about the origins of the Dean boar, they may descend from just a handful of the 15 individuals released in 1997 and the 65 released in 2004. That said, they probably had more founders than the boar of Lille Vildmose, Denmark – a population that began in 1926 with just two males and two females, and has endured for a century so far.

Regardless, other ecologists and wildlife photographers I've spoken to share Ed's worry about the Dean boar being driven into a genetic danger zone through over-culling. Especially given there are no neighbouring populations to boost genetic diversity. Diversity isn't desirable for its own sake; it is insurance against all the random perils of the world, from disease to climate to predators.

But there are yet more costs of the cull beyond that of genes. Ones that cast long shadows on my mind, and are voiced by Ed and Kieran too: what is the cull doing to the individual boar who survive, and to the boar as a society?

The relationships that females form with their daughters, mothers, sisters, aunts, cousins and other female kin can last for their entire lifetimes – up to around 15 years or more, if they make it that far. They experience a version of love; of this I have no doubt. Think of that sow in the Czech Republic, risking her life for 29 minutes to free her offspring. To believe that only humans are capable of the joy of being with one another, and the pain of being apart, is to deny the biological reality of our kinship with other species. On planet Earth, the continuum of love must be a crowded one. Deer, antelope, bison and other herding animals all belong somewhere on it. Female wild boar society could also be said to be herd-based. Yet the way that females go about this herding seems, to me, to be unique. Although its guiding line is the bond between mother and daughter, this line isn't necessarily followed. A team of French researchers studied a population of boar in Champagne over 12 years, investigating among other avenues 'the decision to stay or leave the natal group'. That use of the word *decision* is important. The team found that most yearling daughters remained with their mothers after weaning, but in some sounders all the female yearlings left to form a new sounder with their sisters. They did so just as their mothers or they themselves were about to give birth. They were more likely to make this decision when they'd been born earlier in the year to older mothers. The researchers thought that females who were born later, and were of their mothers' first litters, wouldn't have had such a good nutritional start in life. So it made more sense for these boar to continue tapping into the protection and knowledge of their natal sounder. But there were no guarantees, no formula that the boar could always be expected to follow. There were anomalies, too; a few yearling females were seen leaving alone, or in the company of their brothers.

A bachelor group is a more ephemeral affair. But if their purpose is to act as a bridge, softening the way to solitary life, to be a young male in one must be to feel a sense of comfort and safety.

The kinships between females, between females and males, and between males and males, all have a conditionality to them. A sense of choosing and being chosen. Physical needs might help to guide these choices. But so it is with us.

What happens, then, when a bullet rips through those bonds?

It's a question mired in uncertainty. Not just because we can't sink into the consciousness of the boar themselves, but because when it comes to the Dean cull, Forestry England publishes no information about the ages of individuals shot, nor sex. Neither do they report how many matriarchs have been among the toll. I'm sure it would be possible to provide the latter information, because if an amateur like me can identify a matriarch, rangers can undoubtedly do so through the crosshairs of their guns.

In 2010, a hunter in East Sussex told Defra researcher Martin Goulding that 'it is our policy not to shoot matriarchal sows'. This policy, apparently adopted elsewhere in the country if the talk on hunting forums is anything to go by, is an import from the Continent along with the boar themselves. It's based on what appears to be a commonplace belief among many hunters that if you kill the matriarch, her sounder will disintegrate, and all the females whose reproductive desires were previously suppressed will go on heat and have lots of babies.

Extensive research has put this to bed. Boar are far more resilient animals than that. Provided the sounder contains other adult females, one of them will step up if needs be. However, the context surely matters. In the woods of Kent and East Sussex, where boar are now much rarer, the loss of a matriarch could be a terrible thing indeed. To find food, shelter and each other they must navigate a maze of roads, housing, farmland and piecemeal woods. To be a boar there is to always be picking your way through a tangle of tripwires. The longer you live, the better you become at helping your kin to live longer.

Much more significant than the killing of single matriarchs is the mass killing of adults while sparing the young. To my knowledge, Forestry England doesn't shoot boarlets, unless they turn to begging. This is different to how we hunted back in the Mesolithic, with bone deposits in archaeological sites from this period including many baby and juvenile boar. They would've been easier to catch, and their meat more tender. Wolves keep the old ways, even if we don't. One study has shown that, at least in northern Spain, about three-quarters of the boar eaten by wolves are young.

I don't know how a sow might feel to realise that one of her babies had been taken. Would there be distress, or would any pain be outburned by anger? Would the emotion be stronger if her litter was only small to begin with?

I feel more certain in suspecting that the loss of a fellow adult female would be worse. They might have been littermates or born in the same year. If she were younger, she would have known the older, fallen sow for her whole life so far. And the pain would be multiplied, would catastrophise, the more females taken. In mainland Europe, it has been observed that when hunting by humans is heavy enough, boar society can reshape under the pressure. Unrelated females who've lost all their kin may coalesce into new sounders, while young males are permitted to stay with their natal sounders for longer − similar changes in customs to those demonstrated by the Orphan Nine. The bursts of stress triggered by hunting can even bring adult females into heat faster and speed the onset of sexual maturity in juvenile ones. This phenomenon could explain why some hunters think shooting the matriarch will trigger her sounder-mates to breed – in periods when especially high numbers of boar are being killed, it's inevitable that matriarchs will be caught up in this, and hunters might then attribute any subsequent boar baby booms to the loss only of those matriarchs. However, if the cull in the Dean is wreaking this kind of hormonal upheaval, it hasn't stopped numbers there dropping.

Wild boar seem as fluid as water in their behaviour. But adaptation, as people changed by the boar know, isn't necessarily free of suffering.

Back in the draughty Forestry England office, Kevin answers all my questions – including those bearing a thorn or two of criticism – with a relaxed air. He has spent years facing off sharp journalists and irate locals. Talking to me must feel like child's play. I ask him if one risk of the cull is picking off the shyest boar and sparing the ones most likely to visit the edges of the villages and towns, given that the rangers concentrate their activities in the quietest parts of the forest for reasons of public safety and opinion. He admits this may be happening to a degree, before pivoting swiftly back to Forestry England's survey method, which I've also pressed him on. 'The value of the survey is that by using the same technique consistently over time, we can map the population trends. And that is more important than the actual figure.'

Cold comfort for those who fear the total population of boar is much lower than Kevin believes.

There are things that could be done to whittle the estimates and speculation into more accurate knowledge. No one knows how many boar are being shot legally on private land, but it doesn't seem beyond the realm of feasibility to set up a reporting system that landowners would be required to feed into as a condition of their gun licences or selling the carcasses on. Poaching events, or estimates for these, could also be incorporated into the kill figures. When the Forest of Dean Wild Boar Cull Saboteurs aren't busy interfering with the cull itself, they do all they can to dissuade poachers. They disarm snares, head out when someone reports a gunshot in the night, keep watch for known poachers' vehicles, and take to the vet injured dogs who've been abandoned after being used to flush boar out. They come across an average of 10 poaching events a year, deer and boar included. Drew says they miss many more.

My own trail camera has sometimes caught the distant reports of gunshots in the middle of the night. The rangers only go out shooting close to dawn and dusk.

As for the population survey, this could be conducted more than once per year, and other methods could bolster it. DNA, even if only collected from a scatter of animals within a population, can be used both to estimate population size and provide a glimpse into genetic diversity. It's a technique becoming commonplace in the conservation world for all kinds of species, from jaguars in Brazil to giant pandas in China. Imagine how much boar DNA you could harvest from all the saliva, skin and hair left on a mud-rubbing tree next to any wallow.

Radio tracking is a much older technology, though it remains a powerful way of improving our understanding of population dynamics by showing where and how far individuals may go. It could also shine light on the social effects of the cull. Forestry England did once conduct a radio tracking study, and Kevin is keen to repeat the exercise on a bigger scale.

'We think the sows will still be following roughly the same pattern year in and year out, but we don't specifically know that. Equally, we want to know how they move from the forest onto private land, and which animals are actually pushing and leaving the forest. The general assumption is that it's young males, but we don't necessarily know,' he tells me near the end of our conversation. Yet, as with most things in the modern world, it comes down to money. There's enough of this for killing boar. Not much else.

I believe Kevin when he insists that he and his agency don't want to exterminate the Dean boar. And I agree that some regular culling is needed. There's one more figure to tack onto the end of my earlier number-poem: 10,000. According to a group of wild boar researchers who once put their heads together on the question, this is how many boar the Dean could support before a population crash. Of course, the rest of the forest – humans included – would be suffering long before this.

In a fully functioning ecosystem, every species has its checks. Other than the odd car, in Great Britain, humans and dogs are currently the only possible predators of boar. With our powers combined, we make poor wolves. But poor wolves are probably better than no wolves at all.

On a different day that November in 2021, a photographer takes me to one of his patches. Hoping for boar, we spend more time tramping through mud and bracken in silence than in conversation. It's only when we return to where we've parked that the photographer finally speaks his mind.

'Why don't they listen to the people who are out in the forest? Fair enough, Forestry England goes into the woods a lot, that's their job. But there are also people who have real-world experience with boar. Give us a listen, talk to us a bit more. We want to speak to you as human beings, you're in our forest, we share it with you.'

Although the photographer is younger than me, he's already a father. He used to prowl the undergrowth for boar with his baby son strapped to his back – a vision that makes me smile. He wants enough of them to be around so that his boy, now six, can choose whether to revel in their being here, as he does.

Environmental philosopher Thom van Dooren uses the term *violent-care* to describe the lethal acts we undertake against certain species to conserve other species. It's a pairing of words that, to me, describes equally well the killing of individuals to ensure that the wider group to which they belong may continue to live. Amid the cacophony of opposing voices in the Dean, boar are dying. For some people, the number feels too high, a sacrifice on the altar of human convenience. For others, the number is too low, a dereliction of duty on Forestry England's part.

We can't know how it feels to be a boar who survives the deaths of their kin in the cull. And we should never lose sight of this. We may yet recognise in them hitherto-unimagined or denied capacities for trauma, just as we learned too late that African elephant culls that targeted only adults left behind a generation of psychologically disturbed youths who weren't ready to be in the world alone. Their wounds never healed.

'It's got to be done right, and I don't think it is being done right,' the photographer says. He sounds close to tears. 'I just want these boar to be safe.'

CHAPTER TEN

The *Torc* of Galloway

In January 2011, the magazine *Sporting Rifle* published an article with a most ominous opening:

> *Our pheasant feeders had been abused, knocked over, muddied, emptied and damaged for a long time before we stopped blaming the badgers. Fred was an old woodsman and part of our rough shooting syndicate; as he was refilling his feeders one day, it suddenly clicked that something a lot bigger than badgers was doing the damage to the hoppers.*

I drive up to Galloway in May 2022 to meet the article's author. Immediately after the Lake District, I turn left. Beneath a light rain I come to find myself in a land that looks as if stone-walled fields from Yorkshire have been carefully peeled away and laid over the bones of Gloucestershire's rolling hills.

Several people, when I said I was going to Galloway, replied with something along the lines of, 'Oh, cool. Where is that?'

'Galloway is unheard of. This south-western corner of Scotland has been overlooked for so long that we have fallen off the map,' writes Patrick Laurie in *Native: Life in a Vanishing Landscape*.

Native was my first introduction to Galloway. I found myself swooning over that book, at its poetry nudged gently into prose. I couldn't believe my luck when I discovered from Patrick's blog that he sometimes has dealings with boar. It was Patrick who put me in touch with Finlay, the *Sporting Rifle* man. But on this Friday, Finlay is busy at his vet practice until the evening, and Patrick has invited me around for coffee and wild boar chat. How could I pass that up?

After negotiating a granite-toothed track, I arrive at the farm and step into Patrick's book. From a pen beside

the house, two black-and-white Galloway cattle look me
over before turning away. Patrick texted earlier to say the
police were late in coming to do a check for his firearms
licence, and they're still busy inside. I spend a few minutes
alone with the cattle, admiring them. In this wide-open
space, I feel far from boar country. Yet dark plantations of
Sitka spruce are bristling along the horizon, like an
approaching army.

A policewoman emerges from the house and leaves.
Patrick gives me a warm greeting, his ginger hair as tightly
curled as that of his cattle. Two Labradors follow us into the
kitchen. I will spend the next hour being petitioned by the
black one, Scoop, for pats.

Patrick loads up a map on his laptop to show me where,
around the time of the foot-and-mouth epidemic of 2001,
the boar in this part of Galloway are thought to have started
out. It's a patchy sprawl of forest not much smaller than the
main part of the Dean.

'You'd call this the stronghold, in here. They just stayed
there for 20 years.' His hand whizzes around the screen as he
points out the pasture areas in the vicinity that the boar have
occasionally hit overnight, raiders who are always gone
before the strike of dawn. He talks of them *irrupting* – how
they'll work an area for a short time, and perhaps not return
there for years.

'But there is this sense that they're suddenly really starting
to spread now. This map perhaps doesn't show how much
woodland cover there is. As soon as they get properly into
Galloway Forest Park, I think they'll be motoring.'

As far as we know, boar have been escaping from farms
in Scotland since the late 1990s. *Torc*: that's what they were
called, in Scottish Gaelic, the last time they were here. As
well as a scatter of splinter groups around the country,
there are currently thought to be two populations of
more than a hundred: one up in Invergarry near Loch
Ness, where Bunloit is, and the other in Dumfries and

Galloway (as the administrative region is called, or D&G
for short). According to a recent NatureScot report on the
status of wild boar – although the Scottish government
insists on calling them *feral pigs* – the D&G population is
formed of two steadily merging groups from the north
and the south. This aligns with what Patrick, and later
Finlay, tell me. But whereas they recall hearing of an
escape around 21 years ago, another Dumfries stalker I've
spoken to on the phone says the boar have been here for
28 years, released for sport. It's possible that everyone is
correct. Only a few boar are needed to spark a breeding
population, and a few boar are easy to hide in a place like
this. According to the NatureScot report, a camera trap
survey has yielded a population density estimate of less
than one individual per km². Despite that modest figure,
the report signals a growing concern at the presence of
what the agency terms a 'non-native' and 'invasive' species.
Yet, in D&G itself, there seems to be a distinct air of
official indifference to the boar. When I enquired as to
whether I could speak to someone relevant from one of
the local NatureScot branches while up here, I received
the following reply: 'We have had no engagement with
the topic of wild boar'. A stark contrast to what's happening
in the Forest of Dean, where both the boar and the killing
of them are impossible to ignore.

Patrick wrote in a 2016 blog post that most local people
don't know boar are here, or else refute that they are. Six
years on, he tells me this is still the case. Even if or when the
boar claim Galloway Forest Park, Patrick isn't sure it'll be
noticed; much of the Park is currently blocked off to public
access, apparently due to antisocial behaviour since the start
of the pandemic. As unfair as this is – and surely in
contravention of Scotland's right to roam – it makes the
Park sound like the promised land for wild boar.

But there's one group of people here who do know the
boar, in their own way: the stalkers. It's them whom I've

travelled up to meet. To get a glimpse into what feels to me, as a non-hunter, to be a shadow world – and to experience a story that is very different to the one playing out in the Forest of Dean.

As in most parts of the country, a shooting infrastructure already existed in Galloway for animals such as grouse and deer. Boar called for a change in tactics, and I'll soon get a good look at these. For now, I cradle my coffee and ask Patrick what it was like, the one time he shot a boar himself.

'Fraught,' he opened with, smiling. 'I borrowed Finlay's rifle, and it was awesome, and I'm really glad to have done it. Not least because we were sitting in a high seat in the dark, and they came in from underneath us, and you could see them without any electric light at all, just from the last glow of moonlight or starlight, and they came in silence. Big things the size of this table, running through fallen bracken in complete silence.'

He shakes his head in frustrated wonder. 'Like, nothing can do that. Don't be stupid. Not even a cat could do that, that's ridiculous. And then Finlay put the torch on and I had three seconds before they ran away. Which was a very high-pressured thing. I remember a glimpse of what I should be shooting at. And then bang. And fortunately it was a fine shot and it was stone-dead.'

The boar had been male and, rather than any feral stink, he had smelled of spruce sap.

Bait stations and high seats are the favoured way around here to shoot boar. Stalking them on foot is nigh unthinkable in a place where the quarry is scattered far more thinly than they are in the Dean.

'They have tried to drive boar here,' Patrick says, after regaling me with his experiences of driven boar hunts in Croatia. 'And they've wasted a lot of time because the techniques you might use in Croatia, in mature deciduous woodland, where the pigs kind of know the drill and they'll run in a certain way and they'll double back on you – I think here if you had a gap of more than a hundred yards between two beaters, the pigs would just go back through the gaps. If indeed you were even in the right parish that day, because they might be miles away.'

I'm glad that I've already schooled myself into expecting not to see boar while I'm up here. They're hard enough to find in the Dean, where their travels are far more constricted.

Patrick radiates enthusiasm for his newish neighbours. He'd take another shot if he had the chance, but the meat is only a small part of it. He treasures the few glimpses he's got of them in daylight, one of which he wrote about for *Shooting Times & Country* with typical verve:

> *Boar do not gallop or sprint; nor do they scamper or bound. Wild boar travel and they do so at a jostling, tireless jog. I watched them go, high-sided and dark as a pirate's sail with a tumult of boarlets alongside them, each one ochre and striped.*
>
> *I laughed aloud to see them; the tall boxy ears of the leading sows, the comic despair of the last boarlet as it tried to keep up with the team. I recalled similar encounters in the forests of Croatia, Sweden, France, and Poland; that same top-heavy lurch that screams excitement, danger, and fun in equal measures.*

In a way, I'm surprised. Patrick's book *Native* is largely about trying to hold on to Galloway's curlews, whose numbers are slipping away. Many of their breeding grounds are being planted over with forestry. The curlew's loss is the boar's gain, for every new plantation is another stepping stone for them. The boar could've easily represented yet another facet of human greed and hubris to Patrick, and besides, his pasture lies vulnerable to them. But as someone who considers himself a steward of both cattle and wildlife, Patrick is already well versed in sharing the land he loves with other beings.

No, that's not quite right. Those other beings are part of the love. And now, the boar are too.

———

The full moon watches as Finlay and I walk through long grass towards his high seat. I'm carrying his rifle on one shoulder. It's far heavier than I expected. It has already been fired once this evening, bringing down a young roe buck in an instant. Through binoculars I watched him fold and fall. An hour has passed since then, plenty of time for the crack of the gun to fade away and the dark to come pouring in.

After passing down an alley between ranks of spruce, we turn right and arrive at the high seat. It's a simple thing of angle iron and, when I climb the ladder after Finlay, a few boards of wood. I am dismayed at how small the space is. Having already passed the rifle up, I squeeze in beside my companion.

'I can't believe you and Patrick both fit up here,' I whisper (no offence meant to Patrick, it's just that I'm smaller than the average man).

'Oh, he wanted that boar,' Finlay replies in an accent far stronger than that of his friend.

Finlay is a mix of affable and intimidating. Quick to smile and quick to refill my wine glass at dinner earlier, yet steely now that we're out on the hunt. I was only going to follow him around, but I seem to have become his apprentice; just a few hours after meeting him for the first time, I was dragging the roe buck by the antlers towards the road while he fetched the car, trying to avoid getting myself caught on the gorse or the body wedged in among the many rocks. All while hoping that none of the ticks that had been tucked in under the buck's belly were crawling their way towards my hands.

I wonder if Finlay was testing me.

I rest my arm on a piece of iron and try to settle into the night. Neither of us speak, although our gurgling stomachs stymie our efforts at silence. Finlay's wife, Lorna, had served us wild boar pastry earlier, the last meat from his most recent boar kill.

Moonlight flicks on and off as the tree that our backs rest against waves its branches in the wind. It's almost bright enough to read by. I recall a paper I read a few months ago, which found boar to be far less active during full moons, for fear of wolves and humans. I already know that our chances of seeing boar, let alone Finlay shooting one, are almost zero. The trail camera he has trained on the bait station 75m away hasn't picked up any of them for weeks. Except, that is, for a few who turned up after 1 a.m.

'Let me tell you, those pigs are going to live, because no way am I staying out that long in the cold for them,' Finlay said over the phone a few days before my trip.

It is cold now, though not unbearably so. I have multiple layers on, capped with a dark green hunter's jacket lent by Finlay after my pink ski jacket failed to pass muster. The foam pad I'm sitting on helps, and not just with retaining body heat. Arthritis has been living in my hips and lower back since my early 20s and, as if on cue, the pain has flared in the last week. Not that I would let it get in the way of this.

With the barrel of his rifle resting on the bar in front of us, Finlay passes me his thermal monocular. We'd used it earlier to spot the roe buck as he grazed on yellow gorse-like broom. Against the dark rocks, he was a bright white figure, as if already made into a ghost. Now, training the monocular on the point where Finlay says the bait station is, I see no movement. Just some distracting flickers to the far left: sheep in the adjoining field.

We pass the scope between us. The moon stares from behind. The wind soughs through the spruce, and there comes the bubbling call of a bird that I've never heard before, a sound whose essence my memory can't hold on to once gone.

'It was an odd thing,' Patrick had said of sitting and waiting for his boar. 'It was quite a solitary sort of just letting go. You go to a place and then you let that place settle down behind you. And you start to notice birds coming out and doing stuff again. And then I would hear lots of cracking and branches and each time I was like, "Oh, shit!" And every time it was a badger because badgers, unlike pigs, make a racket.'

But we don't even have badgers tonight. I shift on the foam pad. My hips need movement to keep the pain at bay, otherwise it comes trickling in like sand through an hourglass.

'I think we'll go,' Finlay says, still whispering. He wouldn't have even bothered tonight if I hadn't been here. Dragging that deer felt like earning my keep.

We pick our way back towards the main track, which glows at us through the trees. I stop trying to stifle my yawns. We've spent something like two hours in the seat, less time than Finlay would usually wait for, but it's around midnight now and I woke at 5.30 a.m. to beat the traffic.

We go back to Finlay's house, share a vanilla-tinted nightcap with Lorna, and then turn in. The last image in my mind before I sleep is the rumen and intestines of the roe buck, pearly blue and wrapped in thin deltas of blood vessels, stranded on the ground at my feet.

———

It's a strange thing, to have wanted a boar to come in the night and put itself in Finlay's sights. I adore the look of them, I laugh at their antics, I know they think and feel in their own porcine ways. But I want to sink the hands of my mind deep into everything about the boar, and that means trying to witness death too. There is, also, a gory curiosity.

When Finlay *gralloched* the buck – the hunter's word for pulling out the entrails and other organs – he narrated for me as he went. He sliced open the dark shining liver to check for fluke. When he got to the heart, he held it out to show the wreckage left by his well-placed bullet. A good boar shot would result in the same, though there would be no rumen nor fore stomach to remove.

After the buck had been partly disassembled, I had time to take him in. I'd never been so close to a wild deer before. Each hair of his brown pelt ended in a tiny arrowhead of white. The bases of his antlers were knobbed and rough like the boles of old oaks. He was beautiful, and young, but there were too many of his kind here, in a place with too few of the right trees for him. And there was no denying that Finlay took pleasure in the deftness of his kill.

Throughout human history, we've crafted ways to reconcile our awe of other beings with the need and desire to take their lives and use their bodies. Many indigenous hunters today cleave to the belief that other animals 'give' themselves up. I could never think this, but it almost goes without saying that such hunters tend to have a far more sustainable and respectful relationship with the rest of the living world. I stopped eating farmed animals some time ago, and on the rare occasions I do eat meat, it must come from an animal killed in the wild. I want to know that he or she was home, and that the agony was quickly done. I don't want to have eaten someone who was herded into a roaring lorry and taken far away to an alien place stinking of endings.

I'm not sure if I'd be able to take the life of an animal like a deer or a boar if the circumstances ever presented themselves. Still, I felt comfortable enough to go to the butcher in my village not long after I'd moved in. My timing was right; he'd just got a fresh boar in. The animals culled by Forestry England are sent on contract to high-end restaurants elsewhere in the country, so I knew the butcher's animal would've come from a private shooter.

I bought a steak. I fried and ate it with roast potatoes, and sautéed leek and mushrooms. The first meat I'd had in months. Tougher than expected, though still pink in places, and deep with flavour. Chewing, I thought of the wild boar I was eating. How far away did he or she live from here? They were nurtured on the same soil that cushioned my feet when I walked.

So I feasted on my Dean boar, and afterwards I went into the woods, fuelled by the flesh of the very species whom I wanted to meet alive. Only later did I learn that around here, there's another way to take a boar: a box trap.

This knowledge came to me from the man who supplies the village butcher. While he was too wary to arrange a meeting, on the phone he was open enough about his work. He mostly stalked on foot or waited at bait stations. But sometimes, he resorted to the ruthless convenience of a trap. In a pained voice he said he didn't like returning to shoot the helpless individual within. He did it anyway.

If I had to make the choice, I'd still prefer to live wild and then die of a gunshot in a trap, rather than the existence we force so many other animals to suffer for our cheap meat. But the phone call left my conscience bruised. I didn't buy wild boar again.

I can't imagine Finlay would take any satisfaction in traps. There's an art in his way. I've heard that some hunters on the Continent turn their noses up at the idea of sitting in wait for boar to come to the bait. It must, I concede, require a degree of nerve to stand ready with a gun for the dogs to flush the boar and send them running out towards you.

But a high seat demands silence, and patience. There is no guarantee of a kill. Finlay's last one was five months ago (the meat we ate came from the freezer). He averages about two per year, a similar success rate to that of other stalkers he knows. It's a gambler's way of hunting.

It also seems to me a far better way for a boar to die. No conflagration of fear rushing through your body as a barking dog chases you from shelter. Far less risk of messy shots that rip through the body without the kindness of swift death. Instead, if all goes as intended by your killer, your head is to the ground and your mouth is full of food when the bullet comes.

There's still a chance of a bait station shot being a poor one. Or that the rifle or the ammunition might be inadequate. In its Guide on Firearms Licensing Law, the Home Office states 'it is recommended that a rifle of not less than .270 [calibre] be used for wild boar'. Note the mere *recommended*; for deer, there is a mandatory minimum calibre for rifles and cartridges.

Even so, the larger .308 calibre seems to be the norm when it comes to boar. Finlay uses this, as do Forestry England's rangers. To ensure their proficiency and keep the public safe, the rangers also undergo rigorous training (and periodic retraining). And reassuringly, the Home Office recommendation seems to be taken as a legal directive in all but name, at least by the Gloucestershire Constabulary – who we can safely assume grant more firearms licences to boar shooters than any other force in England.

'If someone put in an application stating boar as the only quarry and requested say a .243 rifle then yes, it is likely that the application would be refused,' a firearms and explosives licensing officer replies to my emailed enquiry.

There are also two separate laws that could apply in cases of cruelty towards wild boar. The Wild Mammals (Protection) Act 1996 is for when someone has inflicted 'unnecessary suffering' on a wild mammal. I can find no record of it being used to prosecute someone for hurting or killing a boar. However, the Animal Welfare Act 2006 *was* used in the successful conviction of former gamekeeper Luke Rix in 2022, for stabbing a wild boar and goading his dogs to attack them. The Animal Welfare Act mainly applies to domestic and farmed animals, but also to wild animals in certain circumstances, such as when they've been physically restrained. It was helpful of Rix to film himself in the act; I've no doubt that similar crimes in this country have gone unpunished.

———

On my first morning in Galloway, feeling somewhat sleep-deprived, I am turned loose by Finlay for a few hours while he sees some patients. I drive to a spot near to where we were last night and go wandering in search of rootings. The back of my shoulder is sore with the memory of the rifle's weight. I choose a track with a darkness of spruce on one side, and on the other, wide-open sky and the distant bulk of Criffel Hill. Patrick called it a granite plug, an extinct volcano. The gravelly path is lined with the same wildflowers and shrubs of the Dean: gorse, broom, greater stitchwort, dandelion, germander speedwell. Though some of the butterflies and moths are unfamiliar, this place is far more like home than I'd expected.

The key difference is that there are no obvious signs of the boar's existence here. I'm used to an exorbitance of rooting, to tears and lumps in the ground that last for many months. Further on, where the spruce gives way to hazel and hawthorn, I find isolated scrapes. But they're small. When I rendezvous with Finlay at lunchtime and show him photos, he reckons they're from badgers. He speaks their name with distaste.

Finlay drives us to the other side of the valley where I'd been walking. As if he's thinking *I'll show you some* real *rooting*, we walk up the hill to a two-year-old spruce plantation where the boar have passed through like a precise tornado; a straight row of seedlings, each about half the size of a household Christmas tree, have been torn out of the ground and left lying there. Where the disturbed earth this morning seemed too minor to have been boar-made, this vandalism seems too much. An impressive sign indeed. The rootings are by now months old, the craters of soil baked into hard grey crags. The purpose of the boar who did this has Finlay scratching his head. What exactly were they after? I couldn't come up with a suggestion at the time, though I've since watched an interview with a forester from the Dean whose theory is that boar may be mistakenly attracted by the smell of fresh compost around plantings. This would make sense in Galloway too, where the earth beneath the monoculture sprawls of non-native Sitka spruce surely offers paltry fare compared to that beneath native broadleaved forest.

We climb on to the hilltop. Finlay has been walking here for years. It's a place peopled with his memories of picking blaeberries and lingonberries in the turns from summer to autumn. He's brought two of his cocker spaniels with us, Rum and Skye, and they go hurtling through the grasses and scrub. Cotton grass nods in the breeze. Far away, Criffel Hill's bareness is plain. No country for boar there. It's a high point above the steady rising tide of conifer plantations. Finlay doesn't mourn the loss of open land to forestry like Patrick does, though he recently learned that the part of the wood where his high seat is set up is soon to be felled. He's glum about the prospect of having to dismantle it and find another location.

As we turn and begin to loop back around, a cuckoo calls. Finlay stops and grins. He'd shaken his head and rolled his eyes a few minutes ago when I'd stopped by a tree stump to exclaim at the size of the two-banded longhorn beetles crawling over it. His love for nature is a tad selective, encompassing creatures like sparrows, cuckoos and red kites, and excluding ones like foxes and badgers. He questions the wisdom of reintroducing white-tailed eagles and beavers, and perhaps he would've felt the same about the boar if their return had happened with the government's blessing. But unlike eagles and beavers, boar are here for the taking.

'As a shooter, I was pleased to have them around,' he replies when I ask what he remembered thinking the moment it dawned on him that the *something bigger than the badgers* was wild boar.

Finlay's first boar in Britain – he'd shot them in Spain already – remains his most memorable, and not just because of the novelty. The boar has a name: Big Peter. His head is on the wall of Finlay's living room, jaws wide, upper tusks puckering the skin above into a snarl.

Finlay had been in the high seat for two hours on a cold moonlit night when he was seized with a need to empty his bladder. He hung the rifle on the end of one piece of iron and quietly descended. Afterwards, he climbed back up and was just resettling into his seat when he heard a movement to the left. With the rifle hanging in front of him, he couldn't risk reaching forward and scaring off whoever the creature might be. After a taut few minutes, another movement: around 10m away stood a huge wild boar.

'He was stalking me,' Finlay recounts. That may not have been Big Peter's intention, but even 11 years later, Finlay feels the freshness of the shock of knowing that the boar could've been watching him while he was in his vulnerable position at the bottom of the ladder.

The male walked on to the bait station and began to eat. Finlay could finally take his rifle in hand again. Except the scope was fogged from the damp air. His target wandered off and didn't return. After a long and unrewarded wait, Finlay gave up and left. On the half-mile walk to his car through the dark, he was keenly aware that the boar was somewhere around.

'Was I scared? I'd rather not say,' he wrote in *Sporting Rifle*. 'But I did have my rifle held in front, thumb on safety, finger on trigger guard and ready.'

He got back into the high seat two nights later. This time, he had a neoprene cover on the scope to keep it clear. This time, the same huge boar came and lingered long enough.

Finlay fired.

He reckons that after the gralloch, Big Peter weighed around 150–200kg. He hasn't seen a boar as big since, and suspects Big Peter had eastern European ancestry.

Our path down and around the hill takes us to last night's bait station – the same one where Big Peter met his end. From here, I can't see the high seat. It's well concealed from boar and human alike.

Rum and Skye lie in the long grass like little lions as Finlay tops the station up with the maize he's brought along. The hunter based near Dumfries called maize 'crack cocaine for boar' when we spoke. Small boulders are scattered around the station, taken from a crumbling *dyke* – a dry stone wall, in Galloway parlance. Finlay heaves these up to slip stale bread into the hollows beneath, adding to the mouldy bread already there and untouched. There's also a big plastic tube, into which he drops the maize, then wedges the tube into place with a boulder on either side.

'When pigs were visiting the site, I would find the large boulders casually thrown five or six feet away from the depressions in the ground, with no scrape marks indicating they had been pushed or rolled over,' the *Sporting Rifle* article read.

Only boar would be getting at this food. Except they are keeping away at the moment, as doubly confirmed by the trail camera trained on the site. Finlay isn't hopeful of our chances tonight, and says we won't bother sitting out. I would've given it another go. But it isn't my call to make. Sensing his disappointment on my behalf, I tell him it's fine, and I mean it. The boar are a law unto themselves, and that's part of why I love them.

Still eager to give me more proxy experiences of boar shooting, Finlay drives us westwards to drop in for much-needed coffee with a friend (so far he's only had four cups today). The friend, Rohan, has his own bait station. Only he's having a dry spell too. He and Finlay instead spend the time discussing how to keep rhododendrons happy. I nod along, sipping on coffee clouded with oat milk. I'm amused to be served such vegan fare by a hunter.

That night, after a few hours spent crawling commando-style around a field with Finlay looking for badgers through the thermal scope, I'm brushing my teeth in the downstairs loo when he pops his head around the door and holds his phone up in front of my face.

'Got a text from Rohan,' he says with a grin.

It reads: *GOT A BOAR!!!*

'Wharppp!' I exclaim through toothpaste.

The next morning, I'm raring to go and have a look at the kill. Finlay is too, although he has decided that my weekend apprenticeship must include one additional module: tick removal. He brandishes his arm, pointing at a dark dot near the crook of his elbow. Then he hands me a British Deer Society-branded plastic card with a slot in it designed for just this job.

Guts and blood I can handle all day. But show me a tick or any other kind of parasite, and I want to run a mile. Grimacing, I take up the card and use it to twist the tick off Finlay's skin.

'Good,' he says. 'Now, count the legs. If it's a larva it'll only have six. You've got less chance of getting Lyme disease if it's a larva, because you might be its first meal.'

I contemplate the object now stuck to the card. 'But it hasn't got any legs.'

'Eh?'

Reader, it is a scab.

With my lesson in tick (or not) removal out of the way, we drive back to Rohan's. The boar is hanging in his garage, next to two bikes. A bucket sits underneath, full of congealed blood. This, at last, is my undeniable evidence of wild boar in Galloway. They haven't felt real until now.

The boar is a sow. And she'd been close to giving birth.

Rohan imparts this information to us with a wince. He'd assumed she was male – she was alone, she looked big, and it's late in the season for birthing as far as he knows. He slit her open and gralloched her last night. Four dark nipples run down either side of the gape. Her womb had held five fully formed offspring. The small amount of meat on them will go to feeding various animals that he keeps, but it's clear that Rohan wishes a different boar had come last night.

I wonder why she'd been alone. Had her sounder-mates already left to give birth, or was it she who'd left and had wanted one final meal before she tied herself to her defenceless newborns? The bait station with its plenitude of maize kernels may simply have been too much to resist.

I lock my sadness away and try to absorb the physicality of her body. She may be gone, but what's left is still something to behold. With organs removed, she weighs 47kg. The bristles running from the back of her head to her midsection remain erect, enlarging her even more. Her thick black eyelashes look long enough to belong to an elephant.

'Can you smell that?' Finlay asks, taking a good sniff. 'There's no muskiness. She smells sweet, don't you think?'

I put my face closer to her thick brown fur and inhale. He's right. It's a warm, almost summer-hay scent.

While we inspect her, Rohan boots up his laptop to play the video of the shooting. It lasts 1 minute and 44 seconds.

He doesn't have a high seat set up, so he approached on foot. Taken by a thermal camera fixed to his rifle, the picture is grainy, and shaky – an undercurrent of nerves, perhaps? In the black crosshairs, the boar's shape resolves, about 50m away. Eyes glow like little twin moons. She seems engrossed in shoving boulders and turf aside. I would've assumed her to be male too. Rohan holds the rifle steady, but with her body pointing towards him, there's no clear shot to take. Then, at last, she turns. Rohan spends a few more seconds training the crosshairs just behind her neck, halfway between spine and chest.

The shot is muted. The flash is bright. She collapses, legs out straight as if electrocuted. The death looks instant.

Was it? Alick Simmons, vet and author of *Treated Like Animals*, is doubtful when he reads an early draft of this chapter. The shot, he writes to me, 'would destroy the heart and the associated great vessels... The resultant catastrophic drop in blood pressure would cause the animal to drop into irreversible unconsciousness in a short period – 30 seconds to 3 minutes – as the brain becomes starved of oxygen. Quite quick but not as quick as the effect of a captive bolt pistol in a slaughterhouse.'

In spite of that possibility, I'd still take the open night over a slaughterhouse.

Finlay helps Rohan out by cutting away the other parts of the carcass that aren't needed. After sawing off the head, Finlay points at the thick white layer of fat and skin that enwraps bone and flesh. 'It's like they have armour. That's probably why they don't tend to have ticks.'

Every deer that Finlay shoots seems to come with a village of ticks, which can remain on the body for many hours. But this boar appears to have none.

With the head untethered, Finlay takes a moment to inspect the sow's teeth. Her tusks are mere nubs. He and Rohan agree that she can only be a year old. The litter would've been her first.

When the ends of her legs are removed too, I move in for a closer look at one. The black hooves are coarse with dried mud. When I gently part them, a webbing of skin is revealed. Boar do well in wetlands, and their feet are part of the reason. But the real surprise is on the underside. Behind the hooves is a round pad, soft and squishy to the touch, like a leather-bound pocket of gel. I imagine that pad flattening, cushioning and quietening footfalls.

The boar is ready for storage. Finlay and Rohan share the load, though they still struggle to get her into the second-hand Pepsi-branded fridge in the corner. Rohan is getting married in two weeks' time. She will feed his wedding guests.

Before we go, Rohan mentions that he only decided to visit the bait station last night because we'd come to talk to him about boar.

With that, I am forever bound to the sow's death.

Yet despite this, and despite the fact that I came to Galloway because the only people here who brush up against the boar are the ones killing them, when I leave for home I am thinking of life. Although the stalker denied the population five new individuals when he took the sow, who knows how many more have been born this year so far? Boar move in currents across the map in my mind, the lines growing ever thicker. But only gradually. If they've been here for nearly 30 years already – as my Dumfries contact maintains – then it is astonishing that many local people remain unaware. Or don't seem to care.

Their seemingly slow population growth could partly be down to the region's lack of broadleaved woodland, the habitat where boar seek much of their food. The disrupted soils beneath young conifer plantations and the moss-thick soils beneath mature plantations offer thin pickings.

But could it be that Galloway's stalkers have also aided in their stealth, by applying gentle brakes to their breeding, and by teaching them to be wary? If so, it means that time has been bought. Time that wasn't given to the boar and people of the Forest of Dean. Galloway shows that there is more than just one possible trajectory when animals like wild boar come back to a place like Britain. Here, there's a chance to draw on the lessons already learned in the Forest of Dean – and beyond our shores altogether. As Galloway recedes in my wing mirror, I have the distinct feeling that behind me a revolution is quietly underway.

A month later, Finlay emails me:

Last Saturday night, I was out to shoot a roe buck beyond the quarry we passed. All quiet. But as I returned, I saw a black movement below me, and thought at first a roe doe. But no, a boar! Off the knee shot (not the easiest), it fell down. But when I was down at it, I heard more grunting nearby in the trees!

So there are more!

PART TWO

FUTURES

CHAPTER ELEVEN

A *Bamboche* of Boar

Part of me belongs to the Loire Valley in France. As children, my cousins, brother and I spent hot insect-whirring summers roaming the woods and fields around the home of Bonne-Maman and Grand-Père. We plucked grass for donkeys with their soft muzzles, peeked under discarded tiles for adders, found crickets to fling into the webs of wasp spiders, chased in vain after lizards. Popping back from time to time to beg for Orangina and La Vache qui Rit.

There were always boar here. I just didn't pay them any heed. I didn't even know there was an English word for *sanglier*, and I held only the barest idea of the creature. Something dark and shaggy. Something wild.

The adults in my family knew to take care when driving at night. Yet the boar posed no threat to free-range children, so we weren't warned about them (though we probably would have ignored our parents anyway, as we did with the adders). The *sanglier* were unquestioned and barely noted neighbours. A far cry from the reactions they stir in Britain today.

Yet, although wild boar were never annihilated on the Continent, they came close to it. From the seventeenth century to the first half of the twentieth, forest loss and hunting kept the fire of them banked. Their numbers finally began to climb in the 1960s and still show no sign of plateauing. In his book *The Implausible Rewilding of the Pyrenees*, Steve Cracknell states that although no one has worked out definitive figures for the population trend, French hunters in 1970 killed 10,000 wild boar – while in 2018 they killed 750,000. At present, there's thought to be a total of around 10 million boar across mainland Europe, with a fifth of those in France.

People in mainland Europe have always lived alongside wild boar. But the boar are now becoming *alive* in a way they haven't been for centuries.

They are becoming something new.

If we're to live with wild boar in Britain, we need to know all we can. And mainland Europe offers lessons aplenty. The boar started bending the rules there decades before they did here. How are people adapting – or not?

I can't hope to encompass an entire region of the world in my answer. But I can make a start.

———

The train from Paris carries me southwards into a heatwave. It's June 2022, and the pale land beyond my window looks brittle with thirst. Disembarking at Toulouse is like walking into a giant hairdryer. It isn't even 40°C yet.

I'm rescued by my uncle Christophe and his air-conditioned car. Although raised in Norfolk with my mother and other uncles, he's lived in France for many years with my aunt Sylvie, raising three children whose English far surpasses my French. He's eagerly taken on the job of my fixer. He only gives me a minute at his house to drop my bag before whisking me off to his local golf course.

We find the blond-haired owner of the course, Charles, smoking a cigarette in the shade of the clubhouse's pergola. We join him at his table. I start knocking back my ice-cold glass of sparkling water as soon as it's brought.

Our conversation soon finds a rhythm, with Charles speaking and then pausing to let my uncle translate for me. Not being able to instantly understand what's being said, I find myself focusing on the wryness of Charles' expression and voice. For there is a sense of the absurd to his brushes with the boar. When they come, they besiege the fairways, with golfing suspended and revenue trickling away until every last upended clod has been pushed back into its hole and patted down. On a few sleepless nights, Charles has even jumped into his car and driven the boar off, literally. He has now spent €7,000 on electric fencing to keep them out. Another course closer to the city is spending €200,000 on 2m-high steel fencing, having found that the boar are able to jump the electric fence they'd already put in.

I find damage to golf courses hard to mourn, and suspect their days are numbered as Europe stares down the barrel of droughts to come. Nevertheless, some people's livelihoods depend on them, and they provide a useful example of what happens when boar come across well-watered lawns.

The reason that boar love Charles' golf course so much is probably also the reason why I am sweating and wilting in my plastic chair at this moment: climate change.

'Twenty years ago, they came maybe two months a year, in July and August. Because it would be dry, and obviously golf courses have water, so the ground is moister and the boar can dig for worms,' Charles explained. 'But the trouble now is that the winters are getting drier and drier, and already in January, February, March, the ground is already very hard. So from being a problem for just two months of the year, they're basically present all year round now.'

I can understand the boar's attraction. Most of the grass I've seen today so far has been a crispy yellow, while here it's still lush and green. Enjoying it in the distance near a pond are some grazing coypu – big plump rodents who share with beavers a love of water, if not a paddle-shaped tail. They're classed as an invasive species, having been introduced from South America, although they cause Charles far less consternation than the native boar.

Climate change is also helping to spur growth in the boar population, Charles says. 'They used to have one litter. But now with the temperature getting warmer, the majority are having two. Since females will have between five and ten boarlets, you basically double the amount every year.'

Of course, that amount is before the hunters take their share. Hunting now happens on the golf course itself, though special authorisation for this had to be sought from the police. The method used is the *battue* – the flushing of animals from their hiding places, with guns at the ready. But Charles himself has stopped taking part in the shoots. 'It's no longer a pleasure to do it,' he says. 'I'll do it if I have to. I don't get switched on by killing an animal.'

Charles' grim statement is indicative, to me, of a wider pattern of human-made catastrophe. All over the world, ecosystems are in disarray. One result is the mass culling of species that are experiencing runaway success, or have simply managed to maintain their numbers while their habitat and neighbour species shrink away. There were surely more boar in Mesolithic Europe. But at this point in time, there's undeniably a gaping mismatch between their numbers and their human-wrecked environment. The problems that people are experiencing with boar, from damaged golf courses and farmland to car accidents, still pale in comparison to those felt by other wildlife. There are now fears that high boar numbers are preventing the regeneration of oak forests in parts of Europe, while in isolated reserves, boar are proving the final straw for a range of threatened species.

And so, in the absence of any semblance of equilibrium, the conveyer belt of killing goes on.

We leave Charles just after 6 p.m., when the air is still roasting. My uncle shakes his head. In the south of France, high temperatures in summer aren't uncommon. But early June is too early for this. We eat dinner inside his shuttered stone house. Outside, swifts on their vesper flights are screeching. Their calls sound less like joy and more like pain.

There's no reprieve from the molten sun the next day as my uncle and I emerge out of a hatch and onto the roof of a five-storey, seventeenth-century manor house. It sits atop a hill overlooking the entire city. With us is Michel, eyes kind and skin nearly nut-brown from sun. His family has owned the house and 350 hectares of land around it for many generations. Although, much like Charles, he only got a hunting licence in middle age.

During many of the interviews I've done while researching this book, maps have been whipped out, in virtual or paper form. Up here, we are in the map. My eyes drift from the horses grazing below – Michel runs a stable, and has no trouble between his equine charges and the boar – to the hazy glass and greyness at the heart of Toulouse. The land just to the right of this is dominated by the hulk of the Airbus factory, from which so many shiny new planes have issued. Between that place and here, I can see how fields and other open spaces are being nibbled away by construction. Most is for new housing. On the drive to Michel's, my uncle had commented on how the local roads had become busier, even in just the decade or so since he moved here. Roads that have already seen plenty of accidents involving cars and boar.

Michel uses the 360-degree view to point to the different woodlands that the boar like to migrate between over the year. There used to be more horses here, and cattle, which held back the tide of scrub and trees that now grow thick enough for the boar. The woodland in the direction of the Airbus factory is their 'summer residence'. It's there that Michel leads the *battue*, with the aim of taking six to eight boar a year, having roughly calculated that the land can bear 25 of them. He goes into detail about the hunt, which is run in a highly regimented fashion. A horn must be blown to signal its start, and again at its end. You need a certain number of shooters standing outside the wood, stalkers to go in, and dogs wearing bells to do the actual flushing (the ringing of the bells alerts the shooters to the approach of boar with the dogs behind them). The shooters must not aim into the wood; must shoot downward at a 30-degree angle; must be within 25m of the target; must use the right ammunition. They try to shoot only males, sparing any sows with babies at hoof – a practice that probably doesn't help much with controlling population size.

Although Michel hunts by necessity, there's a humour to his voice and words as they come to me via my uncle. The boar are clever; some of the older ones seem to know that their best chance of survival is to stay hunkered down in the woods and ignore the yapping dogs. Once, when the horn had blown to signal the end of the *battue*, a big male emerged from the woods, stared at the hunters, and then walked across the field.

'As if to say, "Missed me!"' Michel's face crinkles even more with a sudden grin.

He isn't afraid of them, and outside hunting season they don't seem to be afraid of him; a pair once strolled past him in daylight. Some years they menace his crops, for which he can seek compensation from the local hunting association. But he is philosophical about the inconveniences. 'You've got wildcat here, you've got wild boar, you've got roe deer. It's part of nature. So you have to live with it.'

And there is another creature, Michel tells us, whose return has not yet been officially recognised: the wolf. It seems incredible that this and other such wild beings could have journeyed to – and are surviving in – this landscape mosaic of urban, suburban and rural. Barely different to the place I call home. And yet, the local Toulouse news is absent of wildlife scare stories.[9]

---

[9] I lie: in 2012, a Toulouse resident discovered that a fox was responsible for stealing 38 *boules* (small balls used in the outdoor French game of the same name) from his garden. *Vilain renard!*

'Many urban French people are only one or two generations away from their rural ancestors. Britons are often centuries away from theirs,' Martin Castellan, a British ecologist now settled in the nearby Pyrenees and involved in a local environmental NGO, writes to me in an email around the time of my Toulouse visit. His statement shines one particular beam of light on why the general populace here isn't up in arms over boar. It echoes the words of Steve Cracknell, who claims that 'The animal is considered no more dangerous than a big dog.' Of course, I cannot presume to know what locals who are neither large landowners nor hunters think, though I note that my uncle and his family never mentioned boar to me until I started writing this book.

Up north in Tours, where Bonne-Maman now lives, the nightly ingress of boar into the city during France's first lockdown in 2020 was reported by a local newspaper with apparent glee and delight – a sentiment shared by Bonne-Maman when she posted the article clipping to me. The headline ran: *'Pour les animaux, c'est la bamboche!'* In English: 'For the animals, it is a party!' My educated guess is that the equivalent headline in a British newspaper would have been something like 'Boar RAMPAGE through city, leaving locals in fear for their LIVES'.

Our interview with Michel concluded, we descend back through his house. The ground below is fissured everywhere with cracks, while the leaves of many of the trees already have an end-of-August fade to them. We've only just reached June. Summer has become a marathon, and not all will make it to the end.

I think, too, of the boar, hunkered down in the undergrowth, perhaps even now hearing our voices on the hot wind as we say goodbye to Michel at the car. Dreaming of cool wallows, tongues rasping with thirst. If they aren't already suffering, they will as droughts become a regular fact of life in this part of the world. Even if they themselves are a symptom, an early warning, of the coming changes.

———

Charles and Michel became hunters by necessity. Not so Daniel, an older man with a classic country Frenchman's belly, whom we meet on the third day. We sit in his cavernous kitchen, with chest freezers humming in the background and a pair of beagles in a pen outside still barking in offence at our presence.

Daniel ignores them. He rolls a cigarette, the first of many. It turns out my need for a translator suits him well, because each time my uncle relays his words to me, he takes the opportunity to roll another cigarette or light one he made during the last long pause.

Daniel is a lifelong hunter, and a *garde-chasse*. This latter role is both voluntary and essential: in a deep voice gravelled by smoking, he explains that he ensures hunters in the local association follow all the rules and regulations. He has the power to fine or ban anyone who fails to comply.

There are also unwritten rules, ones that the hunters choose to apply. 'We usually don't hunt too many. We don't go out to hunt just for the sake of killing them,' Daniel echoes Charles. 'We kill what we can eat.'

Hunters in France aren't permitted to directly sell the meat they harvest, and since few want to bother selling to a butcher via a middleman, they tend to give away to others what they can't eat themselves.

'You'll only find certain meats like boar during the hunt. It's through people you know,' Charles had said before. This is a pleasing notion – that even in a highly developed country like France, some food is still only seasonal and acquired through bonds of community rather than money.

Yet Daniel's insistence on killing only what he and friends can eat means that hunters like him are less effective than they might otherwise be at controlling wild boar. That is, the wild boar of today.

'If you go back in time, the females were only having four or five little boar each time. Nowadays, because of mixture with pigs, they're having litters of eight to ten. And it only takes them three months before they can be pregnant again, so they can have two or three litters a year, which isn't natural.'

Again, this is similar to what Charles said. But whereas Charles insisted that French boar are pure, with no interbreeding with farmed pigs, Daniel thinks otherwise. And he has the science to back him up on that particular point, if not the three-litters-per-year one. Indeed, some researchers claim there are few genetically 'pure' wild boar left in Europe at all. After all, it's been about 8,500 years since humans first brought pigs here from the Middle East. That's a lot of time for mingling. According to Swedish researcher Lara Tickle, some French hunters now call wild boar *sanglochon,* a bastard name born of *sanglier* and *cochon* (pig), an unwanted hybrid.

Genetic analysis of boar from various regions of Europe has found evidence of both historical and recent interbreeding events. Recent as in, happening right now. This is to be expected in places where pigs are still turned out into the woods to fatten themselves, such as the Iberian Peninsula. But most pigs in Europe now live and die without ever going outside. So how are they and boar still managing to mingle? And how much blame can we place on fecund pig genes for the rise and rise of the modernised wild boar?

'Clearly a little bit of the fault is from the hunters themselves who wanted to have more, but it got out of control,' Daniel admits.

That is something of an understatement, not just in terms of how out of control things have become, but also how much blame can be laid at the door of hunters. There is ample evidence that hunters all over Europe have been shuffling wild boar around, without care for preserving local genetics or avoiding the release of hybrid boar who then go on to make more hybrids with the boar already in their new homes. Hunters have also fuelled the animals' maize habit via supplementary feeding. All to have a better chance of a bigger and easier bag.

I very much doubt that Daniel has been involved in any such ecological vandalism, not least because boar have never been his preferred quarry. In fact, up to around 30 years ago, it wasn't even possible to hunt boar in his home village and its environs.

'They just didn't have anywhere to live around here,' he says, describing how it used to be that only the large forests around Toulouse hosted populations, with the odd lone male or sounder of females making a risky journey between these refugia. More habitat has become available to them, and perhaps they truly have become bolder. Regardless, the sharp rise in boar numbers has demanded a response from local hunters. 'It's not a part of how the culture used to be, but it's become so now.'

Yet, in turn, anti-hunting sentiment is growing across France. And people like Daniel are feeling the lick of the flames.

'Hunters get a bad press because the media jumps if there's an accident. When people don't respect the rules, accidents happen. And then they call us assassins.' Daniel swats at the air with the hand holding his current cigarette. 'Well, I've never killed anybody in my life. Many more people have accidents in Paris with the scooters.'

He mentions an accident that happened in a neighbouring hunting association's patch, where a woman was shot dead in a wood after ignoring the signs warning people not to enter because of a hunt. Yet it's impossible to ignore the fact that all across France, people are falling prey to stray bullets or the misjudgement of hunters. In one high-profile case close to Toulouse, a 25-year-old man was killed while chopping wood near his house in 2020 after a hunter apparently mistook him for a wild boar. According to newspaper *Le Monde*, between 2000 and 2022 there was a total of over 3,000 hunting accidents, 421 of which involved deaths. Some of these tragic losses were likely the result of mixing shooting with alcohol, which seems to be an embedded part of hunting culture in parts of Europe.

'They want to ban hunting in France,' Daniel continues. He is no doubt referring to groups such as le Rassemblement pour une France sans Chasse (RAC), 'the Union for a France Free of Hunting'. RAC and other similar groups have used two recent public opinion polls as evidence that the vast majority of French people do indeed want a ban. However, since both polls were commissioned by anti-hunting interests, they should be taken with a good spoonful of salt. They also unsettle me. Practices such as the glue-trapping of songbirds belong to the past. Yet, to call for a ban on all hunting is to deny our responsibility as apex predators. Humans have always been so in the ecosystems they are part of. Surely it's possible for us to find a balance between how much we should hunt and how much of the hunting we should leave to others? Lynx, wolves and bears are trickling back into the predator-parched lands of Europe. We should welcome them. And we should stand alongside them.

Yet, even if French hunters were not facing fierce criticism, the system is creaking. Daniel, who looks to be in his mid-60s, speaks in pessimistic tones about the future. Hunting is becoming less popular among the younger generations. There are still 1.3 million hunters in France, but the number of licences and of hunting association members have both been falling since the late 1970s. One problem with this is that part of each hunter's licence fee goes towards compensating farmers for crop damage from boar. In 2019, the bill came to €60 million – a sum that highlights the threat posed by boar to some forms of agriculture. And if an association loses members, licence fees may be increased in order to maintain pay-outs to the farmers, which in turn forces more hunters out. It's a vicious cycle.

'In certain areas of France now there are not enough hunters,' Daniel tells us. 'And the hunters that are left can't pay the farmers. It's getting critical.'

He, Michel and Charles all share the opinion that a breaking point will come when the government must step in and set up a nationwide culling programme. Whenever this happens, the utmost care will be needed in determining how and when to hunt the boar, given what we know about the potential unintended effects that heavy hunting can have on the species' reproductive rate.

And yet, in spite of the growing challenges, the impression I've long held about the French – that they find themselves able to live alongside boar – remains intact. I see no sign of the kind of terror that grips some back home. But Toulouse is a city where the skin that divides rural from urban feels paper-thin. Wild boar seem to be treated as a fact of life like wasps and storms. How different might it be for citizens of a more sprawling metropolitan region, where the boar are newer and bolder?

I'm off to Barcelona to investigate.

My original plan is to hop straight from Toulouse to Barcelona by bus. However, Covid has other ideas. The symptoms I originally put down to the extreme heat turn out to be my first visit from the virus. So it isn't till September that I find myself in the passenger seat of a Nissan pickup, with an ex-stray dog called Mamba squeezed between my legs in the footwell while vet Carles Conejero drives us slowly through orange-lit streets. In search of the *senglar*.

We're in Vallvidrera, a neighbourhood that perches in the wooded hills of Collserola Natural Park above the concrete flatlands of the city. An edge zone, where the wild waits for no invitation.

Carles' phone lies in the console between us. He heads up a team of vets from the Autonomous University of Barcelona, whose task it is to respond to police callouts for boar-related emergencies. He's on the rota tonight, as he is many nights; he took charge of the team the year before, and he admits to feeling sleep-deprived. But for now, he has the time to drive me around in search of animals whose notoriety is steadily growing. Everyone's heard about when Shakira was 'mugged' in one of Barcelona's parks.

'Look how they left my bag, the two wild boars that attacked me in the park. They were taking my bag to the woods with my phone in it. They've destroyed everything,' the Grammy award-winning singer gabbled in an Instagram story after the event (translation courtesy of *The Guardian*). Perhaps only one boar in Europe can lay claim to greater infamy than the two who set their sights on Shakira: Elsa, a sow in Grunewald Forest in Berlin, who was christened in 2020 after she stole the laptop bag of a sunbathing nudist. He gave determined chase. The rest is viral history.[10]

The place where Elsa picked the wrong naked man to steal from is now, according to reports, devoid of boar. I have a far better chance of meeting the tribe that calls Barcelona its home, and I peer expectantly out through the windscreen as the Nissan prowls the up-and-down warren of streets.

A small shape bobs across the road ahead of us. I jerk forward, think it's a boarlet, but Carles says it's just a cat. And then a boarlet *does* come trotting along, seemingly following the cat. We park, leaving Mamba in the car, and emerge in time to see the little boar and a slightly bigger

---

[10] The photo of the event was later commemorated by a German toy company, who produced a figurine set of Elsa and the naked man, as well as by science writer Josh Luke Davis using embroidery (his masterpiece can be viewed on Twitter).

sibling sliding through a gap in a chain-link fence to reach their mother. The fence is between us now. My boar, the ones back home, would already be bums in the distance. These boar flick their heads up and down and watch us with eager eyes, like children in the sweets aisle at the supermarket.

A scrunching sound. Carles is massaging a plastic bag in one hand. It is a siren call to the family; they trot along the other side of the fence in step with us, excited squeals escaping from the babies. We stop. I crouch, and the smaller one gets as close as they can, pushing the glistening disc of their nose through a gap. A thrilled voice in my head says, *Touch the schnozzle. Touch it.*

I comport myself and take a step back. Though I can't help my grin.

The mother seems warier now that food is clearly not forthcoming. She grunts, trying to call her babies back to her. They linger. 'She is a semi-habituated boar.' Carles looks back down at the boarlets. 'But *they* are completely habituated.'

Their lack of fear towards us foretells the direction their lives will take.

Once we're on the road again, I ask roughly when the boar problem started in Barcelona.

'The wild boar is not a problem,' Carles corrects me, as streetlights slide off his glasses. 'The problem is caused by people's lack of experience with wildlife.'

This became clear to the Barcelona police in 2013, when an officer shot at a boar in the middle of the city with his service revolver, only for one of the bullets to rebound into his colleague's knee. 'That was when they went, "Okay, we need professionals."' Carles explains. 'And that is when the university got involved.'

Over the last nine years, Carles' team has grimly honed its craft. Boar that make calamitous appearances in the middle of the city are taken down with tranquiliser darts in blow pipes. Meanwhile, in places identified as hotspots, planned captures are carried out with cage traps – which tend to be effective only for boarlets, and which boar learn to avoid once they've witnessed them in operation – or drop-nets.

Drop-nets work in exactly the way you'd expect from the name. The design used by the Barcelona team involves erecting four metal stakes around 3m high, from which a 10m × 10m nylon net is suspended. The net is fastened with electromagnets, until the moment that the boar step beneath to eat the bait, and an operator hiding out of sight hits the button to release.

The drop-nets have proven themselves to be more or less 100 per cent effective at catching whole sounders at a time. Given what we know or can surmise about the emotional depths of boar, this may be kinder than picking a few adults off. Even so, the experience must be a terrifying one for the animals.

'The squeals were deafening,' Bernhard Warner wrote for *The Guardian* in 2019, after accompanying Carles' predecessor on a night of trapping. 'Eleven boars were captured in the netting, the nylon strands wrapping tighter and tighter around their thighs the more they bucked and struggled.'

Every boar that the vets encounter is subdued with tranquiliser. Then, after taking blood samples, another injection is administered to kill them. In 2021, this was the fate of 196 individuals.

Non-lethal control isn't an option. Transport them into the heart of the Collserola forest and they'll come back. They don't wander into the city by accident but with intent.

They're hooked on us.

I meet up with Carles in the same area again the next evening. This time it's early enough that the sky is still light, while the bar across from the metro station is already abuzz.

With the jackal-like Mamba on her lead, we've walked the grand distance of 70m when we come upon our quarry. A juvenile not long out of their stripes is wandering along the pavement outside the bar. A woman who has just parked her car pauses to watch, before walking on. The boar ignores her, too busy chewing on what looks to me like an empty plastic pot. When Carles' team analysed the stomach contents of dispatched boar, they found chicken still in its plastic wrapping, intact enough to identify the supermarket it came from.

The juvenile has company. Next along from the bar is a building site, and there an adult with a striking black pelt wanders through the rubble and scaffolding, face tipped to the ground. Perhaps the builders have dropped food or wrappers. The wild boar's gifts of smell and snout were shaped for earth but seem equally useful for sifting through our detritus.

An incensed lapdog yaps from the balcony of a nearby apartment. Other than that, the atmosphere is calm. People are strolling past or chatting on benches. These boar, in this moment, might as well be giant wingless pigeons.

Carles, Mamba and I move on, seeking others. We cross a concrete road pocked with a single line of tracks, where a boar stepped before the concrete could set. A marker of presence, to go with the bars at the bottom of some of the communal bins – which Carles says prevent the boar from toppling them – and the municipal signs warning against feeding them because *Els animals en libertat poden arribar a ser violents*. 'Wild animals can become violent.'

When we circle back to the metro station and cross the bridge to reach a stone track that plunges into a tract of wood, we meet the boar from earlier. There are two black adults now, along with the juvenile. They ply the edges of the track, rustling in and out of bushes. Mamba quivers with want. Carles takes us past them so that we can sit and watch from a distance. Yet the group has already set their course, and they come closer, grunting to each other as they conduct private searches for food. Plastic, tubers, pizza, grubs – these boar are happy to flip between polar-opposite foods.

The juvenile trots from the other side of the track towards us. I can only stare as they stop to turn over the leaf litter within a metre of Mamba. The dog has an iron discipline, neither straining at her lead nor making a sound. While the juvenile has the gingery-brown pelt of a young boar, their tail also has an undeniable domestic curl.

Without so much as a glance at Mamba, they wander on. One of the black ones draws near next. 'That is a half-breed, a cross with a Vietnamese pot-bellied pig,' Carles says, as the bells of a church ring in the distance. 'The snout is shorter.'

He explains that about six or seven years ago, a TV show called *Porca Miseria* came out that made lots of people want to get a mini pig. Inevitably, some of those pigs turned out to be not so mini. And, inevitably, some owners turned them out into the forest. Legislation is now tighter around the keeping of such breeds, but there are still a few domestic pigs wandering Collserola, fraternising with their wilder counterparts.

I ask if this explains the lack of fear, if it's only the hybrids who dare to approach people.

'No,' Carles replies. Then the hybrid snatches up a big white mushroom and the vet surprises me with a gasp of outrage. 'Look! He's eating the Russula! Fuck you!' he tells the boar, who doesn't flick an ear.

I can't help chuckling at his possessiveness, though I mull on it too. 'An animal behaving as a wild boar should behave is not our target. We want those wild boar,' he said on the phone before we met. These boar are not in their geographical, nor biological, places.

Four teenage boys on bicycles appear. They slow as they pass, looking at the boar and chattering away. 'They were saying, "Oh, boar here, okay, take care,"' Carles translates for me. The words seem to reflect how many people here feel about their porcine neighbours. *Okay. Take care.* No fear or panic, just awareness.

But this isn't always the case, as Shakira can attest. The neighbourhood of Vallvidrera is indisputably within the woods, and there must exist some degree of acceptance that things are going to come out of those woods. From where we're standing, however, it's less than two miles before pine needle-strewn earth surrenders to the concrete of the metropolis. No distance at all for a boar. Carles reckons that about a third of Collserola's 1,500-strong population are venturing out regularly, abandoning the dim spaces below the oaks and pines for the open roads and pavements, the parks and gardens; all places where their presence is far harder for us to process. They collide with cars, and cornered ones can knock people over in panic, although biting is the most reported physical encounter.

'Now we have people getting ass bites.' The American inflection that Carles gives to *ass* makes his words infinitely more entertaining, though it's no laughing matter for the Barcelonians who've found their bottoms on the receiving end of boar teeth.

This mode of interaction is a calculated one on the part of the boar. A strategy. 'They're learning that if they see someone carrying supermarket bags, if they go behind and bite the person, the person jumps and drops the bags,' Carles explains. 'They only started doing it in these last few months. They learn really fast.'

Ass-biting: a new cultural practice among the Barcelona wild boar.

'Every time a new "anti-boar system" to protect commercial waste containers is installed, be it cages or locks, boar figure it out within a fortnight. Adult females have even worked out that weight-triggered traps can be evaded by sending boarlets to fetch the bait,' I will learn from an article in *The Telegraph* a few months after my own visit, an article that also features Carles; he seems to spend as much time entertaining journalists and writers as he does wrangling boar. It's another sign of how important it is to him to get the word out, in any way he can.

It is both the ability of boar to learn and our own behaviour that have woven the city's current boar–human entanglements. The endless manna of our food waste, whether left on the ground or stuffed in bins, exerts a magnetic pull. It teaches wild boar that shiny crinkly plastic contains easy calories. Rome presents the most extreme case of this. The Italian capital is fast becoming infamous for its hordes of boar, who have been lured in and emboldened by heaps of uncollected rubbish. In some neighbourhoods, residents have even imposed 8.30 p.m. curfews in response to attacks by the animals. Rome's municipal shortcomings have come back to, yes, bite it on the ass.

Barcelona doesn't have a similar rubbish problem. But here, some people deliberately leave food out for boar. It is for them that Carles reserves the most ire. *Feeders*, he calls them.

'They have a social distancing problem with boar,' he sighs, after the hybrid boar have gone on their way and we've found a park bench to sit on. 'They have a lack of human contact and they prefer to establish relationships with the boar. Some people are feeding 20 to 30 boar in their backyards each year.'

Carles admits that the cuteness of boarlets is hard to resist, especially when they deploy the high-pitched grunts they normally reserve for their mothers. They soon work out that those grunts work equally well on us. But boarlets grow up, and they don't forget the lessons learned in infancy. Stopping people from offering food is an obvious way to address this issue, but it isn't necessarily an easy one. Carles and other experts have worked with the city council to run public awareness campaigns to try to dissuade tourists and residents from offering food to boar. Feeding wild animals is a deeply engrained cultural habit that Britain delights in too. We seem to have a bird feeder for every garden, and on social media the likes always pour in for footage of semi-habituated foxes snaffling snacks left out for them. In the Forest of Dean, despite years of stern announcements from Forestry England and pleas from grassroots groups like The Boaring Truth, some continue to feed wild boar.

Yet there's a stark contrast between our boar and those of Barcelona. Even the group that's known to roam the streets of one town in the Dean after dark, looking for bins ripe for the tipping-over, has held on to the fear of humans. This is good news. Though we mustn't become complacent.

'We don't know how to behave with animals. People don't know how to behave if they see a wild boar. Habituation is happening in both species at the same time.' Now Carles is talking about everyone, not just the feeders. Hunters aren't shooting enough boar, visitors want selfies, and animal rights activists who decry the action being taken against the animals are misguided. Carles seems lost in despair at the human race. He didn't become a vet to kill boar, yet he has had to take the lives of 1,200 of them since 2018.

After we part at the metro station, one of the last things he said reverberates in my head: 'If you kill a healthy animal, it's not euthanasia, it's sacrifice.'

But for as long as we encourage wild boar to seek us out, someone must do it.

I spend the next day hiking alone through Collserola, swapping the concrete jungle for holm oaks and Aleppo pines and the music of the wind soughing through their

boughs. I stick to their shade where I can. The ground is
stone-dry and all streams have been emptied. The drought
this year is thought to have further encouraged the boar to
go out in search of the ever-reliable currents of human food.

It's Monday. The Park is presumably quieter than at
weekends, although it's never long before a cyclist comes
puffing along. Once, I pass an elderly couple. The man is
using his hiking pole to bring the branches of a small tree
closer to him, so that he can pluck small red spherical fruits
from it. I smile and offer a *Buenos dias*. Further along the
path is another of the trees. I take one of the fruits, finding it
to be textured with tiny blunt spikes. Later I will find out it
is called 'strawberry tree'. I pop the fruit into my mouth,
and at the slightest press of my molars, it collapses sweetly.

'They learn by observing each other,' Carles had said last
night.

Collserola reminds me of the Forest of Dean. It is a
blanket of mostly secondary forest riddled with roads and
pimpled with houses. Whenever my path takes me south-
westwards, the gigantic Collserola Telecommunications
Tower breaches the rim of the hills. But in the Park's 8,000
hectares – 2,500 fewer than the Dean – there are perhaps
1,500 boar thriving.

I don't expect to see any. I pause, once, when a cacophony
of rustling comes from the undergrowth in a gorge below.
With every fresh puff of wind, the oaks around me drop
more acorns. Perhaps it's a mast year here, as it is at home.

As the day wears on, the path funnels me back into the
outskirts of Vallvidrera, a labyrinth of hard-surfaced streets.
I'm thirsty, nursing the last bit of water in my single bottle,
cursing the shuttered cafes I've passed and ignoring the
barking of a dog behind a gate. Then I hear the snort – not
the long belching kind I'm more familiar with, but a quick
outburst of alarm. I look up in time to see two boar darting
up a steep bank ahead of me. Heaps of drought-dropped
leaves blanket the pavement, and there's a deep rounded

imprint in them, as if the animals were dozing there before my interruption.

The pair stop at the top of the bank and regard me. I think they're young, and male; they both have the sharp hump near the end of their spine that I'm starting to associate more with males, although I've never seen such pronounced ones before. The russet flanks, muscled shoulders, and black bristles that run from the boar's heads and along their backs give them the flair of mustang stallions. Their tails hang straight, uncurled. No Vietnamese pot-bellied pigs in *their* family trees, as far as I can tell.

The dog is still barking. With a final exchange of grunts, the two males turn and melt into the scrub and trees. They're a world away from the others I've met here. They've chosen to shun the path that others have happily trotted down – and, in the long run, they may stand a better chance of assuring their genetic legacy. For Carles had said two seemingly contradictory things to me:

'The boar are super-plastic,' and, 'The boar cannot be an urban species.'

What he meant is this: wild boar are adept at overriding instinct and altering their behaviour to exploit our surplus of resources. But the siren call of the urban environment is often a deadly one, regardless of whether there's a team of vets waiting around the corner with a drop-net. Many of the boar who enter the core of the city are killed by dogs or cars. While alive, their appetite for human food exposes them to toxic pollutants. This same diet may provide the habituated boar of Barcelona with the extra calories to produce more, and bigger, offspring. But they may still be leading their lineages into a cul-de-sac.

'Barcelona is acting as an ecological sink,' is Carles' conclusion. The city as a black hole, tithing the parts of the population most willing to accept the risk that humans pose in exchange for their gifts.

Yet there will always be boar ready to take up that same mantle, that same way of life. And their descendants might in turn go back into the woods. Such are the possibilities of these 'reversible pigs', as anthropologist Aníbal Arregui calls them.

Boar have been crossing our boundaries from the moment we first erected these.

It's simply in their nature.

CHAPTER TWELVE

Fences of the Mind

Long after I return home from Spain, the boar of Barcelona continue to press on my mind. I find myself drawn again to the place in the Forest of Dean where the closest approximation to them can be found: the scrubby grassland on the edge of the town where the sow once danced in warning to me.

I haven't come back since then, afraid of … what? Overexploiting what appears to be a reliable boar resource? Scaring her and her family away for good? Surely I overestimate myself. Other people must sometimes walk here in the evenings.

Still, I've been saving this place. And now I'm back, on the edge of twilight, trainers crunching the carefully laid gravel that attests to the fact that this is no forgotten wasteland. Warm light glows from the windows of terraced houses on either side. I pad past the spot where I'd hidden among the brambles, and find myself nearing the far end, which is bordered by a 30mph road that everyone howls down at 40mph instead.

My hopes begin to fall. The path bends ahead, rises a little, trees drawing in. Wooden railings have been put in here.

And something is peering around them at me.

At first, under the dimness of the trees, I think it's a fat black Labrador. My brain defaults to the explanation that best fits my location.

But it *is* a boar.

I can only half-see them. And yet, in almost the same way that dreams seem to work, I piece together enough scraps from my senses to fill the gaps: from the way they hold themselves, the boar is wary, worried.

They turn and run.

I walk fast to the spot where they'd stood, and peer into dark tangles of ivy, bramble and tree. But they and any kin have melted away.

The boar in the town are common knowledge. They can bear being near to humans, just about. Somehow they've avoided being culled by Forestry England, perhaps because of their very nearness to the public. They've hit on the same secret that the ancestors of farmed pigs did thousands of years ago, that the Barcelona ones have too – that humans can be worth the risk.

Yet they are not the same as their ancestors. In fact, some people insist that the relative boldness shown by some of the Dean boar is nothing to do with their essential wild-boar-ness, but rather because they *lack* that wild-boar-ness. It's the same story across the country. Wherever boar reappear, the same charge is levelled at them: they are not wild boar.

The Kent and East Sussex population, and the Dean one, have had their DNA analysed. The former were assumed from the start to have a dollop of farmed pig in them, not least because of the unusually pale coats that some of them sport. Detecting hybridisation takes a bit of lab wizardry that includes analysing differences in alleles, mitochondrial DNA and numbers of chromosomes. But tests on the Kent and East Sussex boar by Defra showed them to be 'no more genetically mixed than many European populations'.

Not so when it came to the Dean boar. When zoologist Alaine Frantz and his team examined *their* DNA some years later, they concluded that, based on the presence of both European and Chinese domestic pig genes, the population 'should be regarded as feral rather than a restored native species'. Yet environmental historian Thomas Fleischman has criticised this study for choosing to compare the Dean boar to some imaginary 'pure' wild boar that no longer exists after countless years of relations with humans.

The results from Frantz *et al.* indicate that the Dean boar acquired their pesky domestic genes many branches of their family trees ago, when their ancestors were still held on estates on the Continent. Did these boar choose pigs as mates or did humans pair them? Both, no doubt. Crossing boar with pigs is a way to increase litter size and the growth rate of boarlets, and to blunt the edges of the animals' wildness. Male boar, meanwhile, will think nothing of breaking into pens that aren't fortified enough if they can smell a female in season. Coupling is even easier if the pigs are free-roaming ones.

The traces of such unions remain easy to detect in the DNA countless generations later. But our boar, according to their detractors, betray their origins in other ways. The first is their perceived boldness, their temerity to be seen and not be shy and elusive. Though this is perhaps a challenging task for any large mammal in a small forest stuffed with humans.

The second apparent giveaway is their fertility. I've lost count of the times I've been told that sows in the Dean can produce between 10 and 16 boarlets at a time, twice or even thrice per year (the latter would require a sow to come into season and mate within days of giving birth, given the four-month gestation period).

'I've seen one sow with a dozen young, and that cannot be refuted by anybody. I have seen that with my own eyes,' said one person. But, as you'll recall, sows pool their litters and they babysit for each other.

How many boarlets *are* the Dean boar having, then? Forestry England's 2015 census, which was more generous with its data than later versions, provided the number of embryos found in the wombs of females shot between 2010 and 2015. Even among the heaviest and therefore most fertile of them, the average was six. And not all embryos complete the journey to birth.

This number tallies with many populations in mainland Europe. It has also been observed that the further north you go, the more boarlets you tend to get; this is the same for the clutch size of many bird species, which is thought to be due to the better availability of resources at high latitudes during the breeding season, in comparison to other times of the year. But as with all other aspects of their being, wild boar are fluid in their reproductive habits. Litter sizes ebb and flow depending on how much food is around. In some years a sow may produce several equal-sized offspring, while in other years some of them may be very big and others very small. And while the sows in a sounder all aim to give birth at the same time if they can, some – particularly younger, smaller ones with less energy to spare for reproduction – may not give birth until late summer. A boar may mate and breed again if her first litter is lost early on, but this depends on her being in good enough condition; and the 2015 census reported that many of the sows shot in late summer and autumn were not. Bearing and raising babies is a costly endeavour.

With all that said, it is possible that the Dean boar, and some boar in Scotland, are having bigger litters than the constraints of their environment might otherwise allow thanks to the traces of pig in their genomes. If this is the case, they may continue to do so for the foreseeable future; scientists studying hybrid boar in Italy suspect that even if the domestic genes they carry are reducing their chances of survival compared to purer counterparts, their higher numbers of offspring work to cancel this out. This is one facet of what has been called *hybrid vigour*, where an organism proves better at thriving than its parents from distinctly different lineages. Hybrid vigour is considered one of the key engines behind the rampant rise of the wild boar across both its native and non-native ranges. And the genetic taint of pig in our wild boar is the ostensible reason many officials and members of the public in Great Britain performatively refuse to call them by their species' name.

'They're not wild boar, they're feral pigs,' I have often been corrected.

Feral pig: a name spoken with the hot bite of a branding iron.

The National Pig Association favours it. So do NatureScot (Scotland's government agency for the environment) and NFU Scotland. The latter organisation's Pigs Committee Chair, Jamie Wyllie, has claimed that Scotland's boar are actually pigs whose ancestors were sometimes crossed with their wild antecedents, when the reality is precisely the opposite. 'In the looking-glass world of Scottish law, a wild boar is only a wild boar when it's not wild,' as Fiona Mathews and Tim Kendall put it in their book *Black Ops and Beaver Bombing*.

It's often said that language helps to shape how we each perceive reality. In which case, the aversion to calling our wild boar *wild boar* – even though they have far more wild boar genes than pig ones, they look like wild boar, and they live like wild boar – will make it harder to win over the government and the general public when it comes to any official programme of reintroduction. There is a world of difference between pigs with a bit of wild boar in them, and wild boar with a bit of pig in them. This is something that Kevin Stannard at Forestry England seems aware of, for he tells me his team is consciously moving away from calling the Dean boar 'feral pigs'.

'We think that's slightly demonising them. They are wild boar, that's what they are.'

Even so, Forestry England continues to call them *feral* in its public-facing communications.

It's tempting for me to go into postmodern mode here and have a rant about our fundamental disgust with beings that blur the boundaries we want to keep fixed. Perhaps, for a few people, the thought of boar and pigs coupling triggers true disgust. But for me to wring my hands in frustration at the *feral pig* branding is, in the end, an exercise in futility. The bottom line is that we wouldn't care about the hybrid origins of our wild boar if they weren't so troublesome, and so good at producing additional troublesome boar. No one uses the name *feral goshawks*, even though these raptors only prowl our skies again thanks to escapes and releases of captive-born individuals, mainly of Finnish origin. The comparison isn't a perfect one, given that goshawks were never domesticated in the way that wild boar were, but the ancestors of our goshawks today still passed through our hands. Their descendants surely bear our fingerprints in their genomes.

No one has ever told me that they would have accepted the presence of wild boar had they been 100 per cent pure. Concerns around impurity, if voiced, always come riding on the backs of greater fears − fear of what an overbold boar might do to you or your loved ones, or fear of the damage a population growing out of control might do to the environment. As one resident in the Dean put it, 'If they're not wild boar they shouldn't be here. If they are wild boar they shouldn't be here.'

Wild boar, or the wild boar that exist today, seem to defy all our attempts to control them. They laugh at our fences. So is it any wonder that in the rewilding fervour that is sweeping through the UK, we have turned our backs on them and looked instead to farmed pigs as one of the saviours of our land?

More to the point, can pigs do the job just as well?

As my car trundles down the stony track in second gear, a solitary goldfinch takes flight from a yellowed teasel. My eyes follow it down the hill towards the small quilt of fields and one wood that make up Watercress Farm. Lying in the valley of Wraxall just five miles from the bustle of Bristol, Watercress is already a place alive with memory for me. As part of my wildlife conservation master's degree the year before, I spent a week here in the spring, conducting botanical and pollinator surveys. Few bees or flies wanted to come out in the relentless rain and cold. But there was plenty of treasure to be had – blue comets of kingfishers, comfrey heavy with the purple bells of their flowers, and treecreepers nesting in an ivy-curtained hole in a willow.

Watercress was acquired by the neighbouring Belmont Estate four years ago. Rewilding commenced soon after. At 30 hectares, it's impossible not to think of it as a miniature Knepp. The herd of friendly red poll cattle who watched me and the other students spending days crouched on the ground have, by now, been joined by a gang of gelded Dartmoor ponies. And, most recently, two Tamworth pigs.

Stockman Robin Haynes meets me by the field where the comfrey ran riot last year. A cap with a stag's head embroidered on the side speaks to his former role as a gamekeeper. In the incandescent January sunshine, his eyes are sapphire-blue. We set off in search of the pigs, pausing to ask a passing walker if she's seen them. She hasn't. Although Watercress is a compact site, the many hedges add a dash of challenge to locating its large herbivores. To reach the back fields we walk through the woodland, a former plantation of poplars with the odd renegade oak growing among them.

Having seen the Dartmoor ponies grazing on the slope near to where I'd driven down, I first ask Robin how they get on with the pigs. With a sardonic smile he replies, 'If the ponies are about, the pigs are usually the other side of the site to them. To be honest, I thought the ponies would probably not want to be near the pigs and would go away. But when the pigs first arrived the ponies really went for them, stamping and kicking.'

He'd been scared that the Tamworths might be killed in that first meeting, although they'd proven to be made of tougher stuff. He speculates whether a herd of brood mares would respond differently to them. 'I think it's because the ponies we've got are a bunch of lads. They just act like thugs. They fight among themselves a lot as well. It's more like showing off to each other, I think that's what's happening.'

This is one fascinating side-effect of rewilding with slightly random mixes of species and individuals: new and unexpected interactions.

Robin spots the pigs in the next field to the left. As we follow a trail of flayed pasture towards them, I can see huge chunks of earth flying into the air. The pigs don't bother to look up at us, so focused are they on their industry. Yet when they'd arrived in the summer, they hadn't done any rooting at all, just grazing.

'The grass I guess had enough sugar in it. Then they just switched to rooting. It was almost overnight. And they can go really deep, they go right up to their eyes,' Robin says. Those eyes are barely open now as the nearest pig to me snuffles and shoves with her snout, mouth constantly working to sift and swallow what her sense of smell has led her to. In her book *Pig*, Soil Association CEO Helen Browning is fascinated to watch a pair of orphan piglets skilfully using their mouths to sort food from the debris around it, like tiny terrestrial baleen whales. Although the Tamworths before me are working so fast, I struggle to catch the process myself.

'They were overweight when they got here, and they have lost a lot of weight over the winter,' Robin goes on. 'But their coats are looking really good, they're looking really healthy. They haven't had any breathing problems, which you get a lot with pigs, because of arcs.'

An arc is a curved metal shelter that outdoor pigs are given for shelter and warmth. Their downside is that they collect dust, which can cause those aforementioned breathing problems. I must agree with Robin: these two Tamworths do look healthy. Magnificent, in fact. In the sunshine, their ginger coats gleam, some hairs even glinting iridescent. As if Robin has shampooed them in anticipation of my visit.

However, admiring the pigs' hair makes me realise how much shorter and less shaggy it is compared to that of wild boar. One shortcoming, then: Tamworths probably can't disperse other organisms on the outsides of their bodies nearly so well.

I notice movement in the distance. Two people are walking along the field margin, a dog bounding ahead of them. Footpaths criss-cross Watercress, with locals used to having the freedom of the place. I ask how the Tamworths are with dogs.

'I've not had problems. To be honest, I think most dogs are frightened of them. You get the occasional dog barking at them but I think they don't care. Though I'd quite like to see what would happen if you had a sow and piglets out here.'

I am mindful of Knepp, where dogs sometimes attack the pigs, and those sent to slaughter have in the past been found with shotgun pellets embedded in their skin. It's one thing to turn out livestock to roam semi-freely, another to trust humans to behave around them and to not be cruel.

Here at Watercress, the worst problem they've had is people leaving gates open. The Tamworths have escaped a few times that way. Otherwise, they've so far failed to live up to their species' Houdini reputation.

'I don't think they've got any real motivation to escape,' Robin says. 'Although they tend to follow people. You want them to be a bit tame but you don't want them to associate people with food, which they do.'

Ah. That sounds more familiar.

I want to know if Robin thinks it would ever be desirable to have wild boar instead of a farmed breed on a site like this.

'I don't think the rooting behaviour is much different, to be honest.' Though it still matters which breed, exactly. In the past, Robin was able to observe and compare the foraging strategies of Tamworths with Large Blacks, whose floppy ears help to mark them as even more domesticated. 'The Large Blacks can do more rooting, but they just plough things up. You put them in a pen and they literally just go in a line. Whereas put the Tamworths in that pen and they'd sniff around and be much more targeted.'

Hence rewilding projects in the UK favour Tamworths, or other heritage breeds such as Mangalitsas with their cockerpoo-curly hair.

But not wild boar.

They've been listed under the Dangerous Wild Animals Act 1976 (DWAA for short) since 1984, the law's aim being to ensure the licensing, control and welfare of privately kept animals that could pose a risk to the public. The impetus for the DWAA was the increasing popularity in the 1960s and 1970s for keeping exotic and often large wild animals as pets, especially big cats. One of the criteria used for including a species on the list was its 'armoury', something that might be fair in the boar's case. Though it does seem bizarre that under this law, a wild boar is essentially on a par with a tiger. The result is that obtaining a DWAA licence for boar requires training, fencing, liability insurance and inspections, none of which are cheap. Boar-proofing a rewilding site, even a small one, would be fiendishly expensive. And that's before factoring in whether you might have any public access gates just waiting to be left open by a careless visitor.

Yet, while the societal and legal barriers to boar mean that heritage pig breeds are having a moment in the British rewilding movement, not everyone is satisfied with this status quo – as I learn when I visit the best-known rewilding site in the UK.

With so much already written about it, I had thought to steer clear of Knepp Wildland. Given over to rewilding from 2002, its own website describes it as 'a leading light in the conservation movement' – a bold yet fair claim. Ceasing agriculture and bringing in red deer and farmed proxies for aurochs, wild horse and wild boar have resulted in a place brimming over with biodiversity. At the same time, the *idea* of Knepp has taken on a life of its own, casting out seeds of inspiration across the entire country and beyond.

Yet I found myself holding a kind of ageism towards Knepp; an assumption that this place, and those who work there, have settled too comfortably into the cosy rut of having animals that are both useful and tame.

Rina Quinlan, one of Knepp's wildlife safari guides, cures me of this. Studying for a PhD as well as acting as a rewilding consultant *and* raising two children, Rina is one of those female powerhouses who leave me in awe. She's also co-chair and founder of what is presently called the Large Herbivore Working Group (LHWG). The group is a nascent collaboration of expert practitioners and academics seeking to deliver case studies, reports and recommendations for policy makers in order to progress rewilding with, well, large herbivores (and omnivores). As Rina and I sit by a flooded meadow at Knepp, eating lunch on a freakishly warm November day, she explains to me that there are two key targets in the group's sights when it comes to wild boar: the DWAA, and the Wildlife and Countryside Act 1981 (WCA).

The DWAA made wild boar a no-go for Knepp when owners Isabella Tree and Charlie Burrell were starting the project up, given the costs involved. Meanwhile, the listing of boar under Schedule 9 of the WCA makes it illegal to release them into the wild without a licence. But it's a little more complicated than just that. In 2015, an amendment to Schedule 9 saw the creation of Part 1B, entitled 'Animals no longer normally present' – a curious mix of words. Only two species were translocated to this subsection: the European beaver and the wild boar (the rest remained in Part 1A, 'Native Animals').

Then, just one month before I meet with Rina, the beaver gets taken off Part 1B. It is instead put under the more-established Part 1A, as part of the government's decision to give the species protected status in England.

'Now wild boar are the only animal left on Part 1B,' Rina says before taking another bite of her sandwich. 'Is there a legal challenge to make about why the government didn't move boar from Part 1B like they did with beavers?'

It's a fair point, given that beavers still cannot be released even into an enclosure, let alone the wild, without a licence from Natural England. Such a move for boar would have great symbolic importance. The government shows no inclination to enact it. Then again, they haven't been loudly asked yet, whereas it has taken a concerted effort by campaigners to win legal protection for beavers.

It's worth noting that the wild boar's current treatment under the WCA doesn't completely rule out the possibility of its reintroduction, as is explained to me a few months later by a lawyer supporting the LHWG, Elsie Blackshaw-Crosby. She's from the Lifescape Project, a charitable collaboration with similar though broader ecological restoration interests.

'Part 1B just requires us to persuade Natural England that they should issue a licence for release,' she writes by email. 'I think it would probably be easier to persuade them if wild boar were explicitly acknowledged as native animals and moved to Part 1A but at least they are not listed as non-native!'

So, while the picture may be gloomy, there is the faintest hint of hope that the legal cliff might be surmounted for wild boar – at least in England and Wales. Scottish law, which Natural England holds no sway over, appears more formidable.

'The legal tests for what can and can't be introduced under the WCA is different in Scotland versus England and Wales. It's incredibly complicated.' No disagreement from me there. 'In Scotland, Section Fourteen says you can't release animals into the wild outside of their "native range", which is interpreted by NatureScot as where the species is currently found.'

Which means that in the case of beavers, given that we wiped them out in Scotland as we did everywhere else in Britain, Scottish law considers them to have no native range at all – something that inevitably applies to wild boar too. But oh, I forget: there are no wild boar in Scotland. Just creatures called *feral pigs*. Silly me!

Back in Knepp by the flooded meadow, Rina and I brush crumbs away and head off in search of the Tamworths. I failed to find them on my last two visits. It seems I am to be unsuccessful yet again, as we stroll down paths and through thickets without any sign of the big ginger beasts.

The difficulty of knowing where they are highlights the legal corseting that Knepp finds itself bound by as it seeks to give its farmed animals a quasi-wild lifestyle. By law, the Tamworths must be checked up on every day, which can cost much time and effort. It makes Rina sigh. 'Of course you should check the pigs every day if they're indoors. But here, our pigs have very high welfare.'

The longhorn cattle are generally easier to find. But they are required by law to have ear tags. Which means that although they can go off on their own and give birth without any help from humans – something that cannot be said for most modern cattle breeds, whose robustness has been sacrificed in the name of economic productivity – their calves need to be located as soon as possible, ideally within hours, so that their ears can be punched with tags that they will carry until their deaths. And if they or any of the other farmed animals do die out in the open rather than going for slaughter, under the Fallen Stock rule their carcasses must be immediately removed to avoid the risk of spreading disease.[11] This, as well as the financial imperative for Knepp to sell animals for meat, prevents completion of the circle of life on the estate. Big animals are important to ecosystems even after death, contributing to what scientists call the *necrobiome* – the community of organisms that rely on dead tissue, and channel its nutrients and energy back into the wider ecosystem.

We need to learn how to live with big wild animals. But it's equally important that we learn how to live with big wild *dead* animals.

With no free-roaming Tamworths in the offing for me today, Rina takes me to a fenced field where six young males are being held. They will soon be sent to the abattoir. This is another thing that Knepp is not permitted: to give livestock a better death at home.

As the young pigs trot up to scan us for food offerings, grunting and squealing among themselves, Rina tells me she wishes they could be shot here instead. This is permitted only for Knepp's red and fallow deer, and on the rare occasions that an Exmoor pony is culled. The Tamworths and the longhorns must be caught, transported by lorry and stunned before having their throats cut. Not only is a bullet in the field undoubtedly less unkind to the animals, it's also cheaper, and *safer* for people – it's no casual thing to corral a big and powerful being who isn't so used to being told where to go.

Changing the law to allow for more sensible care of livestock on rewilding projects doesn't seem too difficult a prospect. Yet achieving this will do nothing to change the

---

[11] This law was brought in following the outbreak of bovine spongiform encephalopathy (BSE) in the UK in the late 1980s, even though the disease entered British livestock after they were fed with abattoir waste – not because of carcasses left out in the open.

reality that domesticated beings will always, sooner or later, find their way barred by fences. Virginia Thomas of the University of Exeter argues that rewilding in England has itself been domesticated; it sacrifices some of its ambitions for ecological restoration in order to retain more human control. It is, as ecologist Richard Broughton once quipped on Twitter, 'wee-wilding'.

Thomas goes on to say that this isn't necessarily a bad thing, if a more controlled and thus more acceptable version of rewilding can do a little bit of good instead of no good at all.

But we could do so much *more*.

Places like Knepp, even if bursting with life, are artificial in their island-ness; their large mammals have nowhere else to go and, even if they did, there are no predators to hunt them and keep them moving so that they avoid over-disturbing any particular patch of land. And so we must move or kill them based on the best of our ecological knowledge. This itself can be the subject of disagreement; both Robin Haynes at Watercress and Peter Cooper at Coombeshead tell me when I visit the two different sites that they would move the pigs or the boar on more often if it was up to them.

Not only do fenced rewilding projects, especially those using farmed animals, require close and possibly suboptimal control, but their impact on the wider landscape will always be limited. They can inspire other similar initiatives, and they can provide a spill-over of biodiversity if other suitable habitats are available nearby (a very big *if*). They cannot, however, provide the scale of restoration that is needed to ensure the survival and hopefully the adaptation of many of our species as we all confront a more uncertain future.

Perhaps there's a middle ground to be found in giving farmed animals slightly looser rein in where they go and how long they spend in any place. This could be aided by new practices and technologies like 'virtual fences', which involve putting GPS collars on grazing livestock that deliver a mild electric shock if they stray from their designated zone. In his book *Cornerstones*, conservationist Benedict Macdonald suggests also allowing pigs to roam 'through the farmed landscape'. But they would, without a doubt, breed with any wild boar who happened to be around. With this mingling of genes, the pigs would become more boar-ish, and the wild boar might well increase their own litter sizes beyond a sustainable and manageable level. You could erect robust fencing to keep pig and boar separated – but that would defeat the point of enabling connectivity. Or you could sterilise the pigs, females and males alike – but that would affect the supply of pigs somewhat. It might work for cattle and horses, whose wild equivalents are lost. It wouldn't for pigs. Unless we chose to eliminate our wild boar again.

Putting potential futures aside, I fear that the sole use of farmed animals is helping to reinforce the mindset that 'human' and 'nature' are, and should always be, separate realms. We have erected fences and other hard barriers to keep nature (including people) in or out. Yet so many wild lives depend on the ability to move through landscapes, to take part in ecological cycles of disturbance, rest and renewal. We've forgotten this. And just as we deny the movement of individual animals and of species by creating artificial boundaries, so we deny ourselves permission to belong to the rest of the world. We absorb our fences into our minds.

Maybe that's a core part of why rewilding raises hackles. If your thoughts are constructed using the nature versus human binary, then rewilding can *only* mean wildlife, and never wildlife and people.

You think:

Humans and domesticated animals belong here.
And everything wild belongs over there.

'The more we press ourselves into the argument that pigs can do it, the more we are dewilding ourselves,' Peter tells me, exactly a year to the day before I walk through Knepp with Rina. 'We mustn't lose sight of the wild animals.'

And who are we restoring our landscapes for, if not for all the wildlife as well as ourselves?

I still haven't seen Knepp's free-roaming Tamworths. But when I'm at Derek Gow's farm in Devon with Peter, we glimpse one of the female wild boar kept there. Or, rather, I glimpse her back-end vanishing into a thick stand of trees. 'Did you see the twist in her tail?' Peter asks. 'That's a sign of domestic pig in her family tree.'

Yet, like the town boar in the Dean, she's no less shy for her heritage. And Peter's grin at seeing her is no smaller. To him, she is a wild boar. When he called *Hello, pigs!* to Gerard and his companion up at the top field, it was no slur.

'This area is very contained and has its own artificial boundaries, but you can follow a wild boar trail through and find a beaver dam. There's this wonderful line between the wild and the domestic that's crossed here,' Peter says as we walk on past the trees. 'Boar are an excellent gateway, in the fact that they can survive quite happily in human landscapes, retreat into the wild woods of old, and then forage in pastures new.'

Through Peter's words I imagine wild boar as stitches, joining together a tapestry of different kinds of wild and less-wild. All while genes from different lineages work to stitch the boar into their present unruly forms.

'They're not the boar we had before,' is a refrain I often hear. This is indeed the truth, but a useless one. We can't reach into the past and resurrect the British wild boar of old. Those lives and lineages are gone. Yet it would be throwing the boarlet out with the wallow water to pretend that the ones we have now are not good-enough approximations. It's a strangely limiting view, to say that if we can't have an animal that isn't 100 per cent pure, we shouldn't have it at all. A similar tussle of opinion is happening in North America with bison, a species in which all existing individuals bear cattle genes. We once reduced their numbers so brutally that they might have ceased to exist at all if they hadn't later been cross-bred with cattle.

Rewilding projects using farmed animals have their place. When I say goodbye to Robin at Watercress and drive away up the hill, I look back over my shoulder. The site looks so small, because it is. But Robin believes Watercress can demonstrate to other landowners that giving over patches of marginal land to pigs and other substitutes can make important contributions to biodiversity. I wonder if projects like Watercress and Knepp could also be, in essence, schools of wilding for us – helping us to learn to accept and behave appropriately around big and sometimes boisterous or unnerving creatures.

When I meet with Rina, she voices an opinion so similar to mine about schools that I want to punch the air.

'What do people need to know in order to live with these species?' she asks.

As we search for the Tamworths, there is an awareness always buzzing at the edge of our minds; the fallow deer rut is not quite finished. We keep our eyes open and listen to the clacking of antlers as we tread among stands of sallow. The risk of being gored by a deer is minuscule, but it's there. Further on, we come to a once-grassy ride that is so pocked with the hoofprints of bucks using it as a rutting arena, it looks like Primrose Hill in London after everyone's been up there to watch the New Year's Eve fireworks.

'I really think there is a lot of hope in changing people quite quickly,' Rina says as our boots slip and slide in the mud and our noses fill with the sharp stink of horny and potentially angry deer. Places like Knepp can help to foster that cultural change, she believes. And as for the possibility of a world with fewer fences, she points to examples like the

New Forest, where ponies roam semi-free all year round and people are trusted to get on with them.

'When people say, "You can't do that", you go, "Well, it's being done, just there".'

We laugh at ourselves trying to best the mud made by the deer and the rain, and at the smell they've left. We are both at home here.

'We always say things are impossible,' Rina says once we're on firmer ground. She smiles. 'But I really don't think they are.'

CHAPTER THIRTEEN

Losing Them Again

The Kent and East Sussex region is our wild boar's Blackpool. Much like that coastal pleasure resort with its faded lustre, the woods of Kent and East Sussex no longer hold the promise of wildness first whispered in 1987, when the Great Storm tore down the fencing of a wild boar farm.

Soon after the storm, rumours began to thrive on tales of glimpses in the dark. Denial and disbelief were no longer possible once farmers began producing the bodies of animals they'd shot. Defra dispatched researcher Martin Goulding to reconnoitre; Derek Harman, author of *British Wild Boar*, spent his nights watching families from his portable high seat; the organisers of Rye's long-running Wild Boar Festival rubbed their hands in delight (at least metaphorically); and poachers went on the prowl.

The population seemed to grow, perhaps bolstered by escapes from other farms, or releases by stalkers if gossip is to be believed. Martin trapped a few individuals with Derek's help in order to radio-collar them for his fieldwork – though he once got himself caught in one of the traps and had to phone Derek to be freed, much to the older man's glee.

In 2004, after six years of research, Defra published the report 'The Ecology and Management of Wild boar in southern England'. By that time, the Kes boar – as I'll call them from hereon – were estimated to number 200 individuals, with a few more scattered around the edges of their range. Crucially, it was predicted that if current hunting pressure failed to ease off, they would be wiped out. Again.

Yet Defra shrugged at its own pronouncement when in 2008 it published its action plan for wild boar in England. In this second document, the forecast was reversed: the authors wrote that existing populations 'will probably slowly increase in size' and that the species was likely to spread to much of England within '20–30+ years'.

At the time of this book's publication, we're four years away from that 20-year mark.

The other populations referred to in the later report were the Forest of Dean, Devon, and Dorset ones, with the latter two both thought at the time to number around 50 individuals each. You can just about imagine the line of analysis the authors must have drawn in their heads: 'Well, three new breeding populations have sprung up within the last decade, and we've had a few reports of sightings from other parts of the country, so even though the other report talked about how much hunting was going on, we'll assume the boar are unstoppable.'

The Dorset boar have vanished. A question mark hangs over the Devon ones. In 2017, University of Bristol undergraduate James Blewett interviewed people living in the vicinity of the Exmoor farm where, in 2005, animal rights activists are said to have cut the fence and set 100 boar loose. Sixty of these, a quarter of which may have been pregnant, could not be recaptured. Blewett learned that boar were still being shot as late as 2016. When we speak by email in 2022, he's hopeful that the population is going strong. Yet when I get in touch with an Exmoor National Park local whose contact details he passes on, I learn they're all but gone. There may be just a few wise old boar left, coming out in the dark. Occasionally you'll see a newspaper or magazine article that says boar are doing well in Dorset and Devon. This is the result, I assume, of journalists on tight deadlines and no patience to go beyond the first page of Google.

Equally little attention has been given to the plight of the Kes boar. The original 2004 prediction of their demise seemed to go unremarked by anyone. Defra declined to impose a closed season or any other kind of restriction on their shooting, save that you needed permission to kill them when on someone else's land. No one has kept count of how many individuals have been and are still being shot.

This story, which has barely begun, may already be coming to an end.

On a wet January day in 2022, almost a millennium after William the Conqueror won the Battle of Hastings, I drive into 1066 Country. So christened by some enterprising member of the local tourism industry, the Sussex Weald lands within 1066 Country have seen more than their fair share of pivotal English history. And, most recently, they have felt again the touch of a beast once beloved – of a kind – by King William. With William being the creator of Britain's royal 'forests' for game, I suspect that he would've approved of the wild boar's return, and cursed our carelessness since.

I'm here to explore Brede High Woods, a reserve owned by the Woodland Trust. While the organisation has never declared an official position on boar, it's with an air of enthusiasm that their display board at the entrance to the 260-hectare site tells me, 'VIP residents include great crested newts, dormice, glow-worms, turtle doves and wild boar'. I also learn that some of the oaks are at least 400 years old – sadly not ancient enough to have experienced the boar of old snuffling around their roots.

I'm soon joined by the ranger for the woods, David Bonsall. His salt-and-pepper beard befits the experience he's accrued in his long career with the Woodland Trust, and he has the air of someone who's hard to faze. Even so, despite the fact that plenty of boar activity was already evident in Brede High Woods when the Trust acquired it in 2007, David's first actual encounter was unexpected: his dog Nellie was busying around in the undergrowth when David heard barking and crashing and a boar burst out, Nellie in hot pursuit. No one came to grief. Nor did one of the contracted deer stalkers for the reserve when he first saw boar. Again, there was a crashing below the trees, and then about 12 individuals came running straight at him. He stood unmoving as they parted around him and hurried on.

'He was more excited than worried,' David recalls as we walk into the woods. Already the path is thickening with mud. It wants my boots.

'The boar here tend to be leucistic, they're a bit blonde,' the ranger continues. 'I think that's because of the limited gene pool. They're really quite gingery pale. And with the classic upright ears and straight tail and really narrow faces.'

His description echoes the first Defra report, which also noted the abundance of leucism among the Kes boar, despite the genetic analysis that showed them to be no less pure than the average wild boar on the Continent. Derek Harman saw and photographed them many times; babies and adults alike look as if the ink was running out when their turn came to be printed.

Despite some of them being almost ghost-pale, a sure hook for the eye, David has only seen boar twice in his 15 years managing Brede High Woods. Their rooting tends to be just as sporadic. Irruptive almost, as Patrick Laurie described the behaviour of the Galloway boar.

'I see boar as a totally integral part of the ecology. There's a school of thought that you should control them before they become a problem. Shoot first, ask questions later. But because they come and go quite a lot, I just don't see them as a problem in terms of ecological impact here. And they certainly don't seem to be a problem for people here.'

While boar seem to move through the Dean with the force of a river in constant spate, the Kes ones are but a trickle that at times dries up entirely. David doesn't need to expend much thought on them, and indeed he keeps drifting off-topic into other matters concerning Brede High Woods. As we pass through a patch of grassland and then into a realm of scaly-barked conifers, I find myself putting effort into tugging the conversation back towards the boar. Eventually I give up and simply listen. In a measured voice that hides his hope, the ranger sets out the management approach he and his colleagues are taking with the reserve. It sounds like a daunting job, with so many different mini biomes packed into it – ancient woods, plantations, grasslands and heathlands, and all threaded through with streams in which primeval lampreys lurk.

'We're busy restoring this back to broadleaf,' he says of the Corsican pines we're stepping between. 'Our approach is to go slowly. We do thinning to let a bit of light in, not too much, otherwise you only get brambles, not trees and ground flora. We're using natural regeneration of the trees. Mainly we've got birch coming up. We're trying to restore forwards to a different version of the woodland. We're not going to go back to historic coppice and carpets of bluebells because you can't go back in time.'

But David and his colleagues are up against that most sweet-eyed of foes: deer. As we look and fail to find any signs of boar, new or old, the ranger bends to peer at tree seedlings in their beds of leaf and pine needle litter. He grasps the top of one and flexes it towards me.

'You see all the ends have been bitten off.' A little further on, he touches what I assume to be a very young holly. 'That one's been bonsaied.'

Death by a thousand nips.

You'd think, given all the grief that deer cost David, he might secretly welcome the attentions of poachers. As he puts it, 'The poaching around here has been epidemic at times.' Yet anger and disgust seem to simmer just beneath the crust of his cool demeanour. 'People think we've got a lovely job and we swan about, but actually you have to deal with the best and worst of humanity.'

With people already present in the area who had the necessary firepower and scorn for the law, it was inevitable that the boar would become targets too. This was brought home to David one morning some years ago when he found a 'calling card' hanging on a gate to the reserve.

'I thought it was a big hearth rug at first. Then I saw a leg. So I thought it was from a Highland cow, a big long hairy shaggy thing. Then realised it was the remains of a massive male boar that had been shot, butchered, and dumped. So I called the police. When the firearms officer turned up, he said, "Oh, there's two of them." And I said, "No, count the legs."'

The boar's death had not been quick. After the firearms officer had inspected the remains – 'they'd taken the easy cuts and the tusks as trophies' – it was concluded that the animal had been shot in both the head and the rump. He'd perhaps tried to flee after the front-on shot, or else decided to turn and face his attacker once pain came searing through his hindquarters. He fell, but it wasn't the bullets that killed him. It was the knife that had left a tunnel through his skin and ribcage and into his heart.

'So that's what we have to deal with,' David sums up.

Things aren't as bad these days. Post-pandemic, the deluge of walkers and dogs has put off the poachers. Though the apparent fall in boar numbers has surely had an impact on poaching rates too.

David shows me around a final part of the woods, ruled on one side of the path by old stands of sweet chestnut coppice left to grow to gigantic proportions. On the other side are more pines and, among these, a sign at last: the trunks of several of the trees bear grooves and indents, where boar once rubbed and scraped and bit. The wood-flesh is scabbing over. It's almost as if we're looking at trace fossils, those marks left in the world by extinct lifeforms.

Close by is the wallow that the boar would've visited before rubbing against those trees, although if David hadn't known it from the time it had been in use, I wouldn't have been able to tell its former purpose. It's a mere chain of quagmire-ish dips in the ground. It has only been kept this way thanks to the various springs that give Brede High Woods an inclination to wet and mud. Wallows dry up without the sculpting force of big bodies such as those of boar. I've seen photographs of one such case, sent to me by a stalker in response to a post I left on a forum for UK-based sport shooters, asking about recent sightings.

'I haven't seen any sign of fresh boar activity on my permission in Sussex since 2013 ... around there they were all poached by a known local who boasted of it,' the stalker writes in a preface to the images. There are two, both taken in late autumn. In the earlier one, a muddy pool is cradled between two spidery roots of a chestnut tree. The bole is well plastered. In the later image, leaf litter covers where the pool used to be, and the tree is starting to grow back the moss that furs the bases of its neighbours.

You would never know.

Months later, I check in with David by email: any fresh signs of boar about? The answer is no. He doesn't share his thoughts as to why, though from what he's already told me in conversation, he seems optimistic that they'll be back. In his mind they seem to be as random and vibrant as a flurry of waxwings. And perhaps they will be; perhaps, like the poachers, they've simply been driven away from Brede High Woods by the surge in human and canine traffic.

But where have they gone?

I don't expect any kind of answer to that question when I return to this corner of England in the summer, although hope is an itch that won't be soothed. This time I've come to Orlestone Forest in Kent. It's as hot and dry and awake as Brede High Woods was cold and wet and asleep. We're one week away from the mid-July heatwave that'll break all the records, and the mercury is readying for take-off.

'I'm a tall chap with longish brown curly hair and a beard,' my guide messages me before I arrive at Ashford International train station. For some reason, I'm picturing a retiree, yet Ade Jupp doesn't seem much older than me, and has a bouncy Labrador-ish enthusiasm to boot.

Ade speeds us out of the metal and concrete soullessness of Ashford, to a Forestry England car park somewhere in the middle of Orlestone Forest. Before we set off on our walk, he produces a map. And I see that I've done the woods of Kent a disservice in thinking of them all as mere shreds of green, barely enough to shelter the boar. I spent much of my childhood not far from here, in Sevenoaks, where it was never long before the trees gave way to suburbia or farmland again. But *here* is a place that surely supplies the boar with the refuge they need.

I met Ade on Twitter after he commented on a post of mine that he hadn't seen fresh signs of boar in his patch for a long time. When I got in touch about the possibility of visiting, he said he didn't want me to feel that I was making a wasted trip. Yet being here still feels important. It's a bearing of witness to the killing indifference of the powers that be.

But I've also come to see the life that's still here, that has always been here and wants very much to stay — if we can make the right decisions to help it. As we walk through thigh-high grasses and along tracks shaded by hornbeam, oak and wild service trees, Ade rattles off the names of species like willow warblers, nightingales, lesser-spotted woodpeckers and fen bent-wing, the last a very rare moth. We pass a grey-haired couple waiting beneath a great oak where male purple emperor butterflies have been sparring. While I don't see the butterflies myself, even the commoner creatures and flowers make my moments spent here worth living. Ade has to keep stopping and backtracking to identify things for me when I ask. I soon find myself saying things like, 'Oh, what an impressive crab spider!' and 'Yes, my first

cinnabar moth caterpillar of the year!' to try and avoid Ade
forming the impression that I'm a one-trick pony of a girl
who knows her boar but not her Bombini.

Ade isn't a paid site manager for Kent Wildlife Trust or
the Woodland Trust or Forestry England, all of whom own
blocks of Orlestone. Instead, he's part of a network of
naturalists who are the forest's unofficial guardians, carrying
out flora and fauna surveys, reporting any mistreatment of
the Sites of Special Scientific Interest within the area, and
very occasionally doing a bit of guerrilla habitat management
(he and a friend 'got in a bit of trouble' a few years ago for
taking down a willow that they thought was shading a pond
too much). While a physicist by training, Ade speaks ecology
as if he was born knowing it. It seems to come to him as
easily as breathing.

On the edge of a meadow thrumming with insects, under
the shade of a tree, we sit and snack on apples and Bakewell
tart slices. Ade gets to talking about what he believes places
like Orlestone Forest need if they're to carry their arks of
species safely into the future. Specifically: big animals.
Longhorn cattle have been at work in the field we're now
in, grazing roughly and stomping out muddy bowls in a few
of the corners.

'You get better habitat, with them,' he says as he pours
out cups of ice-cold water from a thermos flask. 'It's a lot
more complex than what we can do with brush cutters or
chainsaws.'

Yet the cattle here are still penned in, a reality that Ade is
all too aware of. 'We just can't cover the area on our own. I
mean, this forest is huge. We're just gardening, really. My
impression of all wildlife organisations is there's more work
than they can do in a year and so you either rely on animals
or your reserves at best stay in stasis. A lot of them aren't in a
good state now and you can tinker a bit, but you're never
going to make a big change. No one seems to have noticed
that it's terrible for wildlife.'

Despite a few odd jewels such as the purple emperor and the nightingales, Orlestone is bleeding, like so many other nature reserves in Britain. Willow warblers teeter on the edge. Their relative, the wood warbler, is long gone, while the small pearl-bordered fritillary vanished around 20 years ago. These three species are ones that Ade mentions to me, although I'm sure more loom in the back of his mind and that the departure of others has gone unnoticed even by him. The loss is no surprise. Not when you consider that the UK has been rated as one of the world's worst performers when it comes to preserving our biodiversity.

All the while, a decent amount of money and a lot of passion and sweat has been poured into conservation and habitat restoration. But the ways we're used to doing these things don't seem to be enough. 'Unless you can get big stuff in to do the job for you,' Ade says, 'it's just not going to happen on the scale we need.'

With sugar on our teeth and worry on our minds, we move on to a patch of land bought a few years ago by a friend of his. 'This is one of the best sites in the Forest,' Ade tells me, joy lending a higher pitch to his voice. He explains that it was overgrown with young trees. With woodland already surrounding it on all sides, he and his friend believed more could be gained by opening it up. Some of the trees have been left, to preside over grasses and wildflowers and islets of scrub. Nightingales nest here now. This is also where the fen bent-wing was found.

'It's really interesting seeing how quickly the meadow flowers jump into the woods here, because it's a really nice source of seed,' Ade continues as we wade through a wealth of green and yellow. I adore his use of the word *jump*.

Then we come upon a spot that Ade told me about earlier. Eight years ago, boar ploughed through it. In the months after, devil's-bit scabious and heath dog violet flourished, the latter scarce in Kent. Violets of all kinds are important to butterflies such as the small pearl-bordered fritillary. The visitation of the boar here was a tantalising hint of what could be.

Ade sighs. 'There's a lot of cover for boar here. And my friend comes down here two or three times a week. So I'd imagine if they were around, you'd disturb them at some point. There are so few sightings of them anywhere. People do run trail cameras but the boar just don't turn up on them.'

With the local naturalist network that Ade is tapped into, news of any sighting quickly spreads. A sow was seen with boarlets last year, proof that some breeding is still happening. Though it's unlikely to be enough in the long run.

Intriguingly, in 2020, another friend of Ade's had a young male shot after he kept hanging around his Tamworth sows – a boar whose pelt was 'sort of yellowy'. The leucism remains strong, it seems. Back in 2013, a shooter wrote to Martin Goulding that he and others were deliberately targeting the paler boar, based on the belief that these were more genetically impure creatures that needed to be weeded from the gene pool. Despite all the odds against them, the leucistic boar and any others are clinging on.

Just.

Heading home from Orlestone on a heavily air-conditioned train, I'm more certain than ever that the end of the Kes boar is approaching fast. They're already functionally extinct – that is, there are too few of them left to have any significant influence on their ecosystem – if indeed there ever were enough of them to reclaim their functions. They are re-fading from human minds, too.

'I don't think people are that aware of them,' Ade replied when I asked if there was much talk of the boar in the area these days. David said something similar. There are simply too few boar here to generate the same thrills and frictions that they do with humans and other species in the Forest of Dean. Those who decry the negative impacts of boar on people would no doubt say this is to be celebrated. But there must be some midpoint to be found between the density in the Dean and that in Kent and East Sussex. One that would keep moments of conflict between people and boar to a minimum, while gifting us the best of what boar can do.

There *must* be something better than what we've left ourselves with here.

CHAPTER FOURTEEN

The Risks of Being Alive

Through July, Britain bakes and cracks. The rain stops coming and the heat keeps climbing. I can turn on any tap and have as much water as I want, but the trees of the Dean have no such reassurance. In my local wood, I walk across ground where, in all directions, the Trio and their babies and likely other boar have been. For the first time, it makes me wince. The soil has been left open to the elements. The boar are doing what they've always done. Our climate is not. And so rootings that should be stirring new kinds of life are instead haemorrhaging precious moisture.

The Trio have stopped coming in the mornings. The drying ground is harder to plough up and must feel like sandy rock to their noses. New rootings instead appear in the spruce plantation next door. Boar don't tend to forage beneath conifers much. Perhaps now, with its moss coverlet holding the water in better, this other ground has become a blessing.

In another wood two miles away, the boar are proving themselves angels instead of demons. This is where my favourite wallow of theirs lies, where for months I've been leaving my trail camera and getting a soap-opera aficionado's glimpse into boar social life. Their activities have kept the wallow deep and restless and, most important of all, wet.

This place has always been a waystation for other wildlife. But at the peak of the heatwave, as we near 40°C, it becomes like Piccadilly Circus. My camera produces hundreds instead of tens of clips. Someone is always drinking or bathing or resting there. One night, as a sow scratches her rump against one of the trees, two pinpricks of light come bouncing along the corner of the screen: a frog, briefly emerged from their muddy refuge. One day, a buzzard comes down from the sky to take a cooling dip. After wading in, they simply stand in the water for two whole minutes. They return five times over those two hottest days. I've never seen a bird look more reluctant to fly, more exhausted with the weight of the heat.

Deer and their fawns pick around the edges of the wallow, lapping where the deeper sections hold the wateriest water. And the boar, when they return, slide with ecstasy into the muddier parts.

That mud is growing drier. The water level is falling. But this is the biggest wallow I've ever found. It'll cling on. It has to.

The second heatwave in early August finishes it. I stand at the crisping edge, appalled. I fantasise about somehow lugging great containers of water here to replenish it. It isn't fair that while we're merrily wasting water on things like golf courses, sports grounds and pipe leaks, the animals here have nothing. I go away feeling useless and powerless. I've put a bucket out in the woods nearer to home, but it's such a small thing.

Dread presses down on me, like a new form of gravity.

'I don't want to look too closely at the possibility that these are the last recognisable days... That we don't know when this thread will snap,' author Sophie Mackintosh writes in *The Guardian* on the day I turn 32. I want to take refuge in the past, in the time before I knew what climate change meant.

Fear becomes immediate on the day that smoke begins to curl into the sky and the valley fills with sirens. The fire is two fields away. The firemen are hidden by a tall hedge, but I watch as a snake of water begins to cast into the huge beech trees at the wood's edge.

The police close the road. My housemate Dave goes to speak to them. They say they'll let us know if we have to leave. There's no gap between the wood and our neighbours' terraces.

Finally, the sirens and the water stop. Disaster has been averted. Dave and I pack grab-bags in case there's a next time.

The beech trees turn the colour of dried blood on the side that faced the flames. In the rest of the wood, in the

Dean, in Bristol, anywhere I go, trees are yellowing and oranging and dropping their leaves early. An eldritch autumn.

When I next visit the wallow, I find that someone has stuck a bucket of water at one end, with a stick poking from it so that small animals can climb out if they need to. And, in the middle, the mud looks gloopier and darker than before. No rain has fallen. How can this be?

The answer waits in the trail cam footage. Over several days, a mother and father with their three children have been to the wallow. Each time, they've all brought with them as many bottles of water as they can carry. It isn't enough to make the wallow drinkable again, but it is to resurrect a single patch of mud. At night, boar luxuriate in it.

A few times, the father looks directly at my camera. The first time he appeared on it, he reassured his wife that it was probably only set to go off at night. But later, he says, 'You know, if this camera works in the day, whoever it belongs to is going to be really sick of the sight of us.'

I grin and laugh. I wish I could meet them. They don't seem to be local; in one clip, the father answers his ringing phone with a *Hello, Dad*, and his wife calls over to ask if the plants are being watered.

If there's a chance that one day, one of them picks up this book, then: on behalf of the boar, thank you.

Rain comes at last in late August. Much of the land, turned kiln-dry, cannot absorb it. The wallow is a different matter. My eyes widen at the sight of it. The deepest parts already cradle new puddles, enough to slake many thirsts. The hard ground all around, meanwhile, looks as if it hasn't been rained on at all.

Although the water in the wallow eventually gave in to the assaults of multiple heatwaves, it offered a lifeline until that point. And even then, the wallow remained empty for

less than two weeks. It is stark evidence that we need these
acts of the boar. We need them now, and we'll need them
even more in the years to come. At least the tide seems to be
turning for beavers, now furnished with legal protections
that campaigners could only dream of when their return
first became apparent. Yet even for them, are attitudes
changing fast enough? Why are we so resistant to bringing
back the species we know we need?

I think it is because too many of us are trapped in the
mindset that nothing matters more in life than eliminating
all risk to it – even at the cost of happiness. Human progress
has long been driven by risk. We fear the possibility of cold,
of hunger, of fangs and claws. Farming bought us a surety
that gathering and hunting couldn't, or so we thought. We
knew crops should grow where we sowed them, and the
livestock were there for the killing.

Yet risk still prowled our borders, in the form of climate,
weather, natural disasters, pests, disease, conflict, and the wild
animals that had found no attraction in brokering a deal
with us to become domesticated. Of those animals, we
hunted the ones who preyed on our flocks, our crops or us,
and we doomed many more as we reshaped entire landscapes
to insure against anything beyond our foresight or control.
Deliberately and unwittingly, we whittled away the wild.

In few places have we been as successful in this as in
Britain. We are among the most nature-deprived of nations,
and we are still letting the haemorrhaging go on, other lives
pouring into oblivion like the water of the Forest of Dean
vanishing into its abandoned mines. We're still living in a
fantasy that we can have whatever we want, and as much of
it as we want, and nature will continue to provide. But the
Faustian mechanics of our modern world are beginning to
show through, like bones under shrivelling flesh. Energy
can't be destroyed, it can only be transferred – the supreme
law of the universe. Why would risk be any different? Every
mouthful of food we've grown using fossil-fuel fertilisers,

pesticides, deforestation and soil loss has been snatched from our descendants. Every molecule of carbon dioxide we've added to our atmosphere is another mark in a planetary loan shark's book. And now the debt is coming to collect itself.

But no one is thinking all this if they lock eyes with a wild boar and feel afraid.

I've suggested reasons some people in Britain fear for their lives when they meet a boar, while others don't. But perhaps the most essential one is this: the boar remind us that we are, like them, animals. That we are bodies capable of pain and death.

'We live behind a hidden membrane through which – at any moment – one of us may tumble to find ourselves on the other side,' Melanie Challenger writes in *How to Be Animal*. 'We face the truth of what we are … a creature of organic substance and electricity that can be eaten, injured and dissipated.'

But there's an elephant in the room here. Or call it a bear. Or a leopard. Or a snake. Because across much of the planet, humans have never stopped living with the risk of wild animals. In Britain we donate money to fund the salaries and guns of rangers abroad to protect those animals. We rise in social media uproar when a radio-collared lion is shot by a trophy hunter in Zimbabwe. Even the United States, hardly a paragon of environmental stewardship in many respects, has managed to retain (or regain) a gamut of big and powerful species: cougar, moose, bison, wolf, black bear, grizzly bear, polar bear. Even if wild boar were native to the USA rather than an invasive species, I can't imagine many would rationally place them in that list. Like so many other species, a boar can physically hurt us – but there is a yawning gulf between *can* and *will*.

I don't presume to know what it's like to live your life knowing there's a reasonable chance you might encounter an animal that might kill you. But I do assume that living such a life requires mental armour, of the kind that we in

Britain have lost. As if our minds possess a shadow-immune system, and when confronted with something unfamiliar like a wild boar, it goes into overdrive as it tries to protect us.

Yet learning to coexist with wild boar isn't as simple as waiting a certain number of years for them to become more familiar. In the Dean, there are people who remain afraid, either for themselves or for their home. I know of one person who loved the boar when we first met in 2014, yet has since changed her mind and moved away. She began to feel that the boar were restricting where she could feel safe walking her dog, which played a part in her decision to leave.

But a *lack* of negative experience can be just as powerful. Rose, who invited me into her terror-soaked memories, who said she feared being eaten by them if she broke her leg and couldn't get away, now feels ... okay. 'I've had so many close encounters, and I always scream at them to make them move on, and they do. So now I don't think they would attack me,' she says as we sit in the house that I first sat in eight years ago. She still wants the boar gone, for the sake of the forest and other people. All the same, she's given me hope.

We should also take heart from the fact that boar have now been back in Great Britain for over 30 years, and in all that time there have only been two apparently intentional attacks on humans – the dog walker who had the pad of his fingertip bitten off in the Forest of Dean in 2018, and another dog walker in Argyll in 2022 (who clutched on to her dog's lead, putting herself in the sow's path and ending up with a bad bruise on her thigh). When I interviewed Dean residents in 2014, nearly all of the so-called anti-boar people said, 'It's only a matter of time before a child gets hurt.'

Anything is only a matter of time. In 2013, American researcher John Mayer collated records of wild boar attacks globally. Between 2000 and 2012 there were 288 in total, averaging out to 24 per year, with a quarter of these occurring in the USA. In spite of a rapidly growing boar population, Europe's share of attacks remains tiny. There appears to be only one report of a child being injured, in Spain in 2022.

These are *good* numbers, when set against the ecological and cultural importance of wild boar in their native range. Society has always made tacit agreements about the acceptability of certain risks. In the UK, pet dogs kill an average of three people per year. That rate increased in 2022, with four children among the victims. But we choose to allow the keeping of dogs anyway. Their usefulness is immediately obvious. Wild boar, less so. But the fact remains that the physical risk boar pose to us is minuscule.

Yet, even if more and more people in the Dean learn not to be afraid of the boar, to find their own ways of negotiating a newly shared home, this should not be mistaken for acceptance. 'We shouldn't have been subjected to having to overcome our fears,' Rose insists.

Various psychology studies have found that people can far better tolerate risks that they've chosen to bear. Conversely, they're likely to rail against a risk if they feel it has been imposed on them by individuals or groups who hold power over them. While Forestry England had nothing to do with the releases in the Forest of Dean, over and over I've heard the phrase, 'We weren't consulted'. Because Forestry England has permitted the boar to remain, the agency is seen as culpable in their existence.

A sense of unfairness also pervades, one that goes beyond the absence of financial compensation for damage such as broken fences and rooted pasture. Quiet tribes of boar may be rummaging through a few other parts of the country, but the Dean is the only place where they visibly live cheek by jowl with a notable number of people. The obvious answer to that?

Bring back boar to as many parts of the country as possible.

It's a hard sell, far harder than cuddly beavers or the demure, neither-seen-nor-heard lynx. It will require spending money, ceding space, and the mental effort of changing how we behave outdoors. We're not used to feeling afraid of wild animals. Neither are we used to imposing limits on ourselves for the benefit of wildlife. This is why people are inclined to react with outrage when certain 'normal' behaviours are questioned – ones like eating meat every day, or letting a dog run loose in a nature reserve, or releasing masses of pheasants for easier shooting.

Other concerns around the return of wild boar are more understandable, chief among them the risks to arable farming and to motorists. We would undoubtedly see some crop damage, which entails the need for compensation schemes. As farmers, conservationists and policymakers look to how we can redesign British food and farming systems to be more sustainable and to make ourselves healthier, there is surely space for us to consider the needs of other species.

As for road traffic accidents – some people would, undoubtedly, die. France's 2-million-strong population of boar is reportedly involved in 30,000 collisions with cars per year. But the risk of injury or death drops in parallel with speed.[12] This is not to pre-victim-blame. It is instead to point out that we can make adjustments to better fit into the world. We cannot design Britain's entire future around high speed limits for cars. We cannot keep insisting that we will not change a single facet of our lifestyles to accommodate wildlife and healthier ecosystems. There is something that

---

[12] It's also much better to hit a boar than a deer. As Kevin Stannard explained to me, a boar is lower to the ground and so is far less likely than a long-legged deer to come rolling over your bonnet and through the windshield.

disquiets me about the way we expect people in other countries to coexist with troublesome species, while we refuse to. Do we consider ourselves too fragile? Dare I say, too *civilised*?

I believe some of us embrace the wild boar because we're aware that we *need* to experience fear of the wild. In human medicine, a growing pool of research is revealing that some of the essential healing and maintenance mechanisms in our bodies can only be activated by exercise or brief periods of hunger. Would it be so surprising if how we think and feel were affected by similar principles?

We don't need animals to run in sheer terror from. But we do need a space in our minds for the unknown – or that which can only be known through other, different beings. As Jay Griffiths argues in *Why Rebel*, 'To be happy, the senses need to be stimulated and, through animals, our senses grow: we can extend ourselves out through their senses into sensory worlds of unquenchable richness.'

In Britain, it isn't only humans who need more wildness. Almost half of our species – or the ones we have enough data for, at least – are in decline, while 15 per cent face the threat of extinction. It is undeniable that this is in part because of the loss of big boisterous animals, including wild boar.

In a way, it seems absurd that the importance of boar to ecosystems in Britain needs to be stated at all. They used to be here until we wiped them out, after all. While ecosystems are never static, they are always coherent; they are the ever-unfolding products of a multitude of living and non-living entities whose combined actions bind each other closer and closer. Wild boar have been in Europe for a million years, returning to Britain whenever the ice has allowed them to. Our living landscapes have not been bereft of them for long enough to stop needing them. In fact, this will take a very long time indeed. The last few decades have seen a flood of new scientific research on how the destruction of most of our megafauna, a project humans started around 50,000 years ago, has impoverished ecosystems across the planet. When these animals existed, they sculpted landscapes, unlocked and enhanced nutrients for other organisms via the factories of their guts, and travelled far and wide over land or sky, or up and down through the layers of the seas. We don't recognise this because of something called the *shifting baseline* – where people in each generation take the world of their childhood to be the normal state of affairs, even if that world was already badly injured. We cannot truly envision the sheer abundance of life that extinct large animals helped to maintain any more than a person can count all the stars in the sky.

This is not to say that wild boar would automatically and only be a force for good if reintroduced across the country. The Anthropocene, the epoch in which we now find ourselves, is a double-edged blade: we have damaged our world so much that the actions of other species that once helped to power ecosystems now have the potential to deepen our damage. This is becoming apparent in parts of Europe where the abundance of boar has fallen out of harmony with the available habitat and population sizes of other species.

In Great Britain an instructive example of the power of wild boar can be found at Knepp. As of late 2021, these were the tallies for its ungulate species: fallow deer, about 400; English longhorn cattle, 290; red deer, 100; Exmoor ponies, 29.

As for the Tamworth pigs? Six.

Those six adult sows do tend to be accompanied by around 15 to 20 offspring each year, but these latter individuals are always sent to slaughter. Knepp's owners originally had more adults around. They've come to conclude that six Tamworths and their successions of litters are an optimal amount to achieve the right balance between disturbance and recuperation for the 445 hectares that the pigs can access. Boar, and their farmed variants, are a true force of nature.

Perhaps Hayao Miyazaki, lauded director and co-founder of Studio Ghibli, understood this when he gave wild boar such pivotal roles in his environmental allegory *Princess Mononoke*. The animated film opens with a village being attacked by a giant demon who turns out to be a once-peaceful boar god, corrupted by a bullet that tunnelled into his heart. Later in the story, the boar amass in a great army to stop humans clear-cutting for iron mining. Many of them give their lives. Yet it's the Forest Spirit, the omni-god, whose fate feels most boar-like and real of all. For when the Forest Spirit is decapitated by the leader of the miners, their body becomes a literal wave of death that kills all the forest-life and humanity that it touches until the heroes of the story return the head.

Mess with nature, and nature *will* mess with you.

The return of wild boar to Britain is an ecological necessity, albeit one that comes with strings attached. As well as adjusting our daily practices, such as keeping dogs on leads, we must carry out our role as apex predators properly. Our hitherto failure to manage deer populations isn't a glowing recommendation for us in this regard. However, both the Scottish and UK governments have recently signalled a desire to do better; in 2022, NatureScot ramped up the number of deer it expects to see culled, while Defra held a consultation on how to improve deer management in

England. With this political acknowledgement that the current system is not working as it should, there is an opportunity for us to reimagine what sustainable hunting could look like in this country. What if we emulated the best of hunting culture from mainland Europe and paired it with the kind of care already taken in places like the Forest of Dean? Could more of us become hunters, ones both mindful and steeped in the lore of wildness? Whatever path we choose, if we're to competently manage deer and boar, new negotiations will be needed in sharing landscapes – especially if the countryside becomes more accessible to all in a much-needed right to roam renaissance.

But we cannot play the role of every different predator. We lack the resources or the knowledge, and always will. For the sake of boar and every other species still here, we must bring back others, beginning with the lynx. While lynx prefer deer, they would pose a threat to boarlets and so their presence might force boar to move on to new grounds more often. The pursuit of deer by lynx would also help boar-inhabited woodlands to better thrive. As for wolves, in mainland Europe they are defying all expectations when it comes to their ability to survive in landscapes dense with humans. We'll never be able to micromanage all the details of natural systems, no matter how much more research we claim must be done before any actual restoration can be allowed. We must give other predators a fighting chance to do what they were born to do.

Reintroductions are not, however, a panacea for our environmental harms. Nor is it a given that returned species will always do everything we expect of them. Conservationist and writer Hugh Webster has been especially vocal in the British rewilding space around the dangers of false expectations. 'Radically altered ecosystems, like disassembled engines, will not necessarily be restarted simply by replacing one component, however integral that component once was,' he explains in an article for *British Wildlife*. We can speak all we like of ecosystems as machines with missing cogs, or puzzles with missing pieces, but life is altogether more complex and unpredictable. How many inter-species relationships have we destroyed over the last thousands, hundreds and tens of years? There's a special kind of ache in knowing that we don't know how deep our damage goes. One thing is clear, however: our presently miniaturised ecosystems, especially those without the balancing forces of a diverse suite of predators, are not functioning as they should. They are not the best we can do. Much of the conservation management we're used to practising in the UK is the equivalent of pouring bottles of water into a dried-up wallow – it helps, a little, for a short time.

Our refusal to restore species to their rightful places is its own form of ongoing assault against the world. And to say that in Britain our landscapes are too changed – in another word, *damaged* – for them to belong here again is to complete the destruction. Wild boar alone cannot be substitutes for all our missing species and connections, but they are a vital start. They represent one groundbreaking step away from our failing status quo and towards more life. By sharing our spaces and filling our senses, they invite us to re-root ourselves alongside them. Rewilding can and must enfold us all if we're to break the pattern of mistakes that have led us to this critical planetary point. It is part of the answer to the most important question that has ever been asked of our species: can we *choose* to live lightly enough?

In one way, it sounds hopeless and self-centred to argue for the money and willpower that will be required to reintroduce wild boar when so many people in this country are struggling to afford basic needs like food and heating. Yet, in another way, asking for boar is the same thing as asking for economic equality. It is to ask for a sharing economy – between humans, and between humans and the other beings who have equal right to this place we call home.

The biodiversity crisis and climate breakdown together demand as much of us as we have so far demanded of the Earth. I don't know if we'll learn to change in time to ensure that our descendants can live good lives. But if we do allow the boar, and others, to be here with us again, it would be proof that we can.

Epilogue

The *ing* in the word *rewilding* is vital. It is process. Restlessness. A story that will never stop unfolding

One day in early September 2022, I leave the house before dawn and drive to a spot elsewhere in the forest. It's been too long since I last saw a wild boar. In the lightening woods I step off the path and wander through bracken, then spruce, and then into a sweet chestnut plantation where dead leaves lie like shredded parchment, crackling under my feet.

When I see the animal ahead, the odds demand they'll be a deer.

No. They are a boar – dark-furred, lean, out of childhood but still young, I think, ploughing through the leaf litter. I crouch behind fronds of bracken, amazed I could get so close, and making so much noise.

I hear more than I can see from my hiding place. The rustling goes on. Then stops. There comes a series of hissing in-breaths. I lean to the right, and through my green-framed arrowslit the boar raises their head one last time before giving a belching snort and running away.

It often happens like this – that I can almost walk into a boar without them seeming to notice, only for their awareness to turn to me once I'm concealed and watching. As if they feel the beam of my own awareness (though, more likely, it's because I've made the mistake of being upwind).

I go home smiling. I make coffee and sit down to write. I let myself spend a few minutes idly clicking through my usual online stomping grounds. A thought rises: Forestry England might publish some updated figures for the population soon, given that they did so around this time last year. I find the bookmark for the right page. It loads. I scroll down.

I read and then re-read the table of numbers on the screen. Since I last checked, a row for 2022/23 has appeared. I absorb what it says. And release a long breath.

Excluding boar killed by vehicles, 770 have been shot. According to the most recent survey, the estimated number of boar is now at 441. Half the number that there was thought to be in 2021/22. So very near, now, to Forestry England's target of 400.

I am stunned. And unsurprised. To everyone in the Dean who goes out looking for the boar, it has felt as if the rain of them has been steadily drying up. We knew their numbers were dropping, though we hoped we were wrong. That it was much more a matter of the boar hiding themselves better.

A short report is provided with the new figures. It tells me that the average number of boar counted per sounder in the survey was three, down from four in the previous survey. Although an average can flatten and hide many realities, without more detailed data on offer I must assume that the sounders are indeed growing smaller. I think again of the boar from a few hours before. I thought they were male, seeing as they were alone. What if I was wrong?

My mind is a Pandora's Box. Because, after the rush of fear and sadness, there is a strange yet undeniable hope. Forestry England is finally on the border of the target it has been trying to reach for years. Some said it couldn't be done. That boar are unstoppable unless you don't let them start in the first place. Yes, it has taken an injection of cash to fund the killing. But it has worked. Those numbers are fragments of proof – not enough on their own, yet essential – that we can manage wild boar.

That we can let them come back.

———

Kevin Stannard told me that the human conflicts around boar are tethered to their numbers. Fewer boar, fewer flames. And the evidence seems to support him. In the Forest of Dean, for the first time since they arrived, the boar finally feel like old news. I hear no talk of them. No articles appear in the local or national media; the focus has shifted to Scotland. I struggle to find fresh rootings, let alone their makers. Although they're still here, this is an utterly different place to the one I first came to in 2014. And while I wish so many boar had not had to die or experience the loss of their kin, perhaps it's better this way.

Like the land after snouts have reshaped it, those people who lived through their terror of boar will not simply be able to forget. It happened. But reprieve has arrived. This moment is a pause, a plateau. When it comes to rewilding, the support for which seems to grow each day, the Forest of Dean is to be heeded: here is how it can play out when a species returns that requires *us* to change. We can't distil it to a formula or a model that will predict what communities will think and do if the boar (or something toothier) is reintroduced elsewhere. But we can learn from it, as so many of the people in this book have – and as the boar themselves have.

Their survival is not inevitable. That's all too clear from Devon, Dorset, Kent and East Sussex. Wild boar may be a fabulous product of evolution, but guns are a power from an alien world. The boar further south of the Dean found themselves in lands with too little shelter and too many people wanting to take their lives. The luckiest seem to be those dwelling further north in Scotland, from Galloway to Ayrshire to Perthshire to Inverness-shire. While many of them have been shot too, the killing is far more scattered and sporadic; there is simply more country and more forestry in which they can conceal themselves. In a report by NatureScot, updated in 2022, boar are estimated to have so far colonised just 1 per cent of their suitable habitat. If they continue to creep slowly across the nation, they have a chance of staying.

But it isn't certain. Patrick Laurie, the Galloway author, emails me a few months after our meeting to mention he's heard a rumour that the Scottish government is planning to take concerted lethal action. Perhaps they'll have come to a decision by the time this book is in your hands. The aforementioned NatureScot report doesn't come out with explicit recommendations, but the tone is clear from the way the authors discuss the feasibility of eradication. For now, it remains to be seen whether the steady angry chorus of farmers' voices will push the state to act. The longer the wait, the more money will have to be spent to tear out every last boar. But that time, however long it may last, is precious. It provides a chance for more people to gain more ecological awareness; for research into the boar's ecosystem impacts; and for them to find their way to the many rewilding projects, old and new, that are blooming across Scotland.

England and Wales, as things stand, offer much less hope for wild boar. Despite much prophesying over the years – one of the latest from 2021, when a researcher from the University of Worcestershire grabbed headlines by saying that the boar might at any moment spread by swimming across the Severn – the reality has proved very different. The Forest of Dean boar seem to be stuck in place. If they are expanding outwards, the pace is glacial, a testament to the ring of firearms around the forest.

One possible plot twist to come is the Severn Treescapes project, which aims to create a corridor of 'enhanced tree cover' stretching 60 miles from the Wyre Forest in Worcestershire down to the Forest of Dean. Boar ears would be pricking up if we could convey this news to them. For this corridor may be their chance to at last slip past the guns and properly colonise beyond the Dean. They could even help to shape the new forest, too. They might bring gifts of mycorrhizal fungal spores, soil mites and seeds. Though they might also uproot fresh-planted trees.

In the absence of self-willed colonisation by boar, some people may again be taking things into their own hands and helping them along. The ex-ranger Dennis has heard from a

Welsh friend over the border that they finally seem to be establishing there, but he wonders if they've been boar-napped from the Dean and trucked over. Regardless, those who've so far aided the return of the boar in this part of Britain may, in the end, find their work undone. I have little fear that Forestry England's current culling programme will drive boar to extinction in the Dean again. The fewer boar there are, the harder it is to find and cull them, so the system comes with its own brakes. And if the population were to shrink to a critical threshold, it would only take a brief ceasefire for them to begin to recover their numbers – though it would take longer for them to rebuild their cultural knowledge.

But Forestry England *is* ready to kill them all. A few weeks after the 2022 data is released, an article finally appears in local paper *The Forester*. In this, Kevin Stannard comments: 'If there is any indication the Forest of Dean's boar pick up Foot and Mouth or African Swine Fever or other contagious diseases … [the Defra] response will be to exterminate that population.'

Given how well the boar have been confined to the forest since their arrival in 1999, it is surely within Forestry England's power to track down and kill every last individual. Or to kill enough that the population goes the same way as others in England have. We can only hope that a vaccine for ASF can be found in time. The sheer scale of economic loss to the global pig industry means that scientists have been showered with funding. Yet the fact that ASF vaccine research has been going on since the 1920s is testament to the tricksiness of this disease. Early field trials in Vietnam in 2019 were beset with problems, and no other country has attempted them since. Eyes have now turned to a vaccine being developed in Spain through the work of a worldwide consortium, with roll-out expected by late 2024. However, many question marks remain around efficacy and feasibility.

In the absence of ASF itself, in Great Britain, the fear of it continues to do its own damage. Even if the legislative hurdles of the Dangerous Wild Animals and Wildlife and Countryside Acts can be cleared, and British society can meaningfully shift its attitudes towards other animals, Kevin Stannard has made plain that while the spectre of ASF looms, Defra will not countenance the official reintroduction of wild boar. In the absence of a working vaccine, until we drastically reduce the number of pigs – the ones kept in larger holdings, where the risk of disease spreading is far greater – we simply won't be able to have large-scale ecosystem restoration in much of Great Britain.

Would I have been bewitched by the boar if there had been other fantastically wild creatures to choose from, like the lynx or the wolf? Perhaps not. And yet, wild boar possess their own undeniable magic. They are portals to other worlds in a way that no other British animals are. They can be followed and found by anyone. They promise danger, just enough to shock us out of the loneliness of our self-imposed separation from the wild. But not so much that the prospect of coexisting with them is unimaginable.

I find it hard, these days, to stop my mind wandering into the futures that may await us all. In one of them, the UK has become a breadbasket for a hot and hungry planet, and the country is smothered in farmland. There is no place here for wildlife, especially not those animals who would steal our crops. Wild boar have been turned into memory again.

In a different future, there are more forests, scrublands, meadows and wetlands. Along with many other countries, we have reformed our food system in a way that has made us healthier and has given wildness far more space in which to be. Across the country, wild boar roam, hunted by lynx, wolf and the occasional careful human.

Perhaps your own descendants will be nourished by those of the boar roaming free in Great Britain today.

After everything I've learned about them, I have no doubt that wild boar will still be busy living porcine lives millions of years into the future. Even if boar here are destroyed again, others of their kind will one day find their way back, somehow.

But why should it have to happen that way?

Why should they have to go *now*?

———

2023. It has taken till January for winter to remember to be cold. I am sitting among bushes, wrapped up in woollies. The trees around me are fang-sharp against the twilight sky.

I am listening to a sounder of boar.

My position is beside a sprawling fortress of brambles, which I've taken to calling Boartropolis since I first discovered it a year ago. A few small tunnels lead into it, ones that even my foolhardy self would never crawl into. The surrounding grass borderland is a reliable place to find both fresh rootings and fresh dung.

I take in the many vocalisations of the boar. Squeals, quick grunts, and longer grunts that – it must be said – sound like an old man's sonorous farts.

They are a chatty sounder. I don't think they know I'm here, although I could be wrong. Or perhaps this is simply what they like to do in the lull between waking and heading out for the night.

My ears pick up new noises: a hard rhythm of steps, and puffing. A man comes jogging along the path that runs alongside one flank of Boartropolis. He doesn't see me. If he often runs this late, I wonder if he ever crosses paths with the boar. It seems likely. In which case, he finds little risk in it. Just as I feel safe enough to be here in the dark, so near to the creatures who have brought me to this forest, to this new path of my life.

I am not alone in having been changed by them. In being enwrapped with them in new becomings. We humans and the boar are two kinds among many, taking part in the writing of each other's story.

I've grown too cold. I stand, and creep away. I will miss the shapes of the sounder as they emerge into the night. No matter. I have basked in the sounds of them being themselves.

It is enough to know they are here.

Acknowledgements

The moment of the birth of this book cannot be pinned down. Was it when Sam Randalls, my professor at UCL, said he liked my idea of going to the Forest of Dean to chat to people about living alongside wild boar? Or seven years later when Sophie Yeo enthusiastically published my essay on my experience in the Dean on *Inkcap Journal* and then told me "Go for it!" when a publisher at Bloomsbury expressed interest? Or was it when that publisher, Jim Martin, wrote me an email that began with "Good news"?

If it takes a sounder to raise a boarlet, then it has taken a surrounding net of family, friends, and all manner of people who are each experts in their own way to help me breathe life into this instalment of the boar's story in Britain. Firstly, thank you to David Bonsall, Carles Conejero, Peter Cooper, Ed Drewitt, Ade Jupp, Patrick Laurie, Scott Hendry, Kieran O'Mahony and Rina Quinlan for sharing your time, and your knowledge and experiences of wild boar. To every person in the Forest of Dean and further afield who did the same, but whom I cannot name here: this book would not be the book it is without your openness.

To the earliest reviewers of *Groundbreakers*, Ian Carter, Nick Carter, Steve Cracknell, Chloë Edwards, Pete Moore, Sotiris Nikias, Rina Quinlan (again!), and Alick Simmons: thank you for the treasure trove of feedback. I am also deeply grateful to Hugh Warwick for taking up the unofficial role of my Emotional Support Author throughout most of the writing process.

To everyone at Bloomsbury who has been involved in creating *Groundbreakers* at some point or another, including the aforementioned Jim Martin, Alice Ward, Heather Bradbury, Elizabeth Peters, Charlotte Atyeo, Angie Hipkin and James Watson: I have dreamed of being a published author since the age of nine, and together you have brought about something that for many years felt like it would only ever remain a fantasy in my head.

A shout-out to my colleagues at Mindfully Wired for being unflaggingly supportive of and enthusiastic about the book, and for not having grown bored yet of hearing me wax lyrical about wild boar (or, hiding it very well).

Depthless thanks to the friends who have been my cheerleaders, reading my writing long before it had any hope of finding its way onto a printed page: Kimberly Appleton, Jacob Gardner, Kat Jones, Sally-Ann Smurthwaite, Nick Phillips, Coco McKeever-Ziff, Ben McKeever-Ziff, Jamie Sawyer and, of course, Sarah Llanham and Sophie Graham.

To Uncle Christophe: thank you for being my fixer and translator in Toulouse. Without you, the chapter 'A *Bamboche* of Boar' would not have been nearly as entertaining nor informative. As for my dear Bonne-Maman, may this book live up to your expectations; *gros bisous*!

Finally, a thank-you of TARDIS dimensions to my brother John and my parents Françoise and Andrew. You may not have read every single poem, short story, and novel; and you may have had to endure more than your fair share of my morosity when the literary agent rejections kept coming back in my teenage years and my twenties; but collectively, you helped me to believe in the legitimacy of my creative efforts and dreams.

Further Reading

Cracknell, S. 2021. *The Implausible Rewilding of the Pyrenees*. Lulu Books, Morrisville.

Goulding, M. 2003. *Wild Boar in Britain*. Whittet Books, Stansted.

Fleischman, T. 2017. 'A plague of wild boars': A New History of Pigs and People in Late 20th Century Europe. *Antipode*, 49: 1015–1034. doi: 10.1111/anti.12217.

Harman, D. 2013. *British Wild Boar: The Story So Far*. Skycat Publications, Brent Eleigh.

Lyall, W. 2004. *The Whole Hog: Exploring the Extraordinary Potential of Pigs*. Profile Books, London.

Macdonald, B. 2022. *Cornerstones: Wild Forces That Can Change Our World*. Bloomsbury, London.

Mathews, F. and Kendall, T. 2023. *Black Ops and Beaver Bombing: Adventures with Britain's Wild Mammals*. Oneworld Publications, London.

Monbiot, G. 2013. *Feral: Rewilding the Land, Sea and Human Life*. Penguin, London.

O'Mahony, K. 2019. Feral bo(a)rderlands: living with and governing wild boar in the Forest of Dean. PhD Thesis, Cardiff University. orca.cardiff.ac.uk/id/eprint/131010.

Tree, I. 2018. *Wilding: The Return of Nature to a British Farm*. Picador, London.

Yamamoto, D. 2017. *Wild Boar*. Reaktion Books, London.

A full list of references can be found at:
chantallyons.uk/references-for-groundbreakers

Index

People referred to by a pseudonym are listed by first name.

acorns 75, 221
adaptability of wild boar 15, 20, 21, 29, 67, 148
adders 31, 68, 69, 70
African Swine Fever (ASF) 167–70, 273–4
Albarella, Umberto 24
Albrecht, Glenn 108
Alfred the Great 22
Alice Holt Forest, Hampshire 24
altruism 144–5
Alves, João Pedro Galhano 65
anatomy, wild boar
    bristles and crest 99, 102, 129, 144, 222
    dew claws 36, 41
    ears 39
    eyes 39
    hooves 195
    snout 35, 99
    tail 53, 217, 222, 240
    teeth 49
    tusks 22, 99
Angela 126
Animal and Plant Health Agency 169
animal rights movements 160–1, 163, 210–11
Animal Welfare Act 2006 188
Anne 134–5, 136–7
aquatic organisms 85, 102
Arregui, Aníbal 223
'attacks' by wild boar, accounts of
    on dogs 55, 120–1, 139
    on humans 32, 66, 130–1, 213, 218, 260–1
    on sheep 63–4, 68
attitudes to wild boar
    complaints 108–18, 120–8
    exhilaration 134–7

fear 65, 123, 125, 126–7, 134, 157, 260, 261
    media influence on 8, 32, 207, 210, 211
aurochs 20, 22, 100
Autonomous University of Barcelona 213

baby wild boar see newborns
bachelor groups 172
badgers 41, 85, 88, 104, 160, 185, 189
Barcelona, Spain 15, 212–22
Barro Colorado Island 119
Basel Zoo, Switzerland 142–3
Baynes, Richard 68
bears 20
beavers 11–12, 13, 31, 86, 89–92, 104–5, 190, 235, 258
Beechenhurst Lodge 146
beechmast 75, 159
behaviours, wild boar
    begging 146, 149, 173
    feeding and foraging 33, 35, 52, 63–87, 109, 115, 216, 231
    food-washing 142–3
    mock fighting 58, 59
    play 143
    sideways stancing 129
    staring 54, 133
    tree biting 38, 96–7, 248
    trotting 132
    urine spraying 37
    wallowing 38, 96–8
    for charging see 'attacks' by wild boar, accounts of
Belgium 68, 168
Belmont Estate see Watercress Farm
Beowulf 22
Białowieża Forest, Poland 57
big cat sightings 132

biodiversity loss   252, 258
bison   241
Black Ops and Beaver Bombing
    (Mathews & Kendall)   228
Blackshaw-Crosby, Elsie   235
Blewett, James   244
bluebells   47, 52, 72–3, 112
The Boaring Truth   162–3, 220
boarlets   50–3, 56, 61, 94, 155, 214,
    216–17
Bonsall, David   245–9
bovine spongiform encephalopathy
    (BSE)   237
Bracke, Marc   65, 97
bracken   92–3
Brazil   175
Brede High Woods, East Sussex
    245–9
Britain
    ecological impoverishment
       12–13, 252, 258
    history of wild boar in   19–30
British Association for
       Conservation and
       Shooting   165
British Mycological Society   114
British Wild Boar (Harman)   27,
    243
British Wildlife   267
Broughton, Richard   238
Browning, Helen   231
Bulgaria   168
Bunloit Estate, Scotland   88–96,
    179
Burrell, Charlie   234

Camargue, France   85, 102
Cannop Ponds   149
Castellan, Martin   207
cattle
    longhorn   236–7, 251, 264
    red poll   230
Challenger, Melanie   259
Charles   202–3, 204, 208, 209
China   168, 175

Christophe   202
City University of Hong Kong
    167
climate change   203, 255, 256
Collserola Natural Park,
       Spain   212, 220–2
colours of wild boar   39, 50, 99,
    140, 222, 246, 253
complaints about wild boar   108–
    18, 120–8
Conejero, Carles   212–14, 216–20,
    221, 222
Coombeshead Rewilding,
       Devon   67, 98–101, 105–6,
    238
Cooper, Peter   98–101, 102,
    103–4, 105, 238, 240
Cornerstones (Macdonald)   239
coyotes   12
Cracknell, Steve   53, 201, 207
Croatia   181–2
cruelty towards wild boar   188–9
culling
    deer   95, 164, 165–6, 265
    wild boar   29, 42, 145, 147,
       148–9, 158–60, 164, 168, 172,
       173, 176, 186, 273
culture and events, wild-boar
       inspired   9, 154, 165, 265
Cumbria
    Haweswater reserve   11
Czech Republic   144, 171

Dan   120–1
Dangerous Wild Animals Act 1976
       (DWAA)   26, 233, 234
Daniel   208–12
Dartmoor, Devon   55, 139
Davies, Greg   65
Davis, Josh Luke   213
dead wild boar   145, 169, 193–4,
    248; *see also* mortality, wild boar
death, awareness of   145
deer   36, 131
    culling   95, 164, 165–6, 265

ecological impact of 95, 164–5,
    247
deer species
    Chinese water   164
    fallow   31, 51, 82, 108, 164, 237,
        241, 264
    muntjac   31, 36, 51, 82, 108,
        164, 166
    red   21, 100–1, 164, 234, 264
    roe   21, 31, 36, 41, 51, 81, 82,
        104, 108, 164, 183, 184, 206
    Sika   94, 95, 164
Denmark   170
Dennis   159, 170, 272–3
Department for Agriculture, Food
        and Rural Affairs (Defra)   29,
        169, 170, 172, 243, 243, 244,
        265, 273, 274; see also Ministry
        of Agriculture, Fisheries and
        Food (MAFF)
Devon   105, 271
    Coombeshead Rewilding   67,
        98–101, 105–6, 238
    Dartmoor   55, 139
    Exmoor   244
Diablo Range, USA   67
diet, wild boar   66–71
diseases, pig   167–70, 273–4
dispersal
    aquatic organisms   85, 102
    seeds   77, 80–1, 86, 87, 90–1
    soil microorganisms   79–80
Doggerland   20
dogs   55–6, 71, 134, 137, 139, 232,
    245
Dolman, Paul   165
Domesday Book   21
domestication process   149–50
Dooren, Thom van   177
dormice   68–9
Dorset   26, 244, 271
Drewitt, Ed   69, 82, 93–4, 101,
    102–3, 149, 159, 166–7, 170,
    171
droppings, wild boar   78–9, 81–4

droughts   11, 114, 203, 207, 221,
    255
Dumfries and Galloway,
    Scotland   26, 63, 178–97
Dumont, Jude   8
dung beetles   78–9, 82, 83

East Sussex   14, 26–7, 68, 116, 154,
    172, 225, 243, 271
    Brede High Woods   245–9
ecological boredom   31
ecological impact of wild boar
    benefits for other wildlife   52,
        91, 101–2, 255–6
    habitat improvement   77–8,
        92–3, 100
    sediment loss   104–5
    soil disturbance   72, 73–4
    see also dispersal
'The Ecology and Management of
    Wild Boar in southern England'
    (Defra report)   243–4
ecosystem restoration and
    reintroduced species   11, 12
Edgehills Bog,
    Gloucestershire   101
environmental degradation   10, 21
Estonia   68
Europe, pigs and wild boar in   23,
    57, 65, 68, 77, 85, 101, 102,
    143–4, 168–9, 171, 181–2,
    201–23, 262
Exmoor, Devon   244
extinction of wild boar in
    Britain   23–4

fallen stock   237
fear of wild boar   65, 123, 125,
    126–7, 134, 157, 260, 261
feeding wild boar   146, 154, 210,
    216, 219–20
female wild boar see sows
fencing   28, 37, 70, 89, 111, 146,
    158, 168, 203, 233, 237, 238–9,
    243, 244, 251

Feral (Monbiot)   13, 32
feral pigs   228–9
Finlay   178, 183–97
firearms licensing   188
Fleischman, Thomas   225
food-washing   142–3
Forest of Dean   14, 26, 75, 93–4,
   96, 107, 162
  Beechenhurst Lodge   146
  Cannop Ponds   149
  Pygmy Pinetum garden
    centre   126, 149
  water loss   103, 255, 258
  woodland composition and
    wildlife   31–2, 41, 112–18
  for wild boar in the Forest of Dean
    see under wild-boar related subjects
Forest of Dean Wild Boar Cull
  Saboteurs   160–1, 175
Forestry Commission   28, 29, 32;
  see also Forestry England
Forestry England   41, 111, 162,
  169–70, 250, 261
  Beechenhurst Lodge   146
  boar culling   29, 42, 145, 147,
    148–9, 158–60, 164, 172, 173,
    176, 186, 273
  boar population estimates   29,
    42, 156–7, 226, 269–70
  deer culling   164, 165–6
  forestry operations   107–8
  forestry policies   70
  land management plans   163–4
  see also Forestry Commission *and*
    Stannard, Kevin
Forestry and Land Scotland   95
foxes   90, 96, 104, 120, 206
foxgloves   93–4
France   168, 171, 182, 262
  Camargue   85, 102
  Loire Valley   201, 207
  Paris   143
  Toulouse   15, 202–12
  Tours   207
Frantz, Alaine   225, 226

futures for wild boar   199–268,
  274–5

Galloway *see* Dumfries and
  Galloway
Gates, Nick   147
genetics, wild boar   139, 170, 209,
  253
Genoa, Italy   143
Germany   68, 168
  Grunewald Forest   213
Gieser, Thomas   6
Gloucestershire
  Edgehills Bog   101
  Nagshead Reserve   70
  see also Forest of Dean
Gloucestershire Wildlife
  Trust   101, 161
golf courses   202–3
Goodall, Jane   143
Gough Island   67
Goulding, Martin   27, 172, 243,
  253
Gow, Derek   98, 100, 240
Griffiths, Jay   263
groups and individuals, named
  Beechenhurst Six   146, 149
  Big Peter   191–2
  Boris   147
  The Boys   58–60
  Elsa   213
  Gerald   146
  Gerard   99, 102, 105–6, 240
  Orphan Nine   150–3, 168, 173
  Pygmy Boar   146, 149
  The Trio   47–8, 52, 72–3, 255
Grunewald Forest, Germany   213

habitat improvement   77–8, 92–3,
  100; *see also* ecosystem
  restoration and reintroduced
  species
Hampshire
  Alice Holt Forest   24
  New Forest   75–6, 242

Harman, Derek   26–7, 60, 243, 246
Haweswater reserve, Cumbria   11
Haynes, Robin   230–3, 238, 241
heatwaves   151, 202, 249, 255–7; see also droughts
hedgehogs   70–1
hefting   152
Helgason, Thorunn   114, 115
Hendry, Scott   88–92, 94–6
Henry III, King of England   23
heraldry   22
The Hidden Life of Trees (Wohlleben)   68
Highlands Rewilding   88, 89
history of wild boar in Britain   19–30
Hogwatch   161, 163
Holocene   20
Home Office Guide on Firearms Licensing Law   188
hoofprints   36, 41, 96
horses
　Dartmoor ponies   230
　Exmoor ponies   237, 264
　New Forest ponies   242
horses and riders   121–2, 126–7, 133
How to Be Animal (Challenger)   259
Howe, General   24
human-boar relations
　co-existence adjustment   113, 124, 125, 136–7, 241, 259, 261–3, 271
　conflicts   154–77, 270
　historical   20–5
　see also complaints about wild boar and fear of wild boar
humbugs see boarlets
Hunt, Nick   49
hunting
　accidents   160, 210–11
　bans   168

driven hunts   181, 204, 205–6
for sport   21–2, 139, 180, 249
subsistence   208
see also poaching and stalking
hybrid vigour   227
hybridisation, pig/wild boar   22–3, 209, 217, 225–9, 240

The Implausible Rewilding of the Pyrenees (Cracknell)   53, 201
insect habitats   77–8
intelligence, wild boar   140–6, 148, 206
International Union for Conservation of Nature (IUCN)   25
Italy   77, 86
　Genoa   143
　Rome   219

jays   76, 92
Jupp, Ade   250–3
juvenile wild boar see newborns and boarlets

Kendall, Tim   228
Kent   14, 26–7, 116, 154, 172, 225, 243, 271
　Orlestone Forest   249–53
Kent Wildlife Trust   69
Kikuchi, Satoshi   131–2
kinship bonds, wild boar   144–5, 171–3, 168, 177
Knepp, West Sussex   56, 77–8, 234, 236, 238, 241–2, 264–5

landscape bonding   152
Large Herbivore Working Group (LHWG)   234, 235
Laurie, Patrick   63, 64, 178–82, 246, 271–2
legislation   26, 188, 233, 234–5, 236
leucism   246, 253
Lifescape Project   235

Lilley, Clive   66
litters   48, 61, 203, 209, 226–7
The Living Mountain
      (Shepherd)   136
Liz   120, 122
Loire Valley, France   201, 207
London Zoo   25
Lorimer, Jamie   37
Lydia   122, 133, 157, 163
lynx   19, 20, 24, 98, 118, 262,
      266

Macdonald, Benedict   20, 35, 69,
      239
Mackintosh, Sophie   256
MacLachlan, Kate   21
male wild boar   37, 57–61,
      109, 120, 126, 222, 248,
      253
Mance, Henry   142
Mathews, Fiona   228
matriarchs   49, 50, 54, 124, 141,
      172, 173–4
Max Planck Institute for the
      History of Science   168
Mayer, John   260
media
   influence on attitudes to
      wildlife   8, 32, 119, 120
   see also 'attacks' by wild boar,
      accounts of
Michel   205–6, 207
Middleton, Arthur   12
Ministry of Agriculture, Fisheries
      and Food (MAFF)   26, 27;
      see also Department for
      Agriculture, Food and Rural
      Affairs (Defra)
Miyazaki, Hayao   265
Monbiot, George   13, 31, 32, 117,
      132
Montesinho Natural Park,
      Portugal   65
more-than-human geography   37,
      39, 122–3

mortality, wild boar
   culling   29, 42, 145, 148–9,
      158–60, 172, 173, 176, 186,
      273
   natural   105–6
   road traffic accidents   157, 158,
      205, 262
   see also hunting; poaching *and*
      stalking
mycorrhizal fungi   74, 80, 83, 86,
      114

Nagshead reserve, Gloucestershire
      70
National Dormouse Monitoring
      Programme   69
National Farmers Union
      (NFU)   169, 228
National Pig Association
      (NPA)   169, 228
Native (Laurie)   178, 182
natterjack toads   102
Natural England   12, 235
NatureScot   180, 228, 236, 265,
      271
necrobiome   237
Neil   33–7, 46, 56, 129, 130, 140–1
nests   48
New Forest, Hampshire   75–6,
      242
newborns   48, 49, 51
nightjars   69–70
nocturnal walks   42–5

Olive   161, 163
O'Mahony, Kieran   29, 148,
      161–2, 168–9, 171
Orlestone Forest, Kent   249–53
orphaned groups   149–53, 168
otters   104
Our Shared Forest project   163–4

Pangea   19
pannage   22, 25, 75–6, 154
Paris, France   143

peregrines 31
Pfeiffer, Dirk 167
phoresy 80, 86
Pig (Browning) 231
pigs
  breathing problems 231–2
  cognitive aptitude 141–2
  diseases 167–70
  interbreeding with wild
    boar 22–3, 94, 209, 217,
    225–9, 240
  Large Black 233
  Mangalitsa 23, 88, 233
  Tamworth 23, 56, 77, 88, 230,
    231, 232, 237, 253, 264, 265
  Vietnamese pot-bellied 217,
    222
pine martens 13, 31, 117
play 143
poaching 24, 146, 147, 149, 158,
    161, 175, 243, 247–8, 249
Poland 85, 168, 182
  Białowieża Forest 57
polecats 104
populations of wild boar
  decreases 15, 243–54, 270
  establishment 24–30, 139, 179,
    180
  in Europe 201
  fluctuation 155–6
  Forestry England estimates 29,
    42, 156–7, 226, 269–70
  impact of climate change 203
pork industry 168–9
Portugal 65
Pretten, Drew 160–1
Princess Mononoke 265
Pullar, Polly 82
Pygmy Pinetum garden
    centre 126, 149

Quinlan, Rina 234, 236, 241–2

Rackham, Oliver 23, 24
radio-tracking 57, 168, 175, 243,
    259

le Rassemblement pour une France
    sans Chasse (RAC) 211
red kites 25
reintroduced species and ecosystem
    restoration 11, 12
reproduction, wild boar
  gestation 48
  inbreeding and
    interbreeding 22–3, 94, 209,
    217, 225–9, 240
  litter sizes 61, 203, 209, 226–7
  mating 60–1
  number of litters 203, 209
  synchrony 50
rescue of kin, intentional 144–5
rewilding 10–13; *see also under
    named rewilding projects*
Richard 108–11, 157
right to roam 266
Rix, Luke 188
Rohan 192, 194–6
Romania 101
Rome, Italy 219
rootings 33, 34–5, 77, 109, 115,
    189–10, 255
Rose 123–4, 127, 260, 261
RSPB 11, 38, 70, 161

Scotland 14, 20, 26, 63, 67–8, 93,
    102, 114, 169, 227, 271–2
  Bunloit Estate 88–96, 179
  Dumfries and Galloway 26, 63,
    178–97
seed dispersal 77, 80–1, 86, 90–1
senses, wild boar
  hearing 46
  sight 46, 130
  smell 46, 59, 72, 142, 216
  taste 72
Serbia 67
Severn Treescapes Project 272
Shakira 213, 218
sheep 63–4, 68, 152
Shepherd, Nan 136
shifting baselines 264
Shinshu University 132

Simmons, Alick   195
size and weight of wild boar   37,
    49, 192, 194
Slater, David   147
smell of wild boar   36–7, 38, 181,
    194
soil disturbance   72, 73–4
soil microorganisms   79–87
solastalgia   108
Somerset   26
    Watercress Farm   229–33, 238,
        241
sounders   49, 52–4, 94, 124, 127,
    140–1
sows   37, 39–40, 46, 47, 51
    defence of young   54–5, 144–5
    matriarchs   49, 50, 54, 124, 141,
        172, 173–4
    see also sounders
Spain   77, 191
    Barcelona   15, 212–22
    Collserola Natural Park   212,
        220–2
squirrels, grey   164
stalking
    in Forest of Dean   148, 159
    in France   205
    in Galloway   180–97
Stannard, Kevin   71, 104, 155–7,
    158, 159, 162, 165–6, 174,
    175–6, 228, 262, 270, 273,
    274
Strange, Alison   93
Sutton Hoo helmet   22
Swanson, Jim   101–2
Sweden   127, 182
Swindale Beck, Cumbria   11
Switzerland
    Basel Zoo   142
Szczygielska, Marianna   168

tarpan   22
Thiébaux, Marcelle   21, 165
Thomas, Virginia   238
Tickle, Lara   209
ticks   193, 195

Torc of Galloway   178–97
Toulouse, France   15, 202–12
Tours, France   207
trail cameras   47, 58, 91, 94, 97,
    144, 145, 151, 156, 175, 180,
    184, 192, 253, 255, 257
trapping and netting   187, 215
trauma from loss of kin   173, 168,
    177
Treated Like Animals
    (Simmons)   195
Tree, Isabella   77, 234
Trees for Life   93
triops   102
truffles   86

University of Bristol   244
University of California, USA   67
University of East Anglia   165
University of Edinburgh   114
University of Exeter   238
University of Worcester   121, 272
urban areas, wild boar in   143, 225;
        see also Barcelona; Rome;
        Toulouse *and* Tours
USA   119, 259, 261
    Diablo Range   67
    University of California   67
    Yellowstone National Park   11

Van Dooren, Thom   177
Vera, Frans   76
Viv   111–15, 117, 164
vocalisations, wild boar   39, 40,
    43–4, 45, 46, 51, 54, 60, 141,
    221, 269, 275

Wageningen University   97
Wales   29, 65
wallows   38, 96–8, 100–2, 105,
    145, 151, 248–9, 255–6, 257
wariness, levels of   146–53, 221–2,
    224, 232
    habituation   214, 216–20
    tamed wild boar   98–9
Warner, Bernhard   215

water
  availability   203
  conservation   103–4
  loss   103, 255, 258
water buffalo   100
Watercress Farm, Somerset
      229–33, 238, 241
Webster, Hugh   64, 266
weight and size of wild boar   37,
      49, 192, 194
West Sussex
  Knepp   56, 77–8, 234, 236, 238,
      241–2, 264–5
Whipsnade Zoo   25
White, Gilbert   24
White, Sam   23
white-tailed eagles   13, 25, 64,
      190
Why Rebel? (Griffiths)   263
wild boar
  adaptability   15, 20, 21, 29, 67,
      148
  body size and weight   37, 49,
      192, 194
  colours   39, 50, 99, 140, 222,
      246, 253
  diet   66–71
  droppings   78–9, 81–4
  genetics   139, 170, 209, 253
  intelligence   140–6, 148, 206
  interbreeding with pigs
      22–3, 94, 209, 217, 225–9, 240
  kinship bonds   144–5, 171–3,
      168, 177

  see also anatomy; behaviour;
      mortality; reproduction; senses
      and vocalisations
Wild Boar (Yamamoto)   58
Wild Boar in Britain (Goulding)   27
Wild Boar Chase bike ride   154
Wild Boar Week festival   154, 243
wild garlic   72–3
Wild Mammals (Protection) Act
      1996   188
wildcats   13, 98, 206
Wilderfest   105
Wilding (Tree)   77
Wildlife and Countryside Act
      1981 (WCA)   234–5, 236
William the Conqueror   21, 108,
      245
Wohlleben, Peter   68
wolves   11, 20, 22, 24, 118, 127,
      206, 266
women's fears   125–6
Worcestershire
  Wyre Forest   272
Woodland Trust   69, 154, 245
Wyllie, Jamie   228
Wyre Forest   272

Yamamoto, Dorothy   58
Yellowstone National Park, USA
      11
young wild boar *see* newborns *and*
      boarlets

zoophobia   65, 119